Conversations with Moctezuma

Conversations with

Moctezuma

The Soul of Modern Mexico

DICK J. REAVIS

Quill
William Morrow
New York

Library of Congress Cataloging-in-Publication Data

Reavis, Dick J.
    Conversations with Moctezuma: the soul of modern Mexico /
    Dick J. Reavis.
        p.   cm.
    ISBN 0-688-10738-9
    1. Mexico—Politics and government—1970– 2. Representative
government and representation—Mexico—History—20th century.
I. Title.
F1236.R45   1990
972.08—dc20   89-34923
                                                                   CIP

Printed in the United States of America

First Quill Edition

1 2 3 4 5 6 7 8 9 10

BOOK DESIGN BY PAUL CHEVANNES

To Miriam Lizcano

Contents

Conversations with Moctezuma

Introduction

Mᴇxɪᴄᴏ is a land of contro-
versy, and a land of extremes. Everything is under contention
there. Any claim to knowledge about the place is subject to
dispute. Even the spelling of the country's name is a matter of
controversy. Indeed, the conflict over Mexico's name presents
a crude model of what Mexico is, and how it works.

The men who conquered Mexico named their colony *Nueva
España*, or New Spain. But informally, they referred to it as
Méjico. Neither name raised eyebrows back on the Continent,
but when people born and raised in the colony began spelling
Méjico with an *x*, as *México*, erudite Spaniards balked. Scholars
at the Royal Spanish Academy, the authorities on matters of
language, still acknowledge *México* only as a barbarized spelling
of the Spanish tongue. Here is what one authoritative modern
dictionary from Spain says about Mexico's name:

MÉXICO. In this word the *x* is pronounced like a *j*: *Méjico* . . .
México is the spelling that *los mejicanos* have wanted to give the
name of their country, and that at their request has spread in

the usage of the rest of the Hispano-American countries. It is an orthographic archaism that has no justification, since today in our language all *j*-sounds are written with the letter *j* (also the *g*, following *e, o,* and *i*). It furthermore has the disadvantage that people who do not know the secret of the *x* mispronounce it as *méksiko*. Unamuno defines this orthographic singularity as an "itching for distinction and independence," "an extremely envious zeal for differentiation." Without any doubt, the best recommendation is to write *Méjico* and to extend the *j* to all the derivatives of this name. . . .

The authorities at the Royal Academy are of course right about the pronunciation of the Spanish *j*, but in an almost colonial fashion, their explanations do not take into account the limitations that Spanish faced in the historical context of Mexico. At the time of the Conquest, central Mexico was ruled by those whom historians call the Aztecs. They called themselves the Mexica, or Mejica, and their realm they called *México* or *Méjico*. But they spoke those names in Náhuatl, their native tongue. They pronounced the name of their empire as English-speakers would pronounce Mé-shē-cŏ. But the *sh* sound did not exist in Spanish. The *j* sound in Spanish is pronounced like the English *h*, as in *he*. Therefore Spaniards read *Méjico* as Mé-hē-cŏ, not as Mé-shē-cŏ. Spanish-speaking natives of the colony tried to compensate for the lack of an *sh* sound—and tried to demonstrate a little independence as well—by spelling New Spain's informal name with an *x*; in Spanish, the *x* sounds much like in English, as in the words *exorcismo*, or exorcism, and *máximo*, or maximum. The *x* spelling should have resulted in an approximation of the Náhuatl word, a pronunciation that English-speakers would read as Méx-shē-cŏ. But the innovation couldn't overcome established habits. People who did not speak Náhuatl referred to the place as Mé-hē-cŏ, even if they spelled it with an *x*, and that mispronunciation is standard today on both sides of the Atlantic. Neither the Spanish nor the Mexican pronunciation of the word is correct, but the *x* spelling was an attempt to cope with the New World inadequacy of a European language. In time, other *sh*-sounding names entered into the ears of Spanish-speaking Mexicans,

12

only to come out of their mouths in various modes of deformity. For example, women named Xochitl, or "flower," are called Sō-chēl, not Shō-chētl, a sort of compromise. But men named Xicotencatl are called Hē-cō-těn-cātl, as if their names began with *j*. The capital of the state of Veracruz calls itself Xalapa, but the rest of the country refers to it as Jalapa, because its name is today pronounced as if it began with a *j*. Conquest by a people who did not know shish kebab from Shinola produced a bedlam of *x*'s and *j*'s in Mexico, and left the country with a name whose spelling is controversial, and whose pronunciation, outside of the circles of surviving Náhuatl Indians, is always distorted. Mexico began its modern life with a twisted name, and its name represents its history in many ways: Mexico is a place where European norms can't be imposed, and compromises with native culture usually fail.

No matter where one turns for a name or a category to simplify the job of understanding Mexico, obstacles stand in the way. For example, the terms "Latin American" and "Hispanic" are helpful in conversations of an informal type, but in the long run their concepts break down. If Mexicans are Latin Americans, then by the same logic, the Cherokee, Sioux, Kiowa, and Pima of the United States are "Anglo Americans," because they, too, have learned the language of their European conquerors, and have bred with them. If the Mexicans are Hispanic, the peoples of the United States, Australia, New Zealand, Jamaica, Belize, Liberia, and Zimbabwe are all Anglos, because the same language and traditions were imparted to them by the empire on which the sun never set. Argentina, whose European currents are strongest, Peru, whose native heritage is dominant, and the Dominican Republic, which is deeply indebted to African folkways, are all Latin American or Hispanic countries. Yet in terms of daily life, they have no more in common than Americans and Liberians do. Mexico is a part of Latin America, but the term is too vague to provide a key to what Mexico is.

In daily life, we often solve the problem of understanding distant locales by letting their economies define them. We might say, for example, that "Texas is an oil state." By themselves, such shorthand statements are rarely comprehensible. The claim that "Texas is an oil state" only makes sense on the grounds of other presumptions about what Texas is, apart from its being a place where oil is found. For example: (1) Texas is a constituent of the United States, whose chief gift to the world has been development of democracy; (2) the United States is an heir to England, whose chief contribution has been the development of the science of acquisition, or capitalism; and (3) England is a setting for Western civilization, whose chief accomplishment has been the development of machine technology. These three observations—democracy, capitalism, technology—provide a context in which the words "Texas" and "oil" form a picture, or make sense. Without them, we might theoretically confuse Texas with a province of Iran, its governor with an ayatollah, and its chief goal—probably the private acquisition of wealth—with the spread of Islam.

Three distinctions—nation, race, and civilization or culture —are necessary to deciding what Mexico is. None of these terms describes eternal or hermetic entities, and all of them are used with different meanings by people in different disciplines. As I will use them, nationhood refers to political divisions based on geographic boundaries; race refers to one of three biological subgroupings of the human species, Negroid, Mongoloid, or Caucasian—black, Oriental, or white; civilization refers to an order, including a state, based on the cultivation of a particular staple, corn, wheat, rice, or sorghum, for example; and culture refers to matrixes of tradition, language, and outlook. By these terms, the Plains Comanches of the United States represented a culture, but because they did not live by planting, they did not represent a civilization of their own. At least until treaties were signed with the United States and other tribes, they also did not represent a nation, because they did not fix the boundaries by which nations are defined. Also by these terms, the Socialist Republic of Czechoslovakia is a nation, though it embraces both the Czech and Slovak cultures, each with its own language and traditions. Despite the cold-war terminology that identified both Czechoslovakia and Mongolia as members of the Eastern bloc, Czechs and Slovaks, but not Mongols, live in cultures of Western civilization. To ask, "What makes Czechoslovakia work?" is primarily to ask how Czechs and Slovaks

14

contribute to the civilization of the West. It is that, or it is to err by assuming that all cultures seek the same ends, i.e., that oil is sought in Texas in order to promote the spread of Islam.

Mexico's staple crop has always been corn, a plant unknown in the Old World at the time of the Conquest. Europe's staple, on the other hand, has always been wheat, a plant formerly unknown in the New World. The influence that agriculture exerts on culture is invisible to modern, urban American eyes, and is one of those subjects that need volumes to explain. But because corn is still the staple of Mexico, anthropologists contend that Mexico cannot form a part of Western civilization. Contemporary Mexican anthropologists are bringing clarity to discussions like this by promoting a new set of terms. For them, Argentina is a part of Euro-America, as is the United States. The Dominican Republic, in their vocabulary, is a part of Afro-America, as is Haiti. Peru, Bolivia, and Guatemala are Indo-American nations. But the new terms only fuel controversy over Mexico, which officially calls its people *mestizo*, or of mixed race, and applies that same term to its cultural matrix. The *mestizo* characterization putatively explains why Mexico's institutions—Christianity, the market economy, and an elected government—take a Western form. But the notion that Mexico is a cultural mix assumes that cultures "mix" as pigments do. It does not distinguish between a suspension, like nutmeg and eggnog, or a blend, like eggnog and whiskey. It doesn't tell us whether the "mix" that is Mexico is a gray or a beige or a polka-dot pattern or check. The *mestizo* characterization of Mexico, like its categorization as Latin American or Hispanic, is too imprecise to be of much use.

It may also be patently unnecessary. Spain was conquered and ruled by Arabs for four hundred years. Do we regard it as an Arab nation, or a *mestizo* nation, or as part of Europe? Is the culture of Haiti more akin to that of its African or French ancestors? The Arabs gave Europe medicinal science, India gave the zero, China gave gunpowder, and America sent the potato. Does European culture need renaming because of these gifts? Most of the peoples of the world have at some time been enslaved or conquered by alien civilizations, and all borrow, beg, buy, or steal accomplishments from the others. Yet distinct

cultures remain. No one seriously questions Japan's Oriental-
ness, even though the country has mastered the technology of
the West. If European civilization survived in Spain, if African
culture survived in Haiti—and in English-speaking Liberia—
and if the Japanese are Orientals, there is no obvious reason
for regarding Mexico as a *mestizo* rather than an Indo-American
nation.

Americans can make relatively short work of the problems
posed by the term *mestizo,* and can derive another model of
how Mexico works by comparing the ways in which the United
States and Mexico define their minority populations. In the
United States, minorities are defined on the basis of race, even
though, ironically, a code for defining race no longer exists.
People who are apparently white are now accepted into the
Caucasian majority, whether or not their pedigrees attest to
lily-white lineage. But those whom white Americans take to be
black, for example, remain suspended in a largely European
blend. It is neither just nor scientific to attach great significance
to race, but the historical truth is that to overcome minority
status, the United States has offered only one sure means: dis-
solution or absorption by the Caucasian majority. Mexico plays
a similar game, based on culture, not on race.

Sources that publish estimates of the racial composition of
Mexico's population, almanacs, for example, usually guess that
it is about 30 percent Indian, 10 percent white, 5 percent Negroid, 5 percent Mongoloid or Oriental, and about 50 percent
mixed. But Mexico does not classify its small Negroid, Mongoloid, or Caucasian populations as unassimilated minority
groups, nor does it keep contemporary racial records of any
kind. The status of minority, ironically, afflicts only its Indian
population, defined by a cultural standard or code as that
group—of 5 million to 10 million, or about 6–12 percent of the
total population of 80 million—whose first language is an indigenous tongue. Though most of Mexico's Indians also speak
Spanish, often better than a native language, they remain on
the fringes of official and public life, suspended in a *ladino,* or
Spanish-speaking blend. To dissolve into official or *mestizo* Mexico, Indians must cultivate or feign ignorance of their culture,

16

something far more important than race. By defining as Indians only the linguistic survivors of a conquest with far broader cultural aims than extinguishing native languages, Mexico's official definition of Indianhood minimizes the importance of indigenous influences in contemporary life. In doing so, it culturally disenfranchises the majority population.

The evidence of wounded Indianhood is everywhere in Mexico. It's what the country is about. Indo-American values show themselves in a preference for art over technology, for local over national affairs, and for family duties over the call of wealth. Indian influence is evident in Mexican piety, in the cult of festivals, in forms of civic organization, in adoration of the dead, and in the persistence of herbalism and witchcraft. Just as Western civilization did not collapse when the barbarians sacked Rome, Indo-American civilization did not end when the Spaniards came. It merely learned to resist totalitarianism.

The Spanish Conquest was undoubtedly, and shamelessly, and nearly fatally, totalitarian. Mexico had experienced conquests before the Spaniards came. The Toltecs and the Aztecs had conquered their neighbors, and the Zapotecs and Mixtecs and Chinantecs were always at war. But there was a difference in the way that Indo-Americans and Europeans conquered. Even the brutal Aztecs did not dethrone the gods of conquered peoples. Instead, they required their subjects to add the supreme Aztec god, Huitzilopochtli, to their local pantheons. The Aztecs also demanded that subject peoples pay them tribute: cotton-producing areas, for example, sent cotton to the Aztec throne. But the Spaniards demanded that all other gods be disavowed, and instead of demanding tribute, they demanded the sort of transformation that we today call development. Mexico's economy was transformed from one with a *milpa* or cornfield base into one based on plantations and mines. The new economy was oriented not toward producing a small surplus of commodities for tribute, but to producing a great volume of chocolate, sugar, and dyes for export. The Aztecs had traded with northwestern peoples for gold, which they consumed only on a small scale, in the production of jewelry and religious artifacts. The Spaniards regarded gold as money, for which

17

there are no limits of use. In the span of a few years, they depleted most of Mexico's mineral veins. When the Aztecs conquered neighboring people, they left local kings on the throne, so long as tributes were paid. The Spaniards unseated the Indo-American hierarchy, granting power only to European-born subjects of the crown. In the name of God and development, the West subjected Mexico to a dehumanizing totalitarianism. Though several Indo-American rulers aided Cortés in his war with the Aztecs, the whole of Mexico soon repented of that, and the bitter experience of trust in the West, and in the sort of earthshaking change Cortés represented, is reflected even today in the adage "Better a known evil than an unknown good."

Five hundred years ago, with the Conquest, Mexico became a country in transition, from a Native American culture to the lifeways of the West. From the first, Mexico's rulers promoted policies to "modernize" the nation, placing her ever more distant from her roots. "Modernization"—actually, Europeanization—is the slogan of Mexico's leadership today. In the remaking of Mexico, they sometimes draw from a Spanish colonial toolbox, like the j of the Roman alphabet, and sometimes from a New World experience, like the x in Mexico. They have reshaped the country, but their efforts haven't yet made a fit. Mexican civilization is still rooted in corn, as much as the culture of Texas is rooted in wheat—not oil—and in the daily life of Mexico, native influences remain strong. If culture is more than language, then the conquest of Mexico by European values is not over—it is merely being waged from within. Mexico is a controversial country because it is a cultural battleground. It is not a "mix" so much as a stack, with a European upper layer and an Indo-American base, like the cathedrals on top of ancient Mexican pyramids. Mexico is a controversial country because it is a country at war with itself.

It is a place where giants stumble, continents collide, and history ignites, showering sparks across the hemisphere. The result of Mexican warfare, materially, has been what we Westerners regard as progress: highways, refineries, skyscrapers, and television. But on another level, what the war has produced is a nostalgic and fatalistic outlook that, contrary to what we normally assume, I take to be wisdom. The philosophy by which Mexico's common people live is what makes the country endure, and that philosophy, I believe, is one from which we can all learn.

—Dick J. Reavis
Xalapa, Veracruz

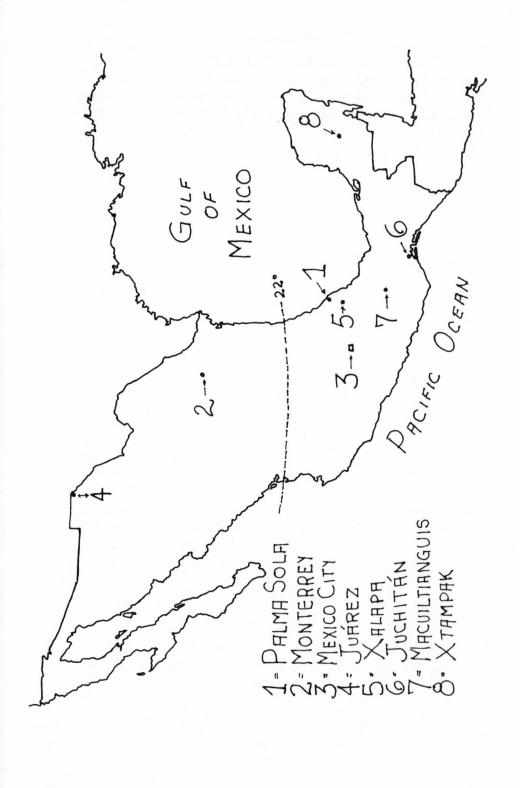

GULF
OF
MEXICO

PACIFIC OCEAN

22°

1 = PALMA SOLA
2 = MONTERREY
3 = MEXICO CITY
4 = JUÁREZ
5 = XALAPA
6 = JUCHITÁN
7 = MACUILTIANGUIS
8 = X TAMPAK

Return to Palma Sola

Iт is a hot, humid Tuesday in late June 1988. For ten years and ten months, I've been watching Mexico wrestle with the chimeras of change. I first watched from guerrilla and squatter camps as its last revolutionary movement declined. Now, I am in Palma Sola, a village on the coast of the state of Veracruz, watching a peaceful demonstration. It is supposed to be peaceful, anyway. But this morning the truckers ganged up to remove the obstacles that block the highway, and they'd have succeeded had the cowboys not rallied to the barricades. Some brows were bruised, but no blood has been shed here yet.

Black-bearded Juan Bozzano, a white-skinned man of thirty-six, is standing on an open patch of pavement about the size of a boxing ring between two trucks, surrounded by a group of drivers. He's wearing Bermuda shorts, thin sandals, and a broad-brimmed hat that he bought last week. His cheeks are flushed from the sunlight. You can tell at a glance that he doesn't belong here, either to the group of drivers, who all wear long pants and gimme caps, or to the local population, whose males are dark-skinned and weathered. Juan is one of those whom the locals call *los ecologistas*, and he's trying to convince the truckers that the antinuclear movement has good reasons for closing the highway.

His opponent in this discussion is a lanky thirty-year-old black Honduran, one of a dozen foreigners among the 150 travelers stranded here, about forty miles north of the city of Veracruz and four miles north of Laguna Verde, the coastal pond where Mexico is building its first nuclear-power plant. To protest rumors that the plant will be opened this year, on Sunday afternoon, forty-eight hours ago, villagers, cowboys, cattlemen, and a handful of outside agitators like Juan B. barricaded the highway leading into and out of the hamlet. Their blockade has halted traffic on the only passable road connecting cities on the Mexican Gulf Coast, the road that is also the main artery for traffic into Central America from the United States. The truckers can't turn around, because the roadbed is elevated and only two lanes wide. They can't go in reverse, because protracted backing is a maneuver too delicate for the double semitrailers in their ranks. Cars, pickups, and passenger buses can't leave, because they're walled in by the big trucks. Nearly one hundred freight haulers and more than twenty-five passenger vehicles are stranded at Palma Sola, and the demonstrators say that their blockade won't end until Mexico's president agrees to hear their arguments against the nuke. President Miguel de la Madrid has been refusing to meet with the *ecologistas* for nearly six years. Nobody expects him to change his mind overnight.

I know Juan B., although right now I'm trying to pretend that I don't. He owns a coffee house on General Zamora Street in Xalapa, the town where I'm living. The coffee house, called the Nahuál, sits between the bank where I cash travelers' checks and the post office, where I must go to claim the newspapers that come for me by mail but that carriers won't deliver. The Nahuál is a vegetarian restaurant, a bookstore, and a folk-art shop, in three rooms. It sells the works of Marx, Mao, and Bakunin, books of poetry and local history, silk-screened greeting cards, fabrics from Guatemala, and baskets from the Huasteca region. I stop in from time to time, just to take a look at the place. It's a typical hangout for Mexican artists, academics, and intellectuals. Juan B. falls into at least one of those cate-gories, because he has a university job and a graduate degree in economics.

I don't want the truckers to know that I'm on speaking terms with Juan because I'm afraid that they are going to attack him and I don't want to share his fate at their hands. I wouldn't defend Juan, not because of anything I do or don't believe about nuclear power, but because I am a foreigner and have no busi-ness taking sides in Mexican tiffs about current events. The Mexican Constitution makes that perfectly clear. "The right to associate or meet peacefully for whatever legal objective cannot be restricted," it says, "but only citizens of the Republic can . . . take part in the political affairs of the country." I'm worried about Juan because of the ire that I know that I'd feel if someone blocked a highway that I needed to travel, and because of the danger I believe that he faces for merely looking out of place. Juan B. doesn't look like a guy who with his knuckles could put new treads on a truck driver's face. The cowboys might jump in to protect him if a scuffle ensued, but I think it's more likely that they would merely laugh. None of them accompa-nied him out to this spot, and I think it's because they're not sure what Juan represents. They don't understand his looks. The cops don't, either, and if they or the army decide to end this blockade, Juan B. is a likely candidate for arrest. He stands out too much.

The blockade is patently illegal, even if it's called a protest. Even the Constitution says so. "The manifestation of ideas," it says, "will not be the object of any judicial or administration inquiry, except in cases where it attacks . . . the rights of third parties, provokes violations of the law, or disturbs the public order." The blockade violates what Mexicans call "the social peace," and Americans term "law and order." But that doesn't mean that any action will be taken soon, or ever. Violations of the social peace in Mexico have in recent years become frequent, and increasingly flagrant. For example, two weeks before the antinuke protestors took over Palma Sola, parents from Monterrey's Tierra y Libertad neighborhood, complaining of a shortage of classrooms for their children, occupied a nearby schoolhouse and barred its 604 students from entering. They were still holding the schoolhouse when the Palma Sola blockade began. In the years since 1968, such takeovers have rarely been repressed by government force. They are usually resolved by negotiations, and negotiations usually take weeks.

The nuclear project that has given rise to this confrontation has been the object of tamer protests for more than a decade. Twice before, the protestors have blockaded the highway, once for four hours, once for thirty-six. Their petitions and protests have not gained so much as an explanation of the plant's necessity. The controversy has been of the kind that brings even newspapers in cities seven hundred miles away to complain that ". . . in Mexico disinformation reaches frightful levels. Society was not consulted about the project; decisions were announced after contracts had been signed that called for the distribution of millions of dollars." What is publicly known about the plant is that it was started in response to a problem that no longer exists. From 1971 to 1974, for the first time in its history, Mexico briefly became a net importer of oil. Geologists at Pemex, the country's government-owned oil monopoly, were already mapping the offshore and coastal reserves that, after 1976, would establish Mexico as the world's fourth-ranked supplier of oil. But for what are vaguely described as "political reasons," the geologists at Pemex kept their findings a secret from Mexico's then-president, the unpopular Luis Echeverría. Alarmed by his country's apparent loss of energy independence, Echeverría approved a plan to transform Mexico's state-owned electric utility, the Federal Power Commission, into an agency based on nuclear, not thermoelectric, production. Equipment orders for Laguna Verde were signed in 1972. The first concrete was poured in 1976. Two years later, in anticipation of an agreement with the United States, the Mexicans began building a thousand-mile pipeline from Chiapas and Tabasco to the northern border. The pipeline carried natural gas that, its builders believed, would in Texas enter lines leading all the way to Chicago. But negotiations fell through. The pipeline got only as far north as Monterrey, where a few industrialists switched from coal to gas-fired operations to take advantage of cheap rates. Mexican natural gas was still being flared in the oil fields when pipeline crews finished work on the *gasoducto*, which on its way north passed a mere three hundred yards from the nuclear plant. Had reactors and other materials not already been delivered, Laguna Verde would probably have been fired by natural gas, and no protests would have been made.

The Laguna Verde plant, if it does become operational, will be powered by some 180 tons of enriched uranium, imported from the United States. Its physical plant includes twin General Electric reactors, each with a generating capacity of 654,000 kilowatts, and turbines from the Japanese firm Mitsubishi. Mexican ecologists say that the plant is a duplicate of one at Zimmer, Ohio, whose completion was abandoned when irremediable defects in construction were detected. They also say that boiling water reactors, or BWRs, like those supplied for Laguna Verde have in the intervening years become obsolete, for safety reasons. Spokesmen for the Federal Power Commission say that any obsolescence at Laguna Verde is the ecology movement's fault, not theirs: The First of Laguna Verde's two reactor units has been ready since 1982. Politics, they say, has been standing in the way of Mexico's development. Not only has Laguna Verde been kept waiting, but nuclear projects at other sites, including one in the border state of Sonora, have been put on hold indefinitely. Ecologists have raised the specter of Chernobyl, saying that an accident at Laguna Verde would make radiation's deleterious effects felt as far away as Oklahoma. The commission's nuclear engineers scoff at such "demagoguery." As one of them explained to me, "Our reactors at Laguna Verde are designed differently from those at Chernobyl. Our plant is more like yours at Harrisburg, in Pennsylvania. If the worst happens at Laguna Verde, it won't be anything like Chernobyl. It will be like Three Mile Island."

The protest at Palma Sola is important for reasons that don't meet the eye. On one level, it is merely an incident in the passage of current events. On another, far more fundamental level, it is a reenactment of the central drama of Mexico's modern history, which began in 1519 when Hernán Cortés and his conquistadores came to the Gulf Coast; in Mexico, nothing, but nothing, happens outside of a long historical context, because unlike the United States, Mexico wasn't born in a historical yesterday. To live in Mexico even today is to have conversations with Moctezuma, the Aztec who was emperor when Mexico fell to the west. Cortés and his soldiers founded Villa Rica, the first Hispanic settlement in New Spain, today a fishing village three miles south of the plant. Tourists don't visit Villa Rica, because there are no monuments or markers there, only a set of neglected ruins. There are no monuments anywhere in Mexico to Hernán Cortés, because literate Mexicans hate him, for reasons that became apparent almost as soon as he dropped anchor in the waters just south of the projected nuclear plant.

His coming had been anticipated by the Mexicans. Two years earlier, an expedition led by Juan de Grijalva had anchored off the coast, and a humble eyewitness had gone running directly to Emperor Moctezuma's palace with a jarring report: "Our lord, forgive me my boldness," he said, "but on the shores of the Great Sea I have seen a small mountain, floating on water. It moved about, never touching the shore. Our lord, no man has ever seen the like of this." The humble witness was correct, insofar as Meso-America's knowledge of the world went: The Aztecs had never seen a sailing ship. The sail was, for them, a new technology, as nuclear power is for Mexicans today.

Scouts dispatched by Moctezuma returned with the additional report that the floating "mountains" or "towers" were inhabited. "Strange men have come to the Great Sea," a scout told the Aztec court. "They were fishing with rods and a net. Then, they returned to their towers out on the sea. We saw fifteen men, some with blue garments and some with red, and others in black and green. . . . They wore red bands on their heads, or fine scarlet bonnets, or large round hats, for the sun."

The description of the men from the "towers" connected the sightings to a second source of anticipation, that of religious prophecy. Among the important gods of Toltec origin that the formerly barbaric Aztecs had included in their own pantheon was Quetzalcóatl, the Plumed Serpent. Quetzalcóatl was at various levels of discourse a priest, philosopher, king, and a god. The historical figure whom he represented was believed to have been a Toltec priest of unusual piety who, among other things,

26

had once passed four years, and later, seven years, in lonely meditations. Friar Diego Durán in his 1581 report, *Historia de las Indias de Nueva España*, reconstructed Quetzalcóatl's routine from surviving legends:

> He had as a duty building altars and chapels for all the neighborhoods, and putting images on their walls, upon the altars. . . . And he would bend on his knees before them and reverence them, and kiss the dirt, sometimes with his mouth and sometimes with his hand, the exercise of which was a complete prayer. . . . He always slept at the base of the altar.

But Quetzalcóatl was not only pious, he was also unorthodox. He did not put stock in the putative powers of human sacrifice. Despite his heresy, in A.D. 977 the Toltec elite elected him to rule. For reasons that remain clouded in the mixture of pre-Conquest history and myth, he was a few years afterward dethroned, or by some accounts resigned after becoming drunk and copulating for the first time, some legends say, with his own sister. In any case, Quetzalcóatl left central Mexico where the Toltecs had reigned, and according to Aztec versions of the tale, either immolated himself and became the planet Venus, or put out to sea in a canoe. He promised, or threatened, to return at the head of an army, to establish a new regime. Friar Durán recorded that:

> He prophesized the coming of strange people, that from the east would come to this land, with a strange suit of different colors, dressed from feet to head and with coverings on their heads, and that that punishment would be sent by God to repay the bad treatment and offense they had given him. . . . With that punishment, children and adults would perish at the hands of those who came to destroy them, even if they hid in caves. . . . He also told them that they wouldn't see the coming of those people, nor would their children, but only the fourth or fifth generation. . . .

In light of these prophecies, Aztec astronomer-priests expected Quetzalcóatl to return in the year *Ce Atl*, or 1-Reed. Juan Grijalva's exploratory mission did not cause panic not only

27

because his men did not establish themselves ashore, but also because he came in the year 12-Rabbit. *Ce Atl* wasn't due to reappear on the cyclical Aztec calendar until 1519, the year that Cortés landed. Moctezuma and his priests were also convinced that Cortés was Quetzalcóatl for the same reasons that colonial missionaries confused him with Saint Thomas. He met the description legend had left: He was opposed to human sacrifice, and like the Quetzalcóatl of myth, he had white skin and a long beard.

Within a week after Cortés dropped anchor, Moctezuma was given drawings and detailed descriptions of the conquistadores and their ships. He ordered that a lode known as the Treasure of Quetzalcóatl, ceremonial objects and regalia that had been kept in trust for the departed king, be taken to the coast. The presents included jade bracelets with gold bells, a mask inlaid with turquoise, animal figurines of gold, jade earrings, a serpent wand, and even a golden bow and arrow. The emperor's messengers also presented cotton cloths, chocolate, corn, and tobacco, products unknown in Europe at the time. But after examining the treasure, Cortés remarked, "Is this all? Is this your gift? Is this how you greet people?" Then he ordered the emissaries bound in chains, so that they would not take flight while his soldiers demonstrated the majesty of the West: cannons, crossbows, muskets, and horses, all them unknown in the Mexico of that age.

But the Spaniards were secretly pleased with the treasure, in a way that their Aztec hosts could not have fathomed. Bernal Díaz, a soldier in the group, wrote in his memoirs:

> The various objects were placed on mats, which they call *petates*, on which were spread other cotton cloths. The first was a disk in the shape of the sun, as big as a cartwheel and made of very fine gold. It was a marvelous thing engraved with many sorts of figures and, as those who afterward weighed it reported, was worth more than ten thousand pesos. There was another, larger disk of brightly shining silver in the shape of the moon, with other figures on it, and this was worth a great deal, for it was very heavy. Quintalbor also brought back the helmet full of small grains of gold, just as they come from the mines and worth three thousand pesos. The gold in the helmet was worth

more than twenty thousand pesos to us, because it proved to us that there were good mines in the country.

The Spaniards appreciated the treasure's cash value, as their weighings showed. The helmet of golden grains was prized because it promised wealth and development for New Spain. But they had no sincere appreciation for their role in Indo-American cosmology. They had not come to restore the grandeur of the Toltecs, but to abolish paganism, and with it, all those Indo-American cultural traits that stood in the way of their plan for riches. Cortés and his lieutenants took stock of the legend of Quetzalcóatl only because it was militarily advantageous. It gave them nearly free passage, and had they not later provoked the Aztecs to rebel, the Conquest would have been mostly a homecoming celebration. When, several months later, Cortés and his troops, both Indian and Spanish, arrived at the Aztec capital, Moctezuma greeted them with these words:

"Our lord, you are tired from your journeys, but now you are here. You have arrived at your city, Mexico. You have come to sit upon your throne; you have come to sit beneath the canopy.

"The lords who have gone before, they were your representatives who guarded and preserved it for your coming again. . . .

"Do these rulers know the destiny of those they have left behind? Are they watching now? If only they might see what I now see:

"This is not a dream. I do not walk in my sleep. . . . I have seen you at last; I have met you face-to-face. I was in agony for many days, with my eyes fixed on the region of Mystery. But now you have come to sit on your throne.

"This was foretold by the rulers who governed your city, and now it has come to pass. You have come back. Rest now, and take possession of your royal house. . . ."

Moctezuma's welcoming speech may have hidden his angst, but he was not a happy man. He was bitterly resigned. When the porters of the treasure of Quetzalcóatl had returned from the coast, they had told him about the instrument that shot out sparks and made a deafening roar and gave off an odor like rotting mud and could destroy a mountain or tree. They also told him, "They have deer which carry them wherever they wish to go. Our lord, those deer are as tall as the roof of a house!" Upon hearing these reports, the Aztec emperor uttered the words that would inaugurate modern Mexican life: "What will happen? Will anyone outlive this? Ah, once I was content, but now I feel death in my heart." Those same formulations— "What Will Happen?" "Will Anyone Outlive This?" "I Feel Death in My Heart"—could well have been used as slogans for the protest at Laguna Verde. They are the slogans of Mexico's contemporary life. The demonstrators at Palma Sola may not be right about the dangers of nuclear power, but they voice the fears of Mexico's ancients, and probably the consensus of its present. The protestors are the Aztecs; the nuke forces, conquistadores from the West.

"Mexico was born of the negation of modernity," says its leading thinker, Octavio Paz. For nearly five hundred years, ever since the Conquest, powerful undercurrents of Mexican life have resisted the techno-centered culture of the West. Mexico's leaders, on the other hand, educated in the Western tradition, have meanwhile prodded their country down the road of modernization: The mystery is that they've done so while being selected by an electoral process. Mexico's modernization has yielded fruit—nobody in Palma Sola complains about having electricity or penicillin, after all—but it isn't overwhelmingly popular, because it's essentially exogenous. Technology is an alien element in the culture, like nutmeg on eggnog or cinnamon in a cup of *atole*. It's a good flavoring, but it's not basic. Mexico has never prided itself on nonagricultural technological innovations; it has adapted to them.

The attitude that most Mexicans take toward machine technology was explained to me by a Mexican intellectual I had known during his political exile in France and the United States. "You Americans," he once chided me, "build greenhouses so that you can have flowers all year around. You think you've done a good thing, but actually, what you've done is to devalue flowers." The critique poses a problem that can't be easily dis-

missed. Mexicans adapt to nature, while technology treats nature as a field for conquest.

The relationship between Mexicans and technology is evident in the simplest of things; for example, in the coins that they use. Mexico's one-, ten-, twenty-, fifty-, and hundred-peso coins, on the face sides, all carry raised metal dots, stating the face value of the coins in Braille. It's a nice sentiment, and a rare one: Compassion is a pronounced characteristic of Mexicans, especially of those in the humbler classes. But the blind don't need the Braille dots to determine the value of coins—they can judge by size—and nobody can feel the dots on the Mexican coins, anyway: the dots are too small. Bigger dots would make the Braille markings readable with the fingertips, but Mexico's coin designers haven't made the change. When

31

one feels the coins, one feels the faces of national heroes. And that's the way life is in Mexico. People are willing to take advantage of technology, especially in ways that touch the heart. X rays, tape players, photographs, and holographic images are treasured, but nobody takes pride in ball-bearing plants. Mexico's cities are industrialized, and can manufacture almost anything the economy needs. But no matter what Mexican technology produces, its quality is almost always inferior to that of the same goods more cheaply sold in the United States and the Orient. As with the Braille-coded coins, it's the thought, and not perfection, that counts. And also as with the coins, the utility or purpose of other things may be dim or poorly expressed, but government leaders and heroes remain prominent. Their images don't wear or fade.

Mexican culture's solace and pride has not been technology, but art, architecture, religion, and color. It's difficult to discourse on topics as subjective and grand as art and religion—though I'll try to deal with the latter at several points in this book—but Mexico's fascination with color is obvious to any passerby. Mexico is a place where cotton candy, Q-Tips, file folders, brooms, and disposable diapers come in six colors, and where houses are not preferably white. It's a place where the plastic flotation balls used in commodes are sold in stripes and swirls of a half-dozen pastel shades, and where young women paint their eyelids with two tones of eye shadow, sky blue or pale purple below, pink above. Technology has contributed to Mexico's culture in many ways, but in recent years its most obvious gift has been fluorescent spray paint. Posterboard signs in Mexico glow in pinks and greens.

Many Westernized Mexicans try to picture their country as a technological power of the first rank, and when they do, they rarely fail to mention that one of their countrymen concocted the world's first color-television set. That's true, but when you think about it, even that was an innovation of an aesthetic kind. Most Mexicans regard machinery only as most Americans regard art: as necessary but not nice; not as meriting a sacrifice but as impossibly overpriced. The plan for a nuclear plant at Laguna Verde tapped a fear of technology that is a factor even in the gadget-happy United States, and in Mexico it tapped a deep and ancient wellspring. The politicians and engineers responsible for the plant may have foresight and wisdom, but like the conquistadores, they do not have an appreciation for their role in popular demonology, where they are viewed as merely new conquerors, with a yet more terrible technology, as the destroyers of Laguna Verde, or the Green Lagoon, and the builders of Laguna Muerte, Death Lagoon. The Federal Power Commission might have made a stronger case for its plant had it adorned its massive walls with a mural depicting the wonders of the atom, or had it established an information center at Palma Sola. But in true centralist fashion, the FPC instead placed its information center in the comfy capital of Xalapa, a hundred miles from the danger site.

Leaders of the antinuke demonstration say that timing is their greatest strength. Mexico's 1988 presidential elections are only two weeks away. Two candidates for the presidency have called for suspending work on the plant until a referendum on its future can be held. The candidate of the incumbent or ruling party, the Partido Revolucionario Institucional, or PRI, has thus far kept mum, but the *ecologistas* don't think that he can hold out for long. They say, and they're probably right, that the majority of the people in the state of Veracruz are opposed to the plant. Xalapa is draped in red plastic bows, the symbols of opposition to the nuke. The state's governor has not promoted the plant, and he is a rising figure in the PRI. The *ecologistas* believe that the governor's agents will persuade the PRI's candidate that in order to carry Veracruz in the elections of July 6, he'll have to declare his opposition to the Laguna Verde plant. The blockade is radical in a tactical sense, but on another level it's merely an attempt to influence a candidate.

But timing works against the protest, too. The national newspapers have assigned their best reporters to the presidential campaign. No television crews have come to Palma Sola yet, and only two out-of-state reporters have stopped in, both on Sunday, during a break in one nominee's schedule. The blockade at Palma Sola is causing financial losses—coastal bus lines, for example, have canceled their routes—but it is largely being ignored in the national press, because it is not on the itinerary of any office seeker.

Timing also works against the blockade because *el año de hidalgo* is coming around again, as it does every six years. *El año de hidalgo* means "year of the nobleman," but there's nothing noble about it. The term is a sardonic reference to the period between the July elections and December 1 of every presidential year, the period between the day a new president is elected and the day the incumbent leaves office. Americans refer to outgoing presidents as "lame ducks," but there's nothing lame about the Mexican presidency, especially during the last days of a president's term. During his 1976 *año de hidalgo*, for example, President Luis Echeverría took lands from the rich and gave them to the poor with such indiscretion that his successor, José López Portillo, felt compelled to nullify the repartitions with a Constitutional amendment. During his own *año hidalgense*, in 1982, Portillo nationalized Mexico's banks. If the blockade presents antinuke forces with their best chance to influence policy, it probably presents them with their last chance, too. Unless the PRI's candidate declares opposition, President de la Madrid can be expected to open the plant before his *año de hidalgo* ends.

"What we want to know," the Honduran trucker demands of Juan B., "is why you had to close the highway. Why didn't you go to the gates of the plant? That's where the problem is."

"My friend," Juan B. says, "we are sorry that this delay had to touch you, but we can't go to the plant. You will see it when you leave here, going south. Please note, when you do, that it is thick with soldiers, carrying machine guns. We are a nonviolent movement, and we don't want anybody to get hurt."

The Honduran doesn't blurt out the word "cowards," but it is lunging against his mind. He's concerned about getting home on time, not about the safety of protestors. He has reason to be concerned: Mexican border officials are strict with Central Americans, and they've given him only three days to make his transit. When he reaches the southern border, what explanation will he give for his tardiness, and how much in bribe money will it cost him to buy belief?

The Honduran backs out of the discussion to cool his smoldering rage in the shady valley between the lanes of parked trucks. Silence comes over the group when he leaves, because the Mexican truckers have little to say. They understand too much about the situation to regard it with anything other than fatalism. I've made an acquaintanceship with one of them, and I ask what is on his mind.

"I don't like it," he says, "because this affair is costing me money; they pay me by the load, you see. But what can we do? These demonstrators won't give up until the government gives in, so it's a case of the stubborn against the bullheaded. The majority is supposed to rule in this country, but who is that?"

The Mexican trucker doesn't know—nobody in Palma Sola is aware—but new forces are coming into play as he speaks. Other Mexican truckers are parking their rigs across the highway at Cardel, about twenty miles south of Palma Sola, and at El Viejón, a truck-stop town two miles south of the plant. They tell policemen and reporters that the object of their "counterblockade" is to cut off the local traffic that has allowed people in the Palma Sola environs to go about their daily affairs, shopping in Cardel, for example, without much inconvenience. But the counterblockade doesn't make any sense: What it really is, is an expression of the drivers' generalized disgust. They want to get moving, they're irritated that the protestors have blocked them and displeased that the government has allowed the confrontation to develop. It is get-mad and get-even time, and the truckers don't care whose interests they hinder.

Their actions have helped the protestors' cause. The truckers have cut off access to Laguna Verde from the south. Now, it is sealed in both directions, inside a three-mile radius. The southern or truckers' cut is more important than that made by the antinuke protestors, because power-commission executives, hotshot specialists, and most building materials come to the plant by the southern route, on roads feeding in from the port of Veracruz. Laguna Verde's blue-collar workers live in a federal housing camp at Palma Sola, and despite the blockade, nobody has prevented them from walking to work. But when the southern route is blockaded, the managers suspend operations at the plant.

The decision to halt work is not merely of local importance. It undoubtedly brings neutrals into the fray. Building the nuclear plant to its present state of readiness has cost the Mexican government from $2 billion to $6 billion, depending upon whose estimate is accepted, that of the Federal Power Commission or that of the *ecologistas*. In either case, every hour of delay is expensive. The interest alone charged on an investment of $2 billion comes to about $1 million a day.

Despite rumors about the plant shutdown, when Tuesday night comes, it's like any other night in Palma Sola during the blockade, like the night of a saint's day celebration or a harvest fair. There's been no traffic on Palma Sola's main street since Sunday, because blockades were set up on both ends of town. From the back of a pickup parked in the middle of the street, cattlemen's wives dispense barbecue and tacos to everyone. The truckers have been surviving on this somewhat luxurious dole, three meals a day, ever since the blockade began. At night the main street fills with peasants and their damsels, who come to town for the dances. A band is playing *música tropical* at the blockade on the north end of the street. It draws townie teenagers and a few truckers, too. At the town's southern blockade, there's a "people's band" composed of two trumpeters and a saxophonist in their sixties, and a drummer, eleven years old. It attracts a handful of aging and potbellied women, and a horde of high-spirited cowboy onlookers. Stores along the highway stay open late to serve the festive crowd, and a few of the town's merchants raise their prices to prey on those who fear that the village will soon run out of its supplies of everything.

The trucks are parked just beyond the blockades, in long files, one truck in each lane, with a passageway in between, marked by the road's white line. Every few hours, both night and day, I walk the truckers' alleyways. They smell like rubber, from the trucks' big tires. The southern alley is shorter, not more than ten trucks in length, and most of its drivers spend their time on the northern alley, three times as long. Drivers on both ends have stretched hammocks beneath their trailers, for napping in the shade. Most of them sleep in their cabs at night, though on the north end a Salvador-bound yellow school bus from Texas has become a sort of hotel. On Monday and Tuesday morning, most of the Mexican drivers take advantage of their idleness by washing their cabs, using buckets of water they filled at a roadside ditch. At night they squat on the pavements beneath the front and rear ends of their rigs, playing cards beneath their headlights or listening to cassette tapes of comedy routines. But the foreigners don't do any of those things. They cluster in small knots, whispering and plotting revenge. Two of them, a Salvadoran and a Spanish-speaking American, point out to me the transformers on Palma Sola's electric lines. If the blockade continues, they say, they're going to put out Palma Sola's lights.

The truckers have an aura in Palma Sola, because they're the heroes of contemporary myth. Most adults in Mexico read comic books, and one of the more popular series is the weekly *Traileros*, a comic of fantasies of the road. A current issue, for example, tells the story of a muscular and lucky young man named Roberto, on his first run as a professional driver. Roberto's orders are to drive a route from Mexico City to Nuevo Laredo, on the northern border. Though he's not supposed to pick up hitchhikers, Roberto is moved by the plight of an old peasant named Julián, who says that he has to go north to pay his last respects to a dying son. While he and Julián are drinking coffee at a truck stop, Roberto encounters an attractive young brunette whose car has malfunctioned. Roberto repairs the malfunction, and when the young woman offers to pay, he asks for a kiss. After a first embrace, the brunette suggests that they climb into the sleeper of Roberto's cab. According to the drawings, they undress, and the comic's text says that "after the moon and stars have returned to their places," both go their separate ways. But Roberto's journey north is delayed again, both when he takes a doctor to deliver a poor woman's baby, and when he stops to deliver a few blows to two thieves who are attempting to hijack another trucker's trailer. Roberto is sure that he'll be fired when he pulls into Nuevo Laredo, because

37

he arrives seven hours late. Instead, he learns that Julián, the old man he aided, was really the company's owner in disguise, and that the young woman who undressed in his cab was really Laura, the company's personnel chief. "You are an undisciplined rebel and an unredeemed womanizer," Roberto's boss tells him, "but you are honorable, charitable, and gentlemanly, too."

The truckers know that tales like these are rank fantasy, but of course they feel complimented by descriptions of them as "undisciplined rebel and unredeemed womanizer . . . honorable, charitable and gentlemanly," and they try to play the part. If nothing else, the myth provides them with dancing partners at Palma Sola, whose young women don't have wide experience at distinguishing grim realities from myth. With their cabs washed and their dancing boots shined, the younger truckers enjoy themselves as the nights pass.

At least one bachelor is among the truckers, a young man in his early twenties, lean and handsome. A girlfriend has found him, a young woman about sixteen who lives in a plastered little house on the north side of the road, about one hundred yards from where the bachelor's rig is parked. Each evening he showers and shaves, and puts on the jeans and western shirt that he will wear to the dance. She dons a Sunday dress of white slinky nylon, puts on her white high heels, and comes to the door of his truck. The bachelor and his driving partner play tapes and sip soft drinks while she chats with them. After the dance she and the bachelor driver return to the cab. The driver sits down inside, and the young woman stands in the open doorway, illuminated by the cab's interior lights. She won't take a seat, because her parents are watching from the house at roadside.

But most of the people who are in Palma Sola because of the blockade are cowboys and cattlemen. It's easy to see that the Palma Sola cowboys aren't like the guys pictured in western comic books. They come into town on foot, not horseback. They come in groups of four, six, or eight, not in ones and twos. They don't have felt hats, either white or black. They wear weatherbeaten straw hats with rounded crowns and narrow, curled brims. Some are shod in sandals with car-tire soles.

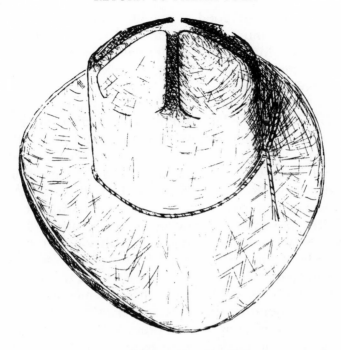

Veracruz Cowboy Hat

Others wear black ankle-high boots with elastic panels on the sides, like British rockers of the sixties. Though a motel has opened two of its rooms for showering and changing clothes, the cowboys didn't bring towels, shaving gear, or extra shirts. After a couple of days on Palma Sola's sunny streets, they look like urban winos. They sleep shoulder-to-shoulder, like dogs, under canopies that are stretched over the sidewalks. Their job is to protect the blockade, in case the truckers should try to break through. Some of them stand guard by day, others by night. Those I talk to admit that they came to Palma Sola because their bosses sent them. They are not conversant about nuclear power, and none of them knows what an atom is. On Sunday one of the reporters approached a cowboy who was holding a sign that said "WE DON'T WANT ANOTHER CHERNOBYL." The reporter asked if the cowboy knew where Chernobyl was.

39

"No, sir, I'm not too good at reading," the cowboy said. It wouldn't matter much if he could read. Rural mail delivery does not exist in Mexico, and there are no bookstores anywhere near. A few newspapers and a lot of comic books are received in Palma Sola, nothing more.

The cattlemen are decked out in narrow-brimmed hats, pastel *guayaberas*, unscuffed boots, and pressed khaki pants. They feel like the generals of this protest, and they act the part: After all, they've provided damn near everything. The pickups and canopies that make the blockades are theirs. The meeting hall where decisions are made belongs to the Cattlemen's Association. The telephone where the *ecologistas* confer with the press and police, and even the cowboy sentinels, are under their control. The whole show is theirs, and they're not averse to taking credit, or buying it. When they spot officials or *ecologistas* at tables in Palma Sola's cafés, they pass word to the managements that the tabs will be paid. The cattlemen are aware of the issues surrounding the plant, and they're opposed partly because the government has not promised to indemnify them if their herds are irradiated. "If an accident happened, I'd have to sell my ranch," one of them complains. "Who would buy it? And where would I get more land?" What he doesn't say is that because ranching requires relatively vast acreages, most Mexican ranches sit on lands that legally belong to dozens of owners, not one. Putting a ranch together is a process that takes years of effort and successive evasions of agrarian-reform laws. In Mexico, ranches can't be bought and sold overnight.

One of the cattlemen repeats to me what the *ecologistas* have said, a charge that condemns the plant on nationalistic grounds. It is founded in a rumor that the electricity produced at Laguna Verde will be channeled to the *maquiladoras* on the northern border, more than a day's drive away. The *maquilas* are foreign, mainly Japanese- and American-owned plants that produce goods only for export to the United States. In the *maquilas*, Mexicans become a part of the American economy, at a substandard or Mexican wage. "Hah, we're building this plant," the rancher says, "so that your countrymen can buy microwave ovens and toys and car parts cheap. If you'd keep your industry within your own damn borders, we wouldn't have to face this risk." There is nothing I can say to exculpate the United States without criticizing the Mexican government as well, because it, too, is a party to the *maquila* plan. I shrug my shoulders and slink away, because in Mexico, when politics are discussed, it's hard for Americans to present a defense. We *have* extended our ideas and our enterprises around the globe, while the Mexicans have largely stayed at home.

About eleven o'clock Tuesday night, the *ad hoc* Anti-Nuclear Blockade Committee of Palma Sola, a group of nine, mostly cattlemen and area gentry, agrees to hear demands from the truckers. I stand in a group of drivers at a window on the north end of the cattlemen's hall, listening to the discussion inside. A broad-faced Salvadoran is doing most of the talking for the truckers. His manner is rude. He says that the blockade is unjust and he bemoans the loss of perishable cargoes—three trucks carrying mangoes are involved—and when a committeeman begins making the *pro forma* responses to these complaints, the Salvadoran bellows, "You guys are just buying time!"—and stomps out. A few Mexicans follow him, but they are quickly replaced by men from the group outside.

A man in a beige polyester suit and a light blue tie rises to speak. He is a representative of the Mexican transport workers union. Though the Blockade Committee has banned the sales of alcoholic beverages, the driver at my shoulder has somehow managed to get drunk. He curses and shouts at the union rep, "Sit down! You don't speak for us!" Others in the crowd join in the protest. The union man is undoubtedly tied to the government, and no one believes that his words can be trusted. He is saying that with his assistance, the truckers can file criminal charges against the committee's members, bringing about arrests, and presumably the reopening of the highway. But nobody is impressed. The committeemen show no fear, and the truckers no interest.

After more than an hour of discussion, a Mexican in jeans and a gimme cap rises at the east end of the meeting table. He's tall and gaunt, and there's a three-day beard on his face. He doesn't remove his cap, but from the deliberate, paced manner in which he speaks, it is obvious that he believes that he

41

is speaking for all Mexicans present, with offense to no one. "Gentlemen," he begins, "we have borne with you. As you have reminded us, we have kept *la patria*, our Mexico, foremost in mind. But we have been here for nearly sixty hours. We have done our part. We have contributed to your cause. Now, let us go in peace. Continue your blockade, but against somebody else. Let another group of truckers take their turn."

There is a murmur in the crowd at the window. The truckers are expressing their approval. I sense that they're going to cheer the gaunt driver, but their congratulations remain at a hum. Everybody wants to hear what the committeemen will say.

There's an old cattleman on the committee known to the drivers as Don Sirenio. He's potbellied and bowed, slow-moving and wary. He's said little to the truckers during this blockade, but he's almost always in sight, buttonholing a cattleman or cowboy. Don Sirenio shifts his straw hat atop his gray head, then turns in his chair toward the driver, who has taken a seat. "Gentlemen," the old man grunts, "we represent different groups, with different interests. We shall never come to an agreement." Then he turns the other way, toward a committeeman. "There's no sense in continuing to talk," he says, "Let's call it a night."

The Mexican truckers gather outside, more than forty strong. Anger isn't their mood. They trade commentaries. Most of them say that nothing is ever produced by talks, anyway. A federal highway policemen sidles into the group, and from him they learn of an event that sends most them to the cabs of their trucks nearly splitting with laughter. The police, it seems, have persuaded the counterblockaders at El Viejón to give up their action. The truckers from Viejón have brought their rigs into the file of stranded vehicles on Palma Sola's south side. The only trouble is, three highway patrol cars were parked at the end of that file. All three are now blocked in by the rigs from Viejón. For once, the truckers have the patrolmen under detention, and until this blockade is over, the cops will sleep on car-seat beds.

After the truckers and cattlemen have adjourned, I sit down to supper with Juan B., in a restaurant that has stayed open to

42

serve the crowd. He is tired and depressed. He left a wife and child back in Xalapa, and he doesn't know when he'll see them again. Dissension has developed inside the Blockade Committee, too. Juan advocated letting the trapped truckers pass, then replacing the blockades. Members of the committee snubbed him, and now treat him, he says, like an agent of the police. His friends on the committee are having their difficulties, too. The cattlemen don't defer to them: It's a case of urban intellectuals against country folk. The cattlemen treat the *ecologistas* like errand boys and peasants, the *ecologistas* regard the cattlemen as rubes. Trust is wearing thin.

On Wednesday morning, the Mexican truckers clean their batteries and cables, merely to pass the time. But while they are diddling away with as much nonchalance as possible, the restless foreigners, most of whom have worn out their welcome among the resigned nationals, are deciding to take separate action, on their own. About noon they rendezvous at the cattlemen's hall to sign petitions asking their embassies to intervene. One of them, an American from New Jersey, asks me to sign, too. But I refuse, on two grounds. The first is that I've developed a sense of Mexico, one that tells me that foreign tinkerings always sound a sour note with officialdom, and I want to stay clear of those guys. The second is that I'm not really stranded here, as my countrymen think. On Sunday night, I drove my Volkswagen through a space between a truck and a ditch. I slept in my bed at home. Monday night I piloted down the alleyway between the lines of trucks and slept at a motel fifty miles up the road. Tuesday I parked my car at a ranch house well out of the way of the blockade. I came to town, had lunch at a restaurant, and rented a room. Others may be suffering here, but I'm not even trapped. I've slept and eaten well in Palma Sola, and I believe that I can leave whenever I want.

To my surprise, both the *ecologistas* and the police welcome the foreign petitions. They go to radios and telephones, relaying the appeals to embassies and the press. Perhaps both sides believe that foreign pressures will aid their causes, but more likely, everybody is ready to go home. The blockade has begun to inconvenience even the locals. Palma Sola is waiting for the inevitable, whatever that might be.

Twenty years have passed between Tlatelolco and the Palma Sola blockade. The cowboys at Palma Sola are lucky, because they don't know what Tlatelolco means. The *ecologistas* know, and they worry, in an almost romantic way. On the night of October 2, 1968, thousands of mainly student demonstrators gathered on Tlatelolco Plaza in Mexico City to hear speeches from leaders who were protesting almost everything: the infringement of university autonomy, anticommunist laws, curbs on labor activity. Troops ringed the plaza and opened fire, killing from three hundred to five hundred. An accurate death count could not be made, because the soldiers whisked their victims away. Demonstrators were attacked again in June 1971, and after that the kidnapping and disappearance of dissidents began. Upon taking office, President de la Madrid had freed some two thousand political prisoners, but nobody in opposition circles was yet ready to breathe sighs of relief: In March a former soldier testified that between 1978 and 1983, when he fled the country, he had participated in the clandestine executions of more than a hundred dissidents, all of whom had been kidnapped, jailed, and killed without facing formal charges. Amnesty International's last report had said that political prisoners were still being held in Mexico, and in Palma Sola the *ecologistas* talked about the possibility that a Tlatelolco could happen again.

When the shooting began on the night of October 2, the leaders of the demonstration were not on the plaza, with the people. They were on the third story of the Chihuahua apartment building, looking down. The chief spokesmen for the movement of '68 were being sought by the police, and on the upper floors of the Chihuahua building they felt safe, because they could control access to the stairways. But they weren't safe. Military units occupied the building, took the stairways, and arrested the leaders, who spent their next years in prison.

Most of the deaths occurred on the plaza, where the people were. Many of the victims, including children, were residents

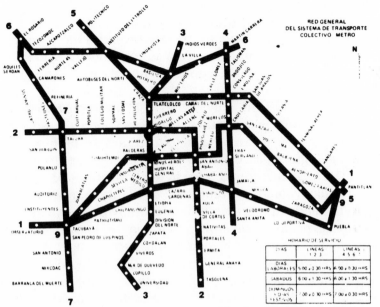

Mexico City Metro System

of the area, people who'd stopped to see the demonstration from motives of mere curiosity. When the shooting started, their instinct was to run. From the third story of the apartment building, the demonstration's leaders could not sense that shots were being fired, and with bullhorns they exhorted the masses to stand their ground. People ran anyway. Most of them ran toward the apartment towers. Some of them slipped inside the buildings to ask for shelter with strangers. Most residents did not answer the knocks on their doors. Several hundred demonstrators ran behind the buildings and escaped onto the streets around the neighborhood. Others tried to enter the cathedral —but a priest bolted its door. A few of the demonstrators jumped down into the ruins, and some ran through the ruins to the thoroughfare on the west; among the stones that their ancestors had laid, those demonstrators found a shelter from the carnage that was being wreaked above. Most of the Tlatelolco dead were commoners in the political hierarchy of the opposition, people who exposed themselves to both a leader-

45

ship and the state on a patch of modern, open political terrain. The lesson that Mexico drew was that open and peaceful resistance was suicidal. Only in the late seventies did Mexicans venture to protest again. As at Palma Sola, nobody who knew the country's history joined a protest without experiencing feelings of dread.

But dread wasn't the only feeling that was spoken among the demonstrators. Some of them expressed hope, though only by telling the type of story that is told around a campfire when people have grown accustomed to one another and the hour is late. The *ecologistas* found hope in the type of legend that not many people would repeat in broad daylight, because its worthiness depends upon something practically unknowable. Or, to be more precise, something that can be known only by closed-mouth PRIistas, Castristas, and perhaps agents of the CIA. The story was that in 1956, when Fidel Castro Ruz and Che Guevara Lynch were preparing their invasion of Cuba, they and some thirty followers were arrested by agents of Gobernación, Mexico's Interior Ministry. They were charged with violating Mexican gun-control laws. The case of the Cuban conspirators was placed in the hands of Gobernación's subdivision for political crimes, and, in particular, in the hands of a political-crimes expert, Capitán Fernando Gutiérrez Barrios. The Cubans were released under the capitán's supervision, and according to the legend, the Cubans won him to their cause. They were able to rearm and launch their successful attack, in part, the legend said, because Gutiérrez Barrios aided them or looked the other way. Capitán Gutiérrez Barrios had remained at Gobernación until 1986. That's when he had become governor of Veracruz. He was governor in 1988. The *ecologistas* believed that Gobernador Gutiérrez Barrios was still a great friend of Fidel Castro, and although he was a member of the PRI, they believed that he secretly sympathized with all movements of protest. Some of them expected Gutiérrez Barrios to lobby for them, and to protect them from massacre and arrest.

About sunup Thursday morning, eighty-six hours after the blockade began, cowboy guards and a couple of sleepless *ecologistas* in Palma Sola heard the muffled sounds of marching feet. They woke their comrades in great alarm. As they did, two lone men came running into Palma Sola, waving machetes. Both ran north, on opposite sides of the highway that is the town's main street. Hardly breaking their pace, they sliced the ropes that supported the canopies that the demonstrators had hung over the sidewalks and street. By the time the two men reached the north side of Palma Sola, some three hundred soldiers and state policemen had marched into town, all from the south. The protestors fell to their knees, symbolizing surrender. The men in uniform ignored them. Instead, with only the strength of their strong backs, the force of law and order lifted aside the vehicles that had formed the blockade. Twelve minutes after the military operation had begun, traffic was moving again. Seeing that they would not be shot, the protestors rose to their feet. As the trucks rolled past, the demonstrators intoned the national anthem. Some of the truckers waved and honked their horns, whether tauntingly or in friendship, no one could tell. The protest was over, and no arrests were made.

I had not stayed for the finale, because I hadn't known when it would come. Instead, I'd left with Juan. To create a second focus of protest, antinuke activists in Mexico City had camped on the Zócalo, a plaza facing the National Palace. On Wednesday afternoon, Juan B. had persuaded his *ecologista* cronies to let him go to Xalapa, spend a night with his family, and then go on to Mexico City, as a messenger to the movement there. I'd volunteered to drive him back to Xalapa. With us rode a young architect from Mexico City, a victim of the blockade. On Sunday afternoon, he, his wife and infant daughter, and a couple of in-laws had been trapped. The young architect had sent the others out on foot, and he presumed that by hitchhiking they had reached Xalapa, whose buses were still running all but their eastward routes. He had remained in Palma Sola until a resident had offered to guard his car. Meanwhile, he'd missed three days of classes and work. Juan B. tried to pacify him, as he'd tried with the truckers, by arguing the antinuke case. But the young man was unpersuaded, and mainly he was tired. When he and his family had set out for a weekend on the coast, they hadn't expected to be taken hostage.

No newspapers had reached Palma Sola during the blockade,

but as soon as it was over, I reviewed what the press had said. National publications carried only short notes. Dailies in the state of Veracruz, though they had crusaded against construction of the nuclear plant, had shown no sympathy for the blockade. Some of their stories were fabulous. The *Dictamen* of the city of Veracruz, for example, published a report headlined FOREIGNER MANIPULATES THE BLOCKADE. The story claimed that a Nicaraguan had ordered the blockade's leadership to concoct Molotov cocktails in preparation for an attack by police. Yet there were no Nicaraguans in Palma Sola.

I ran into Juan B. and others of the *ecologistas* in downtown Xalapa the day after the end of the blockade. I was surprised to find them in high spirits. The nation's secretary of urban development and ecology had agreed to a meeting with opponents of the nuke, and Governor Gutiérrez Barrios of Veracruz had agreed to accompany them. News from Monterrey had also rekindled the ardor of the *ecologistas'* convictions. On Wednesday, June 23, at about the time that the blockade began its seventy-second hour, three gasoline tanks had exploded at a Pemex facility on the outskirts of Monterrey. Seven people were killed, twenty were injured, and ten thousand were evacuated. The explosion, the newspapers said, wasn't the result of lightning or sabotage. It had been caused by the sparks from a welder's rig, by "carelessness," "human error," and "oversight." The *ecologistas* saw in the Pemex accident an argument for the case that nuclear power is unsafe. If human error is inevitable, they reasoned, nuclear accidents are inevitable, too. They might have added that the danger is especially great in Mexico, where not even highways are under control.

Author's Note: In October 1988—during President Miguel de la Madrid's *año de hidalgo*—the Laguna Verde plant began operation.

Return to Monterrey

TODAY is July 6, 1988. It is hot
and dusty, and the streets are almost deserted. Nearly ten years
have passed since anybody in Mexico advocated revolution or
coups. Now, they believe that if they can change Mexico, they
can change it through the vote. Today is a presidential election
day. For the second time in the eighties, I've come to the northern city of Monterrey to watch a Mexican election work.

If I were in charge of Mexico, I'd arrange for these elections
to take place on another day, because a fever is dogging me.
I'd also arrange for the conduct of the elections to be supervised
by an American authority, the Texas Elections Commission, for
example, so that I could more easily make sense of the process.
My fevered mind has just made me remember something that
makes me doubt the sincerity of all Mexican politicians, and I
don't know how I'll dispose of my doubt, or if I will. In the
meantime, I'll do what one always does in Mexico. I'll wait for
my mood or my state of health to change, or for the scenery
to change, or for a surprise or distraction to come along. Mexico
is not a land of immediacy: it is not a place for going directly

49

from point A to point B. It is not a problem in sequential logic, nor is it a machine on a factory conveyor, waiting for the next touch in a purposeful plan. To understand Mexico and what is happening to it, even when you're living here, you've first got to understand that Mexico is a place that has been turned upside down. It's a rubble, and the pieces that fit into any understanding of it may lie yards beneath the spot where you stand.

I'm not even standing, I'm sitting, in the backseat of a red-brown 1974 Ford Maverick. A reporter from a Monterrey daily is riding shotgun, armed with an audiotape recorder, the self-defense weapon of the Mexican press. At the steering wheel is Herminio Gómez Rangel, fifty-three, a man so familiar to Monterrey's readers that in headlines and photo captions he's usually tagged by his first name only.

Herminio stands about 5'6", an average height by Mexican standards, not too tall, like the *gringos*, or too short, like the *indios*. He's slender and smoothly muscled, and his skin is a glistening bronze. His teeth are perfectly white, his fingernails are perfectly clean, and despite his age, there are no dry, weatherbeaten wrinkles in his face; he looks like a man who has spent his life indoors under a sunlamp, or outdoors bathed in oil. If Herminio is physically flawed, it's only because beneath his flashing hazel eyes, on the bridge of his nose, there's a slight depression. Herminio says that it is the stamp of a brief youthful career as a boxer.

In private life, Herminio Gómez is an insurance salesman, a member of the Mexican middle class. He owns a four-bedroom house, paid in full, not financed by the banks. He's the father of four children, all of them adults. One daughter is a schoolteacher, the other a dentist; one son is a contractor in Texas, the other a university student at home. Herminio's wife, Hortencia, or "Tencha," owns a refrigerator and a washing machine—luxuries, by Mexican standards—and devotes her leisure to neighborhood affairs.

Like any sharp salesman, Herminio is always smiling, always optimistic, and always presentably dressed. Today, he's wearing polished gray loafers, thin gray pants, and a white short-sleeved shirt. When introducing himself, he usually says, "Herminio Gómez, *su servidor*"—"Herminio Gómez, your

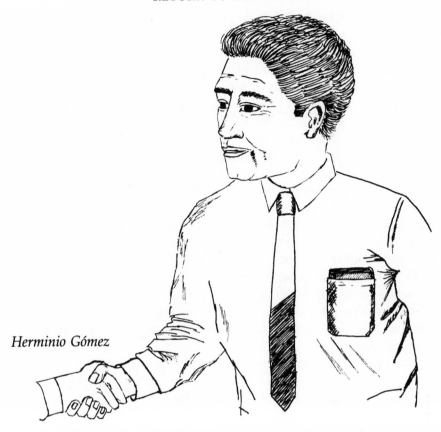

Herminio Gómez

servant"—and then he reaches into his shirt pocket for a business card, or a little book. It's that little book that interests me. Herminio has made himself a local celebrity by quoting that book, especially to officials who don't want to contend with what it says. It's a leatherbound little volume, bigger than a pocket address book, smaller than a New Testament. The gold lettering embossed on its tan front says, *Constitución Política de 1917*, and it's the reason why I am with Herminio today.

In 1983, Herminio founded a regional group called the Movimiento Constitucional Mexicano, or MCM, whose ostensible purpose is to extol and defend the principles of the Mexican

51

Constitution. The MCM is a group of bristling activists, an ACLU with bullhorns. It has broken new ground in conservative Monterrey by staging sit-ins, hunger strikes, marches, and rallies. It has protested election-rigging, clamored for releasing street vendors from jail, and decried hikes in utility rates. It has also helped promote Herminio's career as a political stuntman. In 1985, he went to Europe and unfurled a banner that read IN MEXICO THERE IS NO DEMOCRACY at fetes where Mexico's president spoke. In early 1988, he walked from Mexico's Guatemalan border to the Rio Grande, a distance of some two thousand miles, on what he billed as a "March for Democracy." His forays on behalf of the MCM have landed him in jail a dozen times, but never for long enough to suit his pleasure. Brushes with the law are a tonic for Herminio, who pictures himself as a prophet calling a wayward nation to the path of righteousness. Though much of what Herminio preaches is expounded, I believe, for the sake of agitation, he's made me a convert of a kind. Three years ago, he convinced me that you can't understand Mexico without unraveling its Constitution.

THE CONSTITUTION OF 1917

The Mexican Constitution, formally known as the Political Constitution of 1917, is Mexico's fundamental attempt to define the rules by which its modern society is to operate. Like the American Constitution, it establishes a Senate, to be chosen by popular vote, and a Chamber of Deputies, similar to the U.S. House of Representatives. It also establishes a presidency of six-year terms, or *sexenios*, and a Supreme Court. It defines citizens' rights in a similar, but much broader way than the American document. For example, it mentions the family fifteen times, and the working class more than fifty times. It makes reference to nunneries, drilling rigs, ranch lands, and nursing schedules; the U.S. Constitution doesn't mention any of these topics. The Mexican Constitution is thirty-two thousand words long, four times the length of its American counterpart. The American Constitution failed to resolve at least one important controversy of its day, that of states' rights, slavery, and race. The Mexican Constitution of 1917, on the other hand, encourages some controversies that otherwise might not exist. Some of its passages are flights of mere fancy.

Its greatest delusion is that the State is master of the Church, though its insistence on this point, interwoven throughout the text, may have discouraged the return of the opposite state of affairs. Because the Catholic Church was once the nation's leading landlord, banker, and back-room kingmaker, today Mexican religious organizations cannot own real estate, including their temples of worship. Churches are forbidden to operate primary or secondary schools, religious publications cannot comment on the Constitution or political affairs, all clergymen must register with the Secretaría de Gobernación, Mexico's Interior Ministry, and no clergyman is permitted to vote. Under the guise of abolishing involuntary servitude, the Constitution bans monastic orders. New buildings dedicated to religious purposes may be opened only with the consent of the government, and existing structures may be converted to secular uses at the pleasure of the State. Across Mexico, yesterday's convent or parsonage probably houses a bureaucracy or a bank.

Mexico's restrictions on religion, first written into law in the Constitution of 1857, reflect a long and bitter history that began with the Spanish Conquest. The Inquisition tortured and burned Indians who reverted to idolatry, and priests flogged those who failed to attend mass. The Church financed plantations that deprived Indians of their lands, and most of its professionals opposed independence from Spain. After the Church was castigated by the anticlerical provisions of 1857, it turned to deceit and vengeance. During the Revolution, which produced the Constitution of 1917, some bishops declared that union members were going to hell. When land repartitions began, some priests told their flocks that agrarian reform was a sin; fearing the fires of hell, a few of their rural parishioners—peasants who would have benefited from the land giveaways—fired on government agriculture agents. The government in response launched a campaign to enforce the anti-Catholic provisions of the Constitution of 1917, and civil war ensued. The rivalry between Church and State in Mexico

53

hasn't ended yet, largely because most people in Mexico haven't taken sides.

The neutrality of Mexicans in the Church-State conflict derives more from a deep-seated suspicion of all modern institutions than from any skepticism of a theological kind. The evidence of Mexican piety is so plentiful that it is subject to trivial proofs. The piety of educated Mexicans, for example, is evidenced in bookstores: *The World's Greatest Salesman* by Og Mandino has never left the best-seller list. In Mexico, every blue-collar workplace has an altar, and my wife and I saw obvious evidence of piety even among truckers, who, as in the United States, are not reputedly a pack of choirboys. By custom, Mexican truck drivers are allowed to decorate their rigs with company funds. Most of them hire a sign painter to put a legend on their front bumpers, and sometimes on the back as well. Miriam, my wife, kept a log of these bumper declarations during several of our trips through Mexico, and when we reached 300 listings, we analyzed the list. As might be expected anywhere, the biggest proportion of bumper messages, 114 of them, were those of truckers' names and nicknames. The second most common category, of 92 messages, was a miscellany of women's names, town names, and truck names, like "Dart," "Lightning," and "The Jet." But 62 of the legends on our list, nearly a quarter of the total, bore saints' names or messages like FAITH IN GOD AND ONWARD, THIS CROSS IS MY DESTINY, KNEELING SINNER, and VASSAL OF GOD. Of course, given the perils of highway travel in Mexico—statisticians say that, per vehicle, there are ten times as many accidents as in the United States—Mexican truckers have more reason to say their prayers.

Because Mexicans overwhelmingly profess faith, defendants accused of violating the Constitution's religious controls are Constitutionally denied trial by jury. But for that same reason, many of the Constitution's strictures are ignored, both generally and exceptionally. Protestant missionaries from the United States have evangelized rural Mexico, even though the Constitution forbids foreigners to exercise ministry. Churches operate parochial schools, under the supervision of the State, and religious altars and images are sold everywhere, though private worship is forbidden. Under a Constitutional ban on "external manifestations of religion," it is deemed illegal to wear ecclesiastical garb in public. But when the Polish pope visited Mexico in 1979, he gave a public mass, dressed in his ecclesiastic robes. No one was arrested. Though the president spent a scant forty-five seconds in welcoming him to the country, 3 million Mexicans lined the roads to greet him, some six times more than have hailed any political figure in Mexico's history. The papal visit pointed up a chronic malady of modern Mexican: What is Constitutional or legal is not necessarily what is honored in daily life.

If the Constitution's most unbalanced vision is censorship of the faith, its most troublesome section has been its chapter on agrarian reform. The background to the problem of land tenancy in Mexico is almost the same as Mexico's history as a nation. When the Constitution was written, most Mexicans were peasants, i.e., farmers whose production was largely for family consumption, farmers without enough capital or land to produce a significant surplus for commercial sale. Landless peasants couldn't easily acquire land, and small farmers couldn't easily expand their holdings because suitable land, in Mexico, has always been in short supply: Only 10 percent of the country's surface is arable, compared, for example, to the 25 percent in the agriculturally potent United States. During the colonial period, nobles and the Church owned most Mexican land, and during the period from independence until the Revolution of 1910, most of the best land was devoted to *latifundio,* or plantation production; and in Mexico, big land holdings have almost always been oriented to the production of export crops, not crops for domestic consumption. The result was that Mexico in 1917 was a nation of land-hungry peasants in conflict with big landholders, and foodstuffs were expensive because production was oriented toward foreign markets.

The Constitution's essential approach to the problems of Mexican agriculture is to encourage smaller units of tenancy. During the period of colonial rule, the operant theory of land ownership was that God gave Mexico in trust to the Spanish crown, which had divine authority to appoint and remove landowners. The modern Constitution declares that "Ownership of the land . . . originally belongs to the nation, which . . . has the right to transmit control . . . to private parties. . . . The nation shall always have the right to impose on private property the forms that the public interest dictates." Following that preamble, the Constitution authorizes state legislatures to set acreage limits on land ownership, and forbids the corporate ownership of farms. It also establishes a procedure by which groups of landless peasants may apply for grants of land—either from private or publicly held tracts—not to exceed 10 hectares, or 24.7 acres, per member. In addition to creating these peasant communes or *ejidos*, the Constitution also protects small private farmers, called *pequeños propetarios*, from land seizures to carry out agrarian reform. Today's Constitution defines *pequeños propetarios* as farmers whose holdings do not exceed 247 irrigated acres, 494 dryland acres, or 9,884 acres of pastureland. However, as in all things political, lobbying efforts have produced refinements in the definition, such that today's Constitution also allows *pequeños propetarios* to own as many as 371 irrigated acres—if their land is devoted to cotton cultivation—or 741 acres, if devoted to sugarcane, bananas, coffee, henequen, rubber, and cocoa—ironically, all export crops. But legally, the Constitution's acreage limits ended Mexican plantationism or *latifundismo*.

Investors despise the Constitution's agrarian reform provisions, and evade them at every turn. Nor are peasants pleased by the opportunity it dangles before them. No general review of land titles followed the Constitution's enactment, and therefore most *latifundios* continued as before, legally undiscovered. To bring about the repartition of a *latifundio*, peasant groups must first prove that it exists. Yet the Constitution gives them no right to access to ownership records. To prevent discovery, *latifundistas* parcel out their plantations to relatives or *prestanombres*—literally, name-loaners. Today, as before the Constitution was written, Mexico's most productive lands belong to planters who cultivate crops for export, and as in the period before 1917, Mexico is an importer of staple foodstuffs.

Not only do popes and planters sidestep the Mexican Constitution, but everyone does. Nobody in Mexico fully respects or observes the Constitution, not even the Supreme Court, which has never struck down a federal law on the grounds of unconstitutionality. Lawmakers revise the document capriciously, and its provisions authorize their sleight-of-hand tricks. In the seventy-five years since its enactment, the Constitution has been amended more than 350 times, yet no signs of surgery are visible to the holder of its contemporary text. Changes in the Constitution are made internally, not externally; new wordings simply replace old ones in republications of the text.

THE PAN

Herminio Gómez, like most Mexicans, doesn't subscribe to many of the Constitution's principles. He is a duly reverential Catholic, and an advocate of free-market capitalism, of the opportunities that he thinks have made advancement possible for him. In another age, he would probably have been a revolutionist. But Gómez supports the Constitution because he wants to use its democratic provisions to replace the only government that living Mexicans have ever known. "Our government can't enact the laws we want," he says, "until we teach it to respect the laws we have."

American influence made Herminio a reformer. Though he hadn't finished junior high school, in 1950, when he turned fifteen, Herminio made the first of a dozen journeys into the United States, in search of survival and savings. Sometimes he crossed the Rio Grande as a *bracero*, or legally contracted farm laborer, and sometimes he entered the country as a *mojado*, or wetback, without immigration permits; he usually traveled in groups with other men. During the fifties and sixties, he picked cotton in Texas, Tennessee, and Arkansas. In the South, he witnessed the segregated condition of America's blacks, and he disapproved of it. On newscasts he watched as the civil-rights movement fought for limited goals, and though Herminio is not a bookish or philosophical man—the volumes on his bookshelves are mainly self-help and motivational tracts— he became an admirer of the ethos of nonviolent resistance preached by Dr. Martin Luther King, Jr. While living in East Chicago, Indiana, during the seventies, where he worked as a machinist, Herminio also watched the rise of black municipal

57

power, and was persuaded that electoral systems can work. He wished that oppositionists in Mexico could succeed as he'd seen them do in the United States.

Herminio is like the American idealists of an earlier age. He's the only person I've ever known, for example, to express a sincere desire to read the boy-made-good Horatio Alger tales. Though he's never mastered English, I think it is likely that he would have remained in the United States, had he been able to bring his family, and had he not been the father of two maturing girls. But contemporary American sexual customs scandalized him. His youngest daughter in 1988 married a Mexican physician who had been her boyfriend for ten years. Yet the couple had never been on a date. For the decade in which he completed his studies and founded a career, her suitor sat on the porch every night, merely chatting with his beloved. Herminio has nothing but praise for the young man, and for Mexican sexual prudence in general. "In your country," he once told me, "anyone and everyone can be a boyfriend, girlfriend, husband, or wife. But in Mexico, courtship and marriage still have meaning." When Herminio came home for good in 1976, he came to see his children through adolescence, but he also came back to test the agitational tactics he'd learned by watching American television.

He immediately joined the Partido Acción Nacional, or PAN, a conservative, business-oriented party dedicated to bringing American-style democracy to Mexico. Herminio found only one flaw in the PAN: At the time, it snubbed the tactics of nonviolent protest. He formed the Movimiento Constitucional to bridge the gap. Though no formal connection exists between the PAN and the MCM, Herminio's organization today serves Monterrey's PAN as a corps of shock troops. It provides the demonstrators and the pedestrian appeal that the elitist PAN cannot inspire for itself. In Monterrey, Herminio taught the PAN the value of taking to the streets.

The PAN was formed in 1939 by businessmen and Catholic intellectuals who feared that the ruling Partido de la Revolución Mexicana (soon to rename itself the Partido Revolucionario Institucional, or PRI) was leading the country to Bolshevism. Their fears were largely a reaction to the policies of General

Lázaro Cárdenas, Mexico's Depression-era president. Like Franklin D. Roosevelt in the United States, Cárdenas engaged the Depression with a series of radical measures that, detractors said, were Trojan horses for socialism. Cárdenas was especially taken to task for three measures. First, he honored the oldest wish and promise in Mexican politics, the promise of land. Using the powers and mandates of the Constitution of 1917, he forced the partition of rural estates, and in isolated regions where soldiers could neither enforce the repartitions nor protect their beneficiaries, he armed the peasantry for self-defense. Second, he fostered labor organizations among government employees, industrial workers, even among bootblacks, newsboys, street vendors, and others of the poor-but-self-employed class. He also nationalized Mexico's foreign-owned petroleum industry, whose labor abuses had earned it the ill will of workers, and whose tax evasions had long irritated the government. His actions won such great affection among Mexicans of humble circumstances that they referred to him, not as General or President, but as "Tata" or Grandfather Lázaro.

The affection that ordinary Mexicans, especially peasants, showed for Cárdenas was a measure of Mexico's capacity for gratitude. Neither he nor his revolutionary predecessors parceled out lands with an open hand. Of some 30.7 million hectares—about 75 million acres—distributed between 1920 and 1940, only 1.3 million were irrigated, and 22.6 million, three quarters of the total, were not arable. Despite his socialist reputation, over the years most Mexicans came to regard Cárdenas as a reformist. The landlords and oil companies that he expropriated were, in most cases, paid fair-market indemnities. The union and peasant associations that he fathered, because they owed their existence to political initiatives from above, not to independent struggle from below, became pillars of the PRIista political order, docile servants to the memory of Táta Cárdenas, who—despite their trust—in 1940 turned the presidency over to the first in a series of corrupt, middle-of-the road PRIista regimes.

Cynicism might have eclipsed fond memories of Lázaro Cárdenas had he withdrawn, as other Mexicans have, to diplomatic or private life. But he didn't. First as secretary of defense in

"Tata" Lázaro Cárdenas

the administration that succeeded him, and later as a volunteer on government committees devoted to dams and hydraulic projects, Cárdenas kept in circulation. In closed circles, he opined about current events, and even about the party structure that he'd left in power. After he died in 1970, excerpts from his notebooks were published. Some of his observations would

60

haunt Mexico, among them the following, from one of the last pages in his diary:

> What occurs is that with the process that followed the Revolution, after its pre-Constitutional period, it entered the period of "institutions," and since that time, important official positions have been occupied by men with interests created by the counterrevolution, "peaceful counterrevolutionaries" who deny efficiency to the *ejido*, rights to the worker, socialist education, etc. . . . Though the life of the country is ruled by the Constitution of 1917 which tends to socialism, it lacks a sufficient force to counter the opportunism and abuse of those who want to maintain the capitalist state. The conquests of the *ejido*, of unionism, of education and of the peoples' forces are harmed and halted in their progress.

The PAN in 1940 had backed the candidacy of General Juan Almazán, a popular conservative who bolted the PRI after Cárdenas spurned him. Because moneyed Mexicans were nearly as numerous as the poor in the electoral rolls of that epoch, many historians suspect that Almazán actually won the presidential balloting of 1940, though he was credited with only 6 percent of the vote. But as a moderate PRI took shape, businessmen abandoned the upstart PAN, and the party lost the impetus of its promising beginnings. It fossilized. The PAN became a party of crusty old reactionaries, with a reputation little better than, and little different from, that of the John Birch Society in the United States.

Mexicans most often criticize the PAN for its unapologetic, pro-American advocacy of free enterprise. Herminio Gómez makes no bones about his stance: He thinks the United States is the best model for Mexican democracy. PANista leaders hailed President Kennedy's invasion of Cuba, sympathized with its exile movement, and complained when, in 1973, Mexico granted asylum to socialist refugees from Pinochet's Chile. They were the only important public figures in Mexico to praise President Reagan's aid to the Nicaraguan Contras. When PANista candidates speak on the subject of border relations, they do not assail U.S. immigration barriers; instead, they blame Mexico's mixed economy for the conditions that send immigrants northward in search of work. When Mexican office-seekers and journalists lambaste PANistas for advocating the removal of Mexico's byzantine and innumerable restrictions on foreign investment, the party's stalwarts undauntedly reply that foreign investment is preferable to foreign debt. The PAN's pro-American and right-wing policies clash with educated Mexico's wounded sense of nationalism, and in most Mexican academic and intellectual circles the party is unfairly regarded as a subsidiary of the Central Intelligence Agency.

PANista evangelists like Herminio Gómez say that their critics have been brainwashed. They charge that the ruling party has used the government's Constitutional control over education—in Mexico, all schools, public and private, must provide instruction from federal texts—to create a false and self-perpetuating national myth, in which for all of Mexico's woes, foreigners and free enterprise are to blame. It's a tall and hefty charge, and one that's rarely weighed at its base.

The Mexican public-school system, administered by the federal government, is designed to provide four years of preschool or kindergarten care, six years of primary schooling, and three years of secondary instruction, roughly equivalent to that of American junior high schools. This series can be followed by three years of normal, preparatory, or trade-school education, after which students may begin university careers.

Civic education, as in the United States, begins at the primary-school level, with the teaching of pledges and anthems, and the commemoration of national holidays. It reaches the level of adult discourse in secondary-school texts that, as in almost every country, glorify the existing government and its chartering document. In Mexico, civics texts are written from a social democratic perspective that is absolutely global in scope. Before visiting Herminio in Monterrey, I asked a boy in the Mexican neighborhood where I was living to show me his texts. Here's what he was being taught about the Russian Revolution.

> Lenin was the leader of this revolution. The banks, industries and the railroads, that is to say, the principal services and means

of production, came under the control of the government of the workers. Land was taken from the big planters and put in the hands of the peasants, who exploited it collectively. That is to say, a group worked and then shared the harvest. The big houses were given to poor families, and there ceased to be any rich.

With all these changes, customs also were modified. In a short time women entered factories and farm work, and, as education improved, they became engineers, doctors, mechanics and physicists. Schools and day-care centers were built where children were cared for and educated while mothers studied and worked.

A first-year civics text describes the Eastern bloc in these words:

Various historical events produced by the two world wars, particularly the second, provoked a great number of European nations—those of the Eastern zone—liberated from Nazism by the Soviet Union, to convert to socialism.

The same text, simply titled *Civic Education*, tells students that in Asia:

With the exception of the socialist countries, who in certain measure have resolved the basic problems of their people . . . there is no glimmer of favorable solutions to the problems faced.

For more advanced students, there's the third-year text's discourse on "Social Contamination."

We call social contamination the permanent influence exercised by the alienating factors of human conduct, that generally are introduced, or copied from, foreign countries, that do not correspond to our idiosyncrasy, and whose exercise brings as a consequence the negation and the perversion of the most precious values of society, twisting life, health and social well-being.

The Constitution, of course, gets sympathetic treatment in the texts. Students in a second-year course learn that:

State intervention augments in the measure that the rich minority continues its abuses and violation of the respective laws.

And:

> The *Constitution of 1917* . . . is a dynamic and perfectible code. . . . It is one of the most advanced fundamental laws in the world. This is proved by, among other things . . . the new decrees and laws promoted in this presidential term, all of which also have a humanistic, democratic and revolutionary character that follows the path of social justice.

I believe that the general purpose of passages like these is not to promote Marxism, but is instead to justify the Mexican government's "regency," or general authority, over economic life, a power granted in the Constitution of 1917. But I think that it is unlikely that the texts have greatly influenced the Mexican masses, as the PAN believes. They have instead colored the thinking of those Mexicans whom elite PANistas are most likely to encounter: journalists, bureaucrats, and teachers, the home-grown intelligentsia, the *minority* of the Mexican population that has received extensive formal education. For the same reason that most Mexicans aren't familiar with the Constitution of 1917, they're also not familiar with textbook indoctrinations on nationalism and economics. Many rural settlements lack primary or secondary schools, and even in urban areas, most Mexicans end their schooling on or before turning fifteen, the age of mandatory enrollment. Twenty percent of the voters registered for Mexico's 1988 elections had never attended any school, and in 1980 the Mexican Census Bureau reported that only a fifth of the nation's adults claimed to have completed secondary school; a fourth of the nation's children, the census found, were not attending school. What most Mexicans learn from their brief sessions of schooling are basic word and math skills, not the mental tricks needed to digest fifty-five-word sentences about "Social Contamination," or official attitudes toward affairs of state, culture, and history.

Because the issues it picked were not of mass relevance, the PAN might have withered on the vine had it not been for the victory of a stubborn internal struggle that surfaced in 1976, when the party was too deadlocked to pick a presidential candidate. A younger and more daring corps of PANistas—the

right-wing equivalents of the generation of the sixties—had
come into the party, and they were demanding change. Their
essential stance was that the PAN's traditional anticommunist
and papist policies should take a backseat to issues with a more
popular appeal. The smoke did not clear from the abortive 1976
convention until years later, but by 1980 it was evident that the
PAN's new current was gaining ground. Formerly dominated
by ideologues, the PAN began to attract a following of Mexicans
with everyday concerns. It attracted supporters, as all Mexican
parties do, not on the basis of the personality or competence
of its candidates, but by committing itself to an agenda for
reform.

LA MORDIDA

Its first broad crusade, nascent in the electioneering of 1981,
dominant by 1985, took corruption as its enemy and Constitutionalism as its ideal. The campaign was in many ways a
critique of the economy of Mexico's oil-boom years, 1977–82,
when foreign bankers rushed to Mexico with financing for petroleum projects. Mexicans, as a people, are not prone to debt:
In the daily vocabulary, to say *"está drogado"* is to say that
someone is either drugged out of his mind, or in debt. "It's
better to go to bed without supper," an adage says, "than to
wake up in debt." Most Mexicans are ineligible for credit—
retail credit is a feature of elite life, nothing more—and live
entirely from their pocketbooks, without either savings or
credit. The country's majority took a dim view of the government's borrowings from foreign bankers; but on the other hand,
the people did not feel responsible for government policy, and
when the loans came, flush times began.

Pemex hired workers by the thousands, across the country.
If there were no oil fields nearby, it flew them to the boom
towns of the Gulf Coast, quartered them in hotels, and paid
their air fare home on weekends. Its purchasing agents scoured
the nation in search of materials, signing contracts and stim-
ulating growth everywhere. University enrollment reached
new heights, as a generation of students prepared for the social-

service and bureaucratic opportunities promised by a government expanding under the pressures of new oil wealth. The construction industry mushroomed, and even those Mexicans who had previously been regarded as destined to lead the life of the Eternal Poor—the peasantry and the ragtag elements of urban society—found jobs awaiting them, though not always at home: Texas and Louisiana were booming, too, and in numbers greater than ever before, Mexicans streamed north to work. The country was riding an oil boom. Dollars were everywhere.

"Oil money was flowing out of our ears," observed Adrian Lajous, former director of the nation's bank for foreign trade. "Instead of using oil money to pay our debts, we used it as a come-on to borrow more, ever more. . . . We became inebriated by too much money. We even complained among ourselves about the burden of managing wealth." But the bonanza was not evenly shared. Employment kept pace with population growth, and thousands found work at the minimum wage, but the purchasing power of most Mexicans increased by only some 15 percent. Prosperity, for most Mexicans, meant that almost everybody could have a job. It did not mean financial comfort.

Not all of the new wealth was honestly earned. Purchasing agents ordered suppliers to double, even triple the costs shown on invoices; kickbacks were the order of the day. (In universities and among young executives, the question most frequently asked about prospective posts in government service was not, "How much does the job pay?" but "How much purchasing power does it carry?") Ships arriving in Mexican ports with cargoes bound for the oil fields faced weeks of unloading delays, unless bribes were paid. Tankers carried away more oil than, according to official figures, Mexico had produced for export. The state oil monopoly contracted with friendly Mexican firms that, in violation of the Constitution, entered into partnerships with foreign companies, or subcontracted their commissions to them; some Mexican firms were mere fronts for foreign operators. Leaders in the petroleum workers' union sold memberships, and members rented their union cards to workingmen in exchange for half their earnings. The union demanded and got contracts from Pemex for construction projects, becoming an employer itself. During the boom, more

people made more money thievingly than at any time since
Cortés sacked Moctezuma's stores of gold.

The boom died a swift and cruel death with the 1982 crash
in world oil prices. Inflation, already a problem in Mexico's
overheated economy, destroyed personal savings and crippled
the nation's ability to pay its loans. Mexico's banks, nationalized
in 1982, faced the threat of sudden collapse. Because the economies of American oil states were contracting, too, Mexican
immigrants began returning home. To cope with the country's
$100 billion foreign debt, the government began promising to
tighten its belt—and imposed a 15 percent retail sales tax.

The unprecedented federal sales tax was only the beginning
of hard times. Between 1982 and 1988, according to the International Development Bank, the purchasing power of the Mexican minimum wage fell 67.4 percent. The Bank of Mexico
reported that at the end of that period, though Mexico was the
fourteenth-ranked industrial power in the world, twenty nations paid higher wages. The plummet in purchasing power
was felt across the economy. Clothing sales, for example, fell
by 30 percent, as Mexicans skimped even more to get by. The
peso's value went from forty-four to the dollar in early 1982 to
2,270 in 1986. Inflation rates ranged from about 60 percent to
more than 150 percent annually. To keep pace with rising
prices, the national mint abolished the centavo, or cent, and
over the *sexenio,* or six years between 1982 and 1988, placed
twenty-one new coins in circulation. By the end of the period,
a day's wage, about ten thousand pesos, could be paid with
two coins. The government's popularity declined along with
purchasing power, and civic pride suffered, too: Flag sales fell
by 50 percent after the bust.

But corruption didn't shrink with the economy. Instead, it
took uglier forms. Essentially in violation of Mexico's currency-
control laws, many Mexicans had invested the sudden riches
of the seventies in leveraged American real estate. When the
bust depleted their fountains of wealth, in order to stave off
repossessions in Texas, Arizona, or California, they squeezed
harder on their clients at home. Even the humblest of Mexicans
felt the bite. It was evident in, among other events, a wave of
shakedowns aimed at the owners of *fayuca,* or white contra-

band. Television sets and VCR machines that had come into the country, tax-free but usually not bribe-free, were hot items; members of the working class could afford them for the first time. Knowing that these items had been imported with the collusion of higher-ups, petty officials did nothing to stem the trade. But when the bust came, even humble cops on the beat began stopping young men carrying cassette players and women pushing imported infant strollers. Owners were asked to show import receipts, or bills of sale proving that their chrome-and-plastic treasures had been purchased legally in Mexico. Officials claimed that the campaign was aimed at forcing vendors to pay the 32 percent tax on most imported consumer items, but its object was bribes, as far as victims could tell. The word on the streets was that the cops had gone on a craze because their superiors had made exorbitant new demands.

Nobody could deny that corruption had raised the costs of doing business in Mexico. But the charge didn't win the presidency or any Senate seats for the PAN. Even Miguel de la Madrid, the PRI's 1982 presidential candidate, campaigned on a promise of "moral renovation" of the government. His pledge and subsequent housecleaning produced months of sensational stories in the press, to the delight of nearly everyone. But the effort didn't create much of a following. When de la Madrid, as president, jailed a former Pemex director and a Mexico City police chief, rather than looking at the government in a new light, most people reached for an old adage: "A new broom sweeps clean." People saw the conflict over corruption as a battle between novitiate priests of financial abstinence and the invincible forces of sin. Not many Mexicans believed that their nation could be cleansed.

Corruption is a pervasive and probably ineradicable part of modern Mexico. It is a subset of a greater code of behavior expressed by a vague and uniquely Mexican profanity, to *chingar*. The verb has no precise meaning, but it can be understood by example. If you loan your cassette player to a teenage neighbor or your no-good brother-in-law, you warn him, *"No lo chingues,"* roughly, "Don't screw it up." You might add, *"O te chingo,"* approximately, "Or I'll give you a beating." If he ruins your cassette player, you're stuck with another *chingadera,* a useless or noxious object. His excuses for the machine's ruination are mere *chingaderas,* too—in this case, lies. If you hit your thumb with a hammer you might moan, *"Chingado martillo,"* or "damned hammer," or you might simply blurt, *"chingado,"* to describe your dissatisfaction with the whole situation, as if saying "dammit" in English. No insult in Mexican usage is more offensive than *"Chinga tu madre,"* or *"Chinga* your mother," though it does not have the sexual implication of the analogous invective in English. *Chingar* usually implies hatred, dissatisfaction, worthlessness, or the use of brute force. But a *chingo* is a great quantity of things, and anything that is *chingón* is terrific, or marvelous. If a soccer player says, *"Los chingamos,"* what he's probably saying is that his team scored a one-sided victory over its rival, not that it literally whipped or beat the other players: Not all uses of the word are negative or imply violence, and to *chingar* can be an almost respectable goal. The concept of the word is fully expressed in shopkeepers' signs and on T-shirts that summarize Mexican history in the following way: "A *chingo* of years ago, we Indians were very *chingones.* Cuauhtémoc was the most *chingón.* But a *chingo* of Spaniards came and those sons of *la chingada* perpetrated a thousand *chingaderas,* and *chingaron* the Indians. And that's what carried us to *la chingada.* To keep people from *chingando,* we have to learn to *chingar."* The nearest American equivalent to the notion of *chingar* is expressed in the parody that says, "Do unto others before they do unto you." But in Mexico, the idea of *chingar* is taken seriously. Not too many people believe that a more equitable intercourse is possible, outside of family circles. He who gets a chance to *chingar* is regarded as a saint or a fool if he doesn't take it, and permissiveness extends to the government, whose officials are expected to take bribes. Official extortion is best known in regards the police, with whom everyone must deal.

On its simplest and most benign level, bribery is merely an act of cooperation or charity. In most Mexican cities, policemen have to rent or buy their jobs: Bribes must be paid to win and keep appointments. But in many, especially smaller cities, policemen are not salaried. Those who walk a beat go weekly from door to door, asking for donations. Most neighbors contribute, usually twenty-five to fifty cents a week. Such payments are regarded as *propinas* or tips, because no obligation is involved.

If the cop on the beat fails to show on your block for a week or two, when you encounter him, the diplomatic approach is to say, as if meeting a long-lost friend, "Say, there you are! Why, we've been worried about you. Are you all right? Why don't you drop by sometime." He's likely to say, "How about Wednesday? Will you be home then?" as if accepting a social invitation. The exchange tells him that though he is not accountable to you for his recent absence—he is accountable only to his superiors—you'd appreciate his vigilance, probably with a tip. It would be an error to say, "You know, if you'd stop by, we'd be glad to tip you," because that approach imputes financial need or motives to a guardian of the law. In Mexico an important unspoken assumption underlying almost all interpersonal dealings is that the issue at hand is not money, or any material gain, but instead is personal respect.

Salaried officers of the law—traffic cops, immigration and customs agents, and the judicial or investigative police—are employed by the state and federal governments, usually at salaries of from four to five dollars a day. Their biweekly paychecks barely ensure an urban subsistence. To make ends meet, many hold second jobs. Almost all of them supplement their aboveboard incomes by granting favors to those whom they accuse or apprehend. Mexicans refer to the extra-official monies paid to them as *mordidas*, or "bites." A *mordida* is not a tip, but neither is it a bribe.

If you run a red light and are halted by a traffic cop, the substantial conversation begins when he tells you that you've broken the law. The accusation of guilt—never made in situations in which the *propina* is appropriate—sets the scene for a *mordida*. After the accusation is made, most drivers argue their innocence or point to mitigating factors, usually to no avail, and partly just for show. Your duty as a driver is to mention the names of friends and relatives in high places, and to exhibit any credentials indicating that you, in your own right, are capable of influencing judges. Exhibiting one's clout is a duty to the cop, because policemen don't benefit from conflict with higher-ups.

It's a game of chicken, and the driver sometimes wins. When he doesn't, the policeman takes out his pen and citation pad —and begins explaining why he'll have to write you a ticket. The pen and pad are mere cues, saying that it's time for the driver to make an offer.

Since the driver's guilt is established, and the integrity of both parties is presumed, the driver's best move is to save himself the inconvenience of an appearance in court. The possibility is broached by saying something like, "If I gave the money to you, could you pay the fine for me?" The policeman's likely response is, "I guess I could do that out of friendship, but as a policeman, I'm not allowed to accept payments or give receipts." The friendship of the two parties is then sealed by a *mordida*. According to this unwritten script, which almost all Mexican motorists know by heart, the policeman has fulfilled his duty by bringing an errant motorist to justice, but he's a hero, despite his punitive role, because he's helped reduce judicial red tape. The citizen has confessed his guilt, and has shown respect, by trusting the cop to pay his "fine." The only flaw in the script is—the ticket never gets written.

The text of bribery conversations need not be so veiled as in the classic example, however. It all depends on the driver's vulnerability, the cop's boldness, and even the time of the year. Recently, I was halted in Tampico by two policemen in a patrol car. It was mid-December. One of them came up to the window of the driver's side of my car, and I greeted him aggressively. "Just what is the violation?" I said, making it clear that I knew that I'd violated no law. "Just a minute, and I'll tell you," the cop said. He walked around the vehicle, noticed that it was missing its front license plate, and pointed out this putative "violation" to me. "Since when," I asked, "is it an offense in Mexico to lose a Texas license plate?" "But look, it's Christmastime, and we need money!" the cop exclaimed. We then negotiated my "fine" or "tip."

In Mexico morality is judged by motive, sequence, and tense. *Propinas* are paid for services, not for profits received. In *propina* transactions, amounts of money are never mentioned. *Mordidas* are paid essentially in self-exculpation, only after their victims have acquiesced to a charge of guilt. Like fines, they punish the wrongdoer, and therefore serve social ends. But *sobornos* are more reprehensible arrangements, because their usual motive is financial gain, on both sides of the transaction, and they're usually arranged in advance of the offense, not in circumstances of need or self-exculpation. Though the phrases most frequently voiced by bribe-happy officials when negotiating a *soborno* are "You say how," and "You decide," that's a mere pretense: Accepting *propinas* is honorable, taking *mordidas* is no sin, but arranging a *soborno* is immoral. But due to the pervasiveness and complexity of Mexican corruption, the mute rules for assessing the different types of bribery are subject to dizzying permutation. If an unwed mother bribes a vital records clerk to give her child a legitimizing name, she has paid a *propina* if the man she victimizes is an ordinary sort, but she's paid a *soborno* if her aim is to file a paternity suit against a gentleman of means. A smuggler may pay a *mordida* when caught with his first shipment, arrange a *soborno* his second time around, and once arrangements have been smoothed out with all parties involved, conduct business afterward in the *propina* mode.

Corruption in Mexico, and self-financing of the forces of order, are at least as old as the Spanish Conquest. Here, for example, is an excerpt from the memoir of Bernal Díaz, a soldier with conquistador Hernán Cortés:

> Many of us were in debt to one another. Some owed fifty or sixty pesos for crossbows, and others fifty for a sword. Everything we bought was equally dear. A certain surgeon called Maestre Juan, who tended some bad wounds, charged excessive prices for his cures, and so did a sort of quack by the name of Murcia, who was an apothecary and barber and also treated wounds. . . .

Díaz also provided an account of how the conquistadores—who established the first Western government in Mexico—divided the booty they captured:

> First of all the royal fifth was taken. Then Cortés said that another fifth must be taken for him, a share equal to His Majesty's. . . .

72

After that he said that he had been put to certain expenses . . . and that what he had spent on the fleet should be deducted from the pile, and in addition the cost to Diego Velázquez of the ships we had destroyed. . . . Then there were the shares of the seventy settlers who had remained at Villa Rica, and the cost of the horse that died, and of Juan Sendeño's mare, which the Tlascalans had killed with a knife-thrust. Then there were double shares for the Mercedarian friar and the priest Juan Díaz and the captains and those who had brought horses, and the same for the musketeers and crossbowmen, so that in the end very little was left, so little indeed that many of us soldiers did not want to touch it, and Cortés was left with it all. At that time we could do nothing but hold our tongues; to demand justice in the matter was useless. There were other soldiers who took their shares of a hundred pesos and clamored for the rest. To satisfy them, Cortés secretly gave a bit to one and another as a kind of favor and by means of smooth speeches made them accept the situation.

Corruption continued under the established Spanish government. Contemporary historian T. R. Fehrenbach gives the following description of government during the years of Spanish colonialism:

"By the 1640s most offices were being sold, both in old and New Spain. The post of *alguacil* to the *audiencia,* or high sheriff, went for one-hundred-and-twenty thousand pesos. Men would invest such enormous sums, not for the honor, but because they could expect to retire rich from any high office in a few years. Justice was venal. Judges purchased their robes and split imposed fines with accusers. The Holy Inquisition burned few persons . . . but in a single *auto-da-fé,* in 1649, the crown and inquisitors divided some three million pesos in fines and penalties. Money could abrogate almost any law.

"Corruption in the highest places inevitably spread down to the lowest clerk and constable. The time came when no legitimate business could be done, no permit secured, no certificate honored, without a payoff. Corruption made the system work."

I first witnessed Mexican corruption in 1962, when my father took me through the border-crossing process at Nuevo Laredo.

I had made arrangements to enroll in a summer language school in Saltillo, a city in the mountains about a two hours' drive south of Monterrey. The Mexican official who interviewed us asked the name of the college I was to attend, and then reached for a catalog on his desk, the J. C. Whitney catalog, published by an American auto-parts supplier. He thumbed the catalog's pages for a moment or two, and then told us that I couldn't enter Mexico because the college in which I planned to enroll wasn't included on the government's list of institutions approved for foreign students. My father laid a five-dollar bill on the bureaucrat's counter. The official picked it up, and returned to perusing the J. C. Whitney catalog. Apparently, he'd made an error in his first consultation, for this time, he found my college listed, I believe, on the page between the turbochargers and the clutch plates.

In 1984, I made the error of trying to enter Mexico by auto on July 4, a day of heavy border traffic. To deal with the rush of tourists, the customs station at Matamoros, on the Gulf, formed visa applications into three lines. The "free line," composed of those who did not want to pay *propinas* for rapid service, moved so slowly that it took two hours to get a permit. The ten-dollar line took only half an hour. The twenty-dollar line offered immediate service. The arrangement exposed one of the secondary reasons why bribery doesn't go away. Bribery turns the government into a vast convenience store. An unbribed administration would impose delays on all its clientele.

Corruption in Mexico is not confined to official circles. Anybody with power of any kind may try to *chingar* or turn his position to illegal advantage. For example, while living in an apartment building, I one morning found that my lights had gone out. I went downstairs, where two workmen from the electric commission were checking a neighbor's meter. They pointed out that I had no meter, and said that was why they'd turned off my electric supply. I protested that I'd paid all my bills, but I was unable to show receipts because my landlord had taken them the day before in order to demand a meter from the power company. The workmen gave me a hard look and then hung around a while, making repetitive arguments and waiting for me to pay. When I made no offers, they left.

The following day, when my wife and the landlord marched into the power-commission office, they learned, as we suspected, that the two workmen had no order to interrupt our service. The problem, it seems, was that my meter had been removed when a previous tenant had fallen into arrears, and though I'd paid my bills on time—I was being billed a flat rate—I had not been issued a meter because meters were in short supply. Though the visit clarified the problem, we had to wait, without electricity, for another four days before workmen arrived to install a meter. When they did, my wife gave their foreman a hefty tip. He handed the money back to her. "I know that you may not believe me," he said, "but some of us who work for the power company are honest."

Several months later, when our rental contract expired, our landlord demanded an increase of 25 percent for the renewal period. But a wage-price freeze, the Pacto de Solidaridad Económico, was in effect. "What about the Pacto?" I asked. "Ah, that's nonsense from the government," he said. I should have known; the landlord wasn't paying sales taxes on his rental income, either. So I went to him with a copy of the state's rent-control law, which limits increases to 10 percent. "Ah, but that's the law, and you're in Mexico. Nobody in Mexico obeys the law," he said. As much to learn how Mexico works as to contest the rent increase, I went to see a lawyer. "Yes, we have a rent-control law," he said, "but we've never had much luck in getting judges to enforce it." Mexico has many laws, and more evasions. I paid the rent increase, because no alternative existed. "Swindles were born before the law and the thief before the lock," a Mexican adage says.

Corruption in its many and blurred forms is extensive enough in Mexico that the country does not run, and could not run, without it. Because Mexico is a generally poor and undercapitalized country, almost nothing can be done with the ease or speed of business in the United States. Mexican commoners accept delays and poor service as an immutable fact of life. *"Pronto y bien no hay quien,"* they say: "Soon and well done, nobody can do." Moneyed Mexicans pay bribes of different sorts to obtain the sort of service and attention that are routine elsewhere. For example, if they want an appointment with a functionary this week and not later, they will tell the functionary's secretary, "I will gratify you if you'll work me into his schedule"—and when the meeting is granted, follow with a tip. Householders pay "tips" to postal carriers for bringing mail to their doors; to garbagemen for timely pickups, to laundresses for prompt and careful service, etc. The general rule is that if a customer or client wants a job done *"pronto y bien,"* he expects and will pay an extra, unofficial fee of some kind. Not to offer or pay these kinds of gratuities is considered an act of ingratitude.

THE PRESS

The PAN, of course, wanted to avoid the kind of shotgun campaign that would condemn all corruption alike, for that would have provoked the people to vote for other parties, in self-defense. Corruption in Mexico is too widespread to tackle head-on. The party needed to focus its fire on figures in high office. The irony was that within its own leadership circles, it had all the information it needed: Its business and industrial backers had paid bribes and kickbacks for years. But the PAN couldn't afford to use that information. It needed fresh scandals, from the press. But reporters in Mexico rarely investigate official wrongdoing, and like almost everyone else, they have reasons for standing aside.

In the United States, investigative reporting did not become a science until the passage of the federal Freedom of Information Act of 1974, in the wake of the Watergate scandal. The act requires public officials to divulge a wide range of information and records to the public upon request. The public isn't similarly privileged in Mexico. Because a few publishers demanded it, President José López Portillo sponsored passage of a Mexican Freedom of Information Act in 1976. But the law was a ruse. Rather than requiring officials to open the records, it gave them the right to do so. The Mexicans also passed a financial-disclosure law, requiring high officials to file a report of their holdings with the government. But the disclosure act did not require that those reports be made available for public scrutiny. The notion that government should be an open book has not been accepted in Mexico.

The Mexican press can't force openness on the government because it has no clout. Its readership is small. Mexico has no equivalent of *The New York Times*, the *Los Angeles Times*, or the *Washington Post*, each of which claims a readership of three-quarters of a million or more. The biggest newspapers in Mexico are of the size of the *Atlanta Constitution* and *Sacramento Bee*, with about a quarter-million readers. Mexico's principal domestic news service is Notimex, owned by the federal government. The press can't develop as it would like because the poverty of its potential readers stands in the way. The Mexican minimum wage varies by region and occupation, but generally stands between four and five dollars a day. Legitimate newspapers cost twenty-five to fifty cents a day, a sum that weighs heavily on the delicate scales of the poor. In the United States, some 62 million newspapers are printed each day, about one for every four people. In Mexico, some 9 million are published each day, one for about every nine Mexicans.

Were it not for the government, its apologists say, newspaper publishing would hardly be possible. Until recent years, most newsprint was imported from industrial countries whose currencies were strong. To make newsprint available, the government subsidized its importation, and distributed it through a state-owned monopoly, the Productora y Importadora de Papel, or PIPSA. Today, Mexico exports newsprint, even to the United States. But PIPSA's role has not been diminished. Newsprint cannot be bought on an open market, and publishers who assail this arrangement, or the government's operation in general, invariably complain that they are shipped inferior paper stock, or that deliveries from PIPSA come late.

The government's stated policy is one of support for the press. It sets the example for other publishers with *El Nacional*, a knock-off of the American daily *USA Today*. Like its American model, *El Nacional* is relayed by satellite and published in identical regional issues. Because *USA Today* is privately owned, it is sometimes capable of doubting the government. *El Nacional* belongs to the State.

Newspapers live from advertising, but because in Mexico

their readerships are small and represent an elite, only businesses with a high-end clientele advertise with regularity. The most reliable advertisers, and those with the biggest budgets, are the national lottery, Pemex, banks, the airlines, the telephone and electric companies, and the Social Security system, all State-owned enterprises, some of which enjoy monopolies, and therefore have no inherent need to advertise. About 25 percent of the advertising space in Mexican newspapers is sold to government subsidiaries, and the PRI and its affiliates account for an additional 15 percent of the whole. Though the government is Mexico's single largest advertiser, newspapers are not censored. Television programming is. Two television channels operate in Mexico. One is owned and operated by the government. The other, a concession of Televisa, a private firm, draws its foreign footage and relays its domestic programming by means of a government satellite. About half of Televisa's advertising comes from the government, too.

The control that the government can exercise over the press was evident in a 1986 dispute centering on *Impacto*, a mature weekly news magazine. Though it had enjoyed a national readership for more than twenty years, *Impacto*'s profits had always been marginal. It survived in the shelter of fat proceeds from another magazine owned by the same publishers, *¡Alarma!*, a gory analogue to American pulps like *Police Gazette*. *¡Alarma!* was scandalous, but in its own prudish sort of way. It didn't publish nude photos, as second-rate Mexican newspapers do. But each week it printed pictures of decapitations and dismemberments, and burn victims who'd been carbonized. It was carnography.

In late 1985, *Impacto* began to lean toward the PAN. Early the next year, it violated the one absolute taboo of the Mexican press. It criticized the president by name. (The established custom was to assail the president's advisers and Cabinet men, but never the president.) Within a month, the government shut down a half-dozen girlie magazines on grounds that they violated the Constitution's Article 7, which guarantees free speech provided that publications respect "private life, morality and the public peace." *¡Alarma!* was caught in the net. Federal agents who said that they were representing a faction in a stockholders' dispute invaded *Impacto*'s office, forcing its editor to leave. In weeks, nudie magazines were back on the street, *¡Alarma!* was replaced by a lookalike publication with a sound-alike name—but produced by a different publisher—and *Impacto*, politically tame and friendly to the PRI, had begun putting cheesecake photos on its covers.

The greatest obstacle to Mexican journalism, then as now, is the salary scale for even seasoned reporters. Most Mexican reporters, even on prestigious dailies, earn less than twice the minimum wage, i.e., less than ten dollars a day. Reporters on many regional dailies are hired without salary, on a piecework basis. They are usually paid about a dollar for each story they produce. In these circumstances, journalists are prey for sources on the make. It is a Mexican tradition that reporters earn their greatest income from accepting *"embutes,"* envelopes filled with cash, distributed semimonthly by the agencies they cover. A reporter whose beat includes the local office of the Secretariat of Agrarian Reform, for example, expects that once or twice a month he'll be given an *embute* by the agency head's secretary. The reporter's obligation, in turn, is to write stories that announce, explain, and extol the agency's role, and to promote an image of its director as an official meriting promotion. If the reporter's beat includes the national headquarters of an agency, he can expect, in addition to the *embute*, offers of paid junkets, subsidized housing, and medical care. Crime reporters are treated to nights on the town in red-light districts that buy protection from the police.

Many government agencies and state-owned enterprises keep *aviadores* or "aviators" on the payroll. Aviators are people in whose names paychecks are issued, but who do not perform any work. Most but not all aviators are aware of their phantom employment. They may allow their names to be used in exchange for an immediate financial benefit, or to repay a favor, or in hopes of landing a real job when an agency has openings. The cash given to a reporter as an *embute* may come from any of a dozen different funds, but it may also come from checks issued in his name as an aviator, by the agency he covers or by another, sometimes even in a different province; one doesn't look stolen horses in the mouth. The *embute* system puts the reporter in a double bind. It obligates his sense of honor; having been paid, he cannot betray his patron's interests in print. And it also creates in him the fear that in a truly open society, his own wrongdoing would come to light.

Reporters are not the only corrupt elements in pressrooms. Editors sell space on front pages, sometimes sending corporate public-relations bulletins into print without changing a word. Weddings, parties, and anniversaries are publicized because hosts purchase the service from the editors of society pages. Soccer teams and bullfighters pay sports-page editors to ensure that their performances will be heralded in advance and praised in reviews. Men in jail are the only Mexicans whose activities are routinely covered without cost or consent. When arrests are made, policemen force suspects to pose for news photographs, knives, guns, stolen goods, or packets of dope in hand.

The system of press bribery also sometimes involves extortion by the press. In late 1988, the editors of the weekly newsmagazine *Proceso* came upon documentary evidence of press malfeasance, and disclosed what they found. Their report included the text of a letter written in May 1988 to the director of the Nacional Monte de Piedad, Mexico's State-owned pawnshop monopoly, by the enterprise's public-relations chief. The letter read:

> As I opportunely informed you, a strong newspaper campaign to denigrate Nacional Monte de Piedad has been projected.
>
> The start of this came to the surface in a note published on the twelfth of this month in the daily *El Universal*, with the object of unchaining a series of notes. These reports were stopped by talking to one of the reporters who cover the health and police beats. (It was in the latter that the campaign was being managed.)
>
> After conversations held with several people, it was learned where the information came from, resultingly, two employees of the Institution whose names and data are now known to you.
>
> In order to learn the names and dates involved in this "campaign," it was necessary to offer different economic compensations.
>
> Newly in this situation we were informed in a timely way of

the "meeting" of twelve newsmen in a capital city restaurant, where they received envelopes containing cash, to attack the Monte de Piedad.

To stop this offensive it will be necessary to pay "equalizers" and an extra amount to the person who is directing this movement, and in that way to know (according to the offer made us) who is behind this situation, and in that way, to detect and stop it.

Up until now, this is costing us five million pesos [about $2,200] which should be turned over without receipt to the aforementioned people. For this reason, I am asking you to allow me to withdraw this amount from the fund for special distributions authorized for these purposes by the Honorable Board of Trustees of the Institution.

A copy of this letter was also sent to Monte de Piedad's comptroller!

The establishment press, or press of record, is manipulated in Mexico by advertising placements and *embutes*, but there exists below it an alternate press composed of thousands of tabloid weeklies, and subject to almost no controls at all. The PANistas could have bought or won the support of this press, in the trade known as the *pasquín* or "comic book" press—but nobody wanted to take the risk. *Pasquines* are dangerously sensationalist newspapers, incomparable to any publications sold on American newsstands. Sensationalist weeklies in the United States take celebrities and scientifically dubious events—the birth of two-headed babies and landings by flying saucers—as their subject matter. *Pasquines* make local figures their targets. Because they sell for about half the price of legitimate newspapers, *pasquines* are the newspapers of Mexico's poor.

Pasquines have names like *The Scorpion* and *The Mosquito*, and mottoes like, "The Truth Is No Sin, but It Sure Discomforts." They are infallibly regionalist, intemperate, and written in the slang of the streets. A *pasquín* I purchased in a northern bordertown, for example, carried a headline reading HELP YOUR COUNTRY, KILL A *CHILANGO*; a *chilango* is a resident of Mexico City. The story beneath was not an exercise in satire, but a listing of serious complaints. "If city buses cost 300 pesos in

81

the north, why do they cost 100 pesos in Mexico City?" the *pasquín* asked. "We pay the cost of gold for electricity," it continued, "while *chilangos* enjoy life, paying less. In Mexico City thousands of products and all public services are much cheaper, while in the north prices keep going up. All because if you raise prices for the *chilangos* by one peso, they make a frightful fart, and to calm them, THEY RAISE PRICES TO THOSE IN THE NORTH." As *pasquines* frequently do, the newspaper predicted a revolution, this time of northern Mexico against the "monstrous D.F.," or federal district.

Pasquines are popular because of their boldness, as well as their price. In them, cops and officialdom get their due. Not many newspapers in Mexico, for example, would resort to opening paragraphs like, "The corruption that is manipulated in the Traffic Department is such that traffic policemen, like spoiled children, get what they want by merely stomping on the ground." Nor would many newspapers publish a four-inch headline, for a story about the U.S. Border Patrol, that says "THE GRINGOS HAVE US IN THEIR SIGHTS," though the term *gringo* has been in general use for a century.

Immoderate journalism is sometimes necessary, and it certainly played an important role in Mexico's past. But the *pasquines* take matters too far. Stories from some of the *pasquines* in my files cannot be quoted without infringing American libel protections. One of them, in which, for obvious reasons, I've changed the principal's name, is headlined JOHN DOE ROE (THE CLUTCH MAN) SEXUALLY ABUSES HIS FEMALE EMPLOYEES. The text opens with, "John Doe Roe is a subject who knows neither morals nor decency and who, as if it were natural, sexually abuses his female employees, converting them into his concubines in a humiliating and shameful way." The victim of this report is a married man and the owner of a business cited in the story, a private citizen who had not been charged or convicted of any crime. If it is likely that there is some element of truth in the report the newspaper made, as in any gossip, it is also likely that the story was published because John Doe Roe refused to pay a blackmail demand. The power of the press, like that of any weapon, can be turned to crime, and Mexico is dotted with newspapers of criminal intent. And that, finally, is why political parties don't seek the support of *pasquines:* One doesn't know what ends the relationship might ultimately serve. During the past decade, some thirty Mexican journalists have been murdered by unknown parties. The most illustrious of them were killed because they were trying to do an honest job, but the likelihood is that some of the others were killed by those they blackmailed.

Perhaps the millionaire members of the PAN, and they are legion, could have created a parallel press, a chain of newspapers in which reporters paid bribes to government employees to obtain information damning to officials. But it would have taken a decade to buy or found such newspapers, and government permits are needed to import printing equipment. The PAN instead had to be content with an anticorruption campaign confined to the government's lowest levels.

THE POLICE

If the PAN's offensive against corruption didn't win elections, it at least aided the press. Mexico entered a period in which readers expected a few scandals to be reported, and in which officials sometimes presented reporters with documented evidence of malfeasance in government. Public disclosure became a tactic of political control. When an official offended a rival, the rival felt free to report the official's misdoings to the press. If a superior needed an excuse to fire a subordinate, he reported the subordinate's crookedness to the press, etc. But none of the institutional barriers to public airings were removed. Journalists worried that the impetus for exposing scandals always came from within the government.

Some of them tried to make the process work in reverse. For example, in early 1988, when customs inspectors in the state of Nuevo León impounded a dozen tractor-trailers loaded with some $45 million in contraband cattle feed, instead of merely writing reports that lauded customs agents in the interior, reporters in Monterrey asked how the trucks had entered Mexico without being inspected at the Texas border. Perhaps because Mexican feed producers with links to the PRI also demanded an answer, the newsmen's inquiry turned up a paper trail documenting the legendary corruption of border customs agents.

Gains made by the press became obvious in a series published in May 1988, when astute reporters followed up a relatively routine story about some dead policemen. On the weekend of May 14–15, Mexico City dailies carried a back-page story reporting that on Friday, May 13, two policemen had been found shot to death in an unmarked car. The story attracted little notice, because police deaths are common in violent Mexico. For example, between the years 1960 and 1987, 147 lawmen were killed in the state of New York, whose current population is about 18 million, and 119 were killed in Illinois, whose current population is about 12 million. But in Mexico City, whose population is about 20 million, 126 policemen were killed in 1987 alone, more than twenty times the number that American statistics would predict.

But the details of the May 13 deaths were intriguing. Witnesses said that the two policemen had been waiting in traffic in their Dart K for a stoplight to change when, for unexplained reasons, the Dart K's driver shifted into reverse and slammed into the car behind, a red Ford Topaz. Down-home Mexican insults like "big billy goat" and "ox" were hurled between the occupants of the two cars, and two men descended from the Topaz. They walked up beside the Dart, more insults were exchanged, shots rang out, and the Topaz sped away. One of the dead cops in the Dart had been the son of a police-department executive. The investigation became a matter of secrecy.

A little more than a week later, in the early hours of Sunday, May 22, another cop was found dead in a car, this time in the parking lot of the Mexico City station house on Topacio Street, home to the executive offices of the city's judicial, or investigatory, police. The dead man, Estanislao Aguilar, had been a chief of the judicial police in the state of Mexico, which surrounds the capital city. Initial reports said that he had died of a heart attack, but that story didn't last long. Two police forces had fatally locked horns over the Dart K killings—or whatever gave rise to them—and members of both were telling at least a part of the secrets they knew.

Witnesses to the Dart K killings had provided the Mexico City police with the license-tag number of the red Topaz that fled the scene. The investigation that had begun at Topacio pointed toward another police headquarters, in the suburb of San Agustín, outside the city's jurisdiction, in Mexico State. A leading suspect was a cop named Adolfo Alanís, who worked at the San Agustín station house. On the night of May 19, as he was driving home from work in his Datsun, Alanís was forced to the roadside by two autos, one of which repeatedly bumped his car from the rear, while the other tried to crowd him off the road from the front. Alanís stepped out of his Datsun, showed his identification—and was kidnapped.

He was blindfolded, driven to an unknown location, stripped, bound, and confined to a room. When he asked his captors to identify themselves, they told him that they were military policemen who specialized in extracting confessions from guerrillas. Then they doused him with water, stretched him onto a board, and tied his limbs. "We want you to tell us everything you did on May 13," one of them said, "without forgetting about the two murders that you already know about."

When he denied any knowledge of the killings, his tormentors crammed a rag into his mouth and poured water into his nose. More dousings followed, supplemented by treatments of electrical shock applied to the testicles. Alanís endured about two hours of this fairly standard interrogation before confessing that two of his fellow officers at the San Agustín station were involved in the Dart K affair. He was then unbound and taken to a police station, where, after four hours of apparently civilized questioning, he signed a statement about the May 13 murders.

About 11:00 A.M. on the morning following the abduction of Alanís, three men in a red Ford Topaz left the San Agustín police station to witness an eviction of urban squatters in the suburb of Chalco. On their way back, about three hours later, the Topaz slowed as it approached a tollbooth. A Chrysler New Yorker with smoked windshields pulled in front of the Topaz, and a Dart K closed its path from behind. Two armed men got out of the New Yorker, approached the Topaz—and three more cops were kidnapped.

All three were taken to a house near the Mexico City airport, where they were blindfolded and beaten. But two of the captive officers, both named Gerardo, were separated from the third. They were told that the third officer was the object of the abduction. Nevertheless, they were tortured until they declared that their chief, Estanislao Aguilar—the third captive officer— was guilty of killing the Dart K cops. Though Aguilar was being interrogated out of the sight of the two Gerardos, he was not out of their earshot. They heard the hiss of a welding torch.

About 11:00 P.M., some eight hours after the interrogations had begun, the three officers were taken to the Topacio police station. The two Gerardos were locked in cells. Aguilar was carried into the parking lot—he had fainted—and tied to a stray piece of office furniture. His interrogation resumed.

A few minutes later, a crime reporter drove onto the lot. He saw what was happening, and fearing that he might be in danger, too, he immediately left. The cops continued their labor, undisturbed by either the reporter's arrival or departure. Some two hours later, just seconds after the cops removed a plastic bag from his head, Aguilar's body began to convulse, and he died. The investigating team placed his body in the red Topaz, which had been brought from the torture house. This done, one of Aguilar's captors went inside the station. He telephoned a superior to report that the subject had died of heart failure. The two Gerardos were released from their cells, given their clothing and guns, and told to go home. When they had dressed themselves, they found that their pockets had been robbed! They had to beg taxi fare from the cops at Topacio.

In the wake of Aguilar's death, Mexico City's police chief, Jesús Miyazawa, whose predecessor was still in jail on car-theft and corruption charges, was accused of foreknowledge of Aguilar's interrogation, and of protecting the flight of several policemen who vanished when Aguilar's corpse was discovered. Miyazawa and a half-dozen other police executives were fired. Their departures coincided with publication of a rumor that was making the rounds of criminal circles. According to jailhouse and Mafioso scuttlebutt, the May 13 altercation at the traffic light had not been the result of mere happenstance. The Topaz was shadowing the Dart K, the rumor said, in connection with a row between the city and state police forces over the division of fat *mordidas* paid by the leader of a notorious bank-robbery gang. The rumor was never run to the ground.

PANistas were delighted by the scandal anyway. On May 19, when the Dart K killings had still been clouded by mystery, the PAN had published a tantalizing and defiant quarter-page ad in newspapers across the country. Though the ad caused grumbling in the party's most conservative quarters—its detractors said it made the PAN look like a party of the left—it was probably the most popular piece of propaganda produced during the campaign year. Shopkeepers taped the ad to counters and doors, office workers passed it from desk to desk. In bold-faced letters three quarters of an inch tall, the ad asked, WHO DO YOU FEAR MOST, THE POLICE . . . OR THE THIEVES? Its fine print included a call to elevate the professional levels of lawmen, but the fine print isn't what struck the nation's nerve. The ad was popular because it made public the then-unpublished truth: that *mordidas* and *sobornos* are merely the polite forms of virulence. In Mexico, it's hard to tell the difference between the forces of law and crime.

To test this hypothesis, for several months following the Dart-Topaz killings, I kept a clippings file on crimes committed by the police. My research was not exhaustive. I merely read newspapers that happened to come my way in the process of what amounts to casual reading. My file for the first month after the killings included these reports:

On May 25, the missing mayor of a town in the state of Michoacán turned up just across the border, in the state of Jalisco. He said that he'd been kidnapped by the federal police.

On June 8, Alfonso Maza, father-in-law to a prominent Mexican politician then serving as ambassador to Belgium, attended a Mexico City lineup in which all the suspects were policemen. He said that he'd been kidnapped by uniformed city officers, who had burned him with his auto's cigarette lighter and then had taken the car.

On June 12, two cops were arrested in Guadalupe, a suburb

of Monterrey. They were charged with the killing of a robbery suspect whose body had been found in the backseat of a patrol car the day before. Guadalupe's police chief said that the two officers, both drunk at the time, had collared the suspect to collect a *mordida* payment, and had killed him when he resisted paying. The cop who confessed to the slaying admitted that he'd been drunk, but denied that he was trying to collect a bribe. According to the cop, the suspect knew where the cop's ex-wife lived, and the cop was trying to extract that information when his pistol misfired.

On June 20, in San Nicolas, in the state of Nuevo León, another Monterrey suburb, a cop, a truck driver, and a brick-layer were arrested on charges of stealing and stripping several cars, burglarizing a store, and mugging a pedestrian on his way home from work.

That same week, the Mexico City newspaper *El Universal* reported that "Four uniformed officers of the Auxiliary Police, assigned to the Mexico City International Airport, were arrested by fellow officers on suspicion of responsibility for dozens of assaults on international and national tourists, especially from the south. . . . It was established that the assailants intercepted their victims in the terminal and accused them of being illegal aliens, drug traffickers, or simply suspicious persons, to carry them outside of the airport, where they took money and the valuables they carried."

On June 21, two Mexico City policemen were arrested in connection with an investigation whose purpose, it was alleged, had been literally perverted. Earlier in the month, the two cops had been dispatched to a home in Cuernavaca, an hour's drive away, to investigate a robbery. According to the charges made against them, instead of investigating, they stole two cars from the home, kidnapped the homeowner, and held him in Mexico City until they collected a three-thousand-dollar ransom from his son.

On the night of June 21, between Orizaba and Fortín de las Flores, in the state of Veracruz, a federal highway patrolman halted a motorist and fired a machine gun at the captive's feet, forcing him to dance. The cop was disarmed and taken into custody by a second motorist. Doctors who examined the patrolman, a Veracruz newspaper reported, said that he "was drunk in the third degree."

The prize clipping in my file didn't come until early September 1988, after the furor of elections was past. On Monday, September 5, Mexican newspapers reported an incident that had occurred two days earlier. On Saturday morning, two policemen from Mexico City's traffic and crowd control force, Protección y Vialidad, had been arrested by *judiciales,* or investigatory police, and jailed at the Topacio headquarters, the place where Aguilar had died. The two cops were charged with having mugged a pedestrian. Several hours later, some seventeen police cars and a half-dozen tow trucks from Protección y Vialidad sealed the streets around the Topacio station. A news vendor closed his kiosk and ran; prostitutes on a street corner vanished. Some sixty traffic and riot-control cops dismounted from the vehicles, occupied the basement and roof of Topacio, and posted armed guards at the building's entrances. A group of them, wielding automatic weapons and shotguns, went into the station's operations office and demanded that the two captive cops be set free. After their two comrades had been sprung, the command group took two pistols and five walkie-talkies from the officers at Topacio and led the invading force into retreat. In the days that followed, the Protección officer who led the takeover was booked, but none of the other marauders was disciplined. Justice had met its match in firepower.

THE NORTH

The importance of police scandals to analyzing Mexico is simple: Good governments don't tolerate bad cops. By the time of the police scandals of 1988, I'd already developed doubts about the Mexican government, because three years earlier, I'd watched Mexico vote, in Monterrey. I'd gone there in the wake of the PAN's first important victory, winning the mayoralty of Mexico's fourth-largest city, Ciudad Juárez, Chihuahua. The Mexican northlands had always sympathized with antigovernment movements of the center and right, and most observers predicted that in the gubernatorial elections of 1985, the PAN in Monterrey would triumph at last.

The north of Mexico—north of the 22nd parallel—is nearly a different country. South of the 22nd, Mexico is lush and tropical, and except for the Yucatán Peninsula, it's mainly mountainous, with overcast skies. In the south, there are two seasons, rainy and dry. Rainfall is relatively plentiful, and temperatures rarely cold. In some southern locales, farmers harvest two corn crops a year.

The north is nothing like that. Its four seasons are sharply marked, like those in the United States. Winter is windy and sometimes freezing cold. Summers are parched and scorching; spring and fall are truce times between men and the elements. The northern terrain is mainly flat, sparsely covered with grasses, scrub brush, and mesquite. Northern Mexico is like southern Texas. If southern Mexico resembles any American region, it is California's Pacific Coast.

The staple food in all of Mexico is the tortilla, a flat cake of toasted grain, but in Mexico south of the 22nd parallel the tortilla is made of corn. In the north, it's made of wheat, a plant from across the Atlantic, unknown in Mexico before the Spaniards came. Northern Mexico adopted the flour tortilla because in the north there's not enough rain for corn to grow; most of the area receives less than twenty inches a year, about ten inches too little for dependable corn cultivation. The flour tortilla is a symbol of the north's distinctiveness: flour ties the region to the essentially European culture of the United States as much as its tortilla form ties it to the Mesoamerican culture of Mexico.

Mexico's arid northern landscape is dotted with cattle, red-brown Herefords, as on the American plains. To the south, the dominant breed is Cebú, floppy-earned animals of white or gray whose resistance to disease is superior, and whose flesh is flavorless and tough. Like Americans, northerners prefer beef, and they consume plenty of it. Southerners prefer pork, but its price is beyond their reach; poultry is the dish of the south's laboring classes, as it was for their pre-Hispanic ancestors.

The diet of the north is more than a question of taste and

convenience. It's also a question of culture, class, and caste. The elaboration of corn is the basis of dozens of local cuisines. Mexico has evolved 124 different ways of preparing corn on the cob, 166 types of tortilla, 86 kinds of tamale, more than 100 puddings, pastries, and candies of corn, and 17 different corn-based drinks. Corncobs are used as kindling, and are ground with a glue to prepare a molding material like plaster of Paris. Leaves are cured like rope to be used as plaiting. Corn silk is the basis of medicinal teas, and like I-ching sticks, grains are used in telling fortunes. In some indigenous areas, a newborn's umbilical cord is cut upon an ear of corn, which is then soaked in the blood of the placenta and saved for planting time; its grains become the basis of the field that the child will cultivate for the rest of his life. In Mexico, wheat is an import, devoid of these traditions.

Statistics show that the lower half of Mexico's population, in terms of earnings, consumes twice as much corn per capita as the upper half. It consumes only half as many vegetables, and a quarter of the meat. Though most northern workers preserve a lifestyle similar to that of their ancestors from the south, the north's access to and preference for beef and wheat are a testimony to its prosperity, and its Europeanization. Skin color, corn consumption, and income form similar patterns in the Mexican population, and in the north, people are richer, whiter, and more familiar with wheat and meat—in a word, more Europeanized. Even the radio tells you that the north is distinct. *Norteño* songs are westerns in verse, ballads about bad men, Texas Rangers, and the drug trade. In the south, people prefer the Afro-Caribbean rhythms and baby-let's-dance lyrics of what is called *la música tropical*.

In the south, to say "Indian" is to say "grandmother," or to make reference to a nearby community that still lives by the mysterious, but respectable and seemingly immutable dictates of tradition. In the north, "Indian" is equivalent to "African" in the American parlance, a reference to something the minorities left behind. To the south there are bicycles and electric fans, and all the institutions of ambulatory life, tailored to a street-level scale. But to the north there's an air conditioner in every downtown window and a speeding pickup in every traffic lane. If Mexico is to perfect the ways of the West—national democracy is a Western invention—the momentum will come from the north.

Monterrey is a town of 3 million that Andrew Carnegie would have liked. It sprawls on the flat bottom of a bowl whose sides are the mountains of the eastern Sierra Madre. It's an industrial town like Puebla, Guadalajara, and Juárez, sister cities in the PANista fold. Monterrey is dedicated to heavy industry. Steel mills belch fire into the night, covering it with a blanket of fog. Glass, plastics, and cement are made there, too. Big industry's workers belong to "white" or company-sponsored labor unions. These organizations provide them with cheap housing, sports activities, vacation plans, and transportation to work. Members of the white unions live more comfortably than most of those who belong to the mainstream unions, and, in general, the city's living standard is high. Only 20 percent of Monterrey's workers earn less than the legal minimum wage, and 15 percent of the workforce earns more than twice as much.

Monterrey is also a banking and trade center and, less important in its own eyes, a government seat. A part of its downtown district has been restored and converted into a pedestrian mall. Skyscrapers have been stacked on the rest. The business district begins at a vast square called the Macroplaza, where a towering orange obelisk, the Lighthouse of Commerce, shoots a green laser beam above a half-mile of flagstone walkways, straight into the eyes of the national symbol—an eagle perched on a cactus, with a snake in its mouth—that crowns the capitol of Nuevo Léon. Monterrey's businessmen are so tightfisted that in Mexican slang to say that someone is from Monterrey is to call him a skinflint.

They are careful men, too. During the mid-seventies leftist hit squads roamed the city, on hunts for capitalist game. Their trophy kill was Don Eugenio Garza Sada, the city's leading industrialist, a Mexican Mellon or Du Pont. Following his death in 1973, the rich built turreted walls around their homes, and put a guard at every door. Prosperous neighborhoods in Monterrey became armed camps.

Monterrey owes its character to its locale and to official neglect. Mexico's northern reaches, because of their aridity, were only sparsely settled at the time of the Conquest. Nomadic tribes lived there, peoples whom the settled Aztecs called *chichimeca*, or "sons of dogs." For centuries after the Spanish came, the north was useful mainly as a lode. Its mineral wealth was exploited, but when the veins wore out, almost no one stayed. It was the central government's disdain for the north that led, in 1596, to Monterrey's founding by a company of seven hundred Spaniards of dubious loyalty, exiles from Mexico City. The region's climate was discouraging, but the city's founders couldn't turn back. The Inquisition suspected them of professing Judaism, the penalty for which was death.

Monterrey's development was due not to any Mexican impetus, but to the city's proximity to the United States. During the American Civil War, it became a hub of commerce as a supplier to the Confederacy. The city's first railroad line in 1882 tied Monterrey to Texas, not to the Mexican south. Coal and ore were both near at hand; Monterrey built Latin America's first steel plants. Its Cuauhtémoc Brewery, founded in 1890 and home to Carta Blanca beer, developed plants to produce glass for bottles, sheet steel for bottlecaps, and packing materials for boxes. By the seventies it had become an industrial conglomerate with two hundred thousand employees. Until oil production eclipsed the value of all other Mexican enterprise, Monterrey was credited with a fourth of the country's gross national product and almost a third of its export income. The view frequently taken in Monterrey is that while southern Mexico was still wrapped in the folkways of the pre-Hispanic past, and central Mexico was still wrestling with the traumas of the Conquest, the north followed the lead of the industrial West into an age of reason. The gods of Greek mythology frolic in the principal fountain of Monterrey's Macroplaza. Elsewhere in Mexico, Aztec deities adorn public works.

The city is only three hours' drive from the Texas border, and the influence shows. Convenience stores sit on almost every corner, and traffic is dense. There are neighborhoods in Monterrey like the cushy Contry, where if men wear shorts, nobody snickers, and when women wear shorts, nobody stares, and where in collegiate circles flirting in fluent English is part of the dating game. Graduates take pride in landing jobs with big corporations, and in the business community appointments are set by the quarter hour. The city is so much like an American city that it's possible for a visitor to believe that he's in Houston. Sixty percent of Monterrey's homes have television, and the Super Bowl is practically a municipal event. The Lion's Club is the city's prestige organization, and the coast of Texas is its favorite resort. Department stores in San Antonio and Laredo advertise their sales in Monterrey's dominant daily, *El Norte*. The newspaper's reporters earn the highest journalistic salaries in Mexico—about four hundred dollars a month—and receive professional instruction in classes taught by professors from the American Midwest. When you read *El Norte*, you think you're at home: Almost every day the newspaper reprints feature articles from the *Wall Street Journal* and *Business Week*. Its society pages carry headlines like OFRECEN BABY SHOWER PARA ARACELY RIOS. Popular restaurants carry names like Marshall's Star and Smile Burger, the latter home to the world-famous "Rock and Dog" hot dog.

Monterrey's business leaders don't always say so, but they despise the Mexican government and the PRI. Most government works programs, they'll tell you in private settings, are aimed at generating kickbacks, employing troublesome social scientists, and dispensing patronage to the dishonest poor. The government's Constitutional regency over economic life, they say, has never amounted to much more than a plan for corruption, rewarding incompetence and hastening ruin. They believe that government trade restrictions, rather than encouraging the development of national industry, drive up production costs, discourage innovation, and retard the development of skills and technology.

Though publicly most of Monterrey's businessmen endorse the PRI, privately many of them finance the PAN, which is usually so flush that detractors accuse it of accepting Republican donations in the United States. The hostility between Monterrey and Mexico's leaders is time-honored and mutual. In 1973, President Luis Echeverría declared that Monterrey was home to Mexico's "profascist" tendencies, and though a truce came in the late seventies, when the government bailed out a Monterrey conglomerate that was in danger of collapse, the enmity resurfaced in 1982 with the bust. Monterrey's industries were trapped between dollar debts and peso earnings, and the pinch was aggravated by three devaluations in a period of less than nine months. Mexican capitalism as a whole was about to take a dunk, but Monterrey's businessmen had decided to go down fighting. A few months before my visit in 1985, the PAN had nominated a thin young industrialist with bushy eyebrows, Fernando Canales, for the governship of Nuevo León.

The PRI had made shrewd preparations for an electoral steal. The state's electoral commission, appointed by a PRIista governor, had inflated voting rolls with the names of voters who actually lived not in Nuevo León, but in Matamoros, a border town in the nearby state of Tamaulipas. The trick was discovered by a PANista who, while casually paging the list, noticed on it the names of friends of his from Matamoros, friends whose names, because they came from a family of plutocrats, were familiar even to Texan foreigners like me. After exposing this patent malfeasance in *El Norte*, the PAN submitted the election roll to a computer scan. It turned up a pattern of false listings, thousands of names: The conclusion reached was that a government computer had been programmed to pad the voting list. The discovery reminded the PAN of the need for vigilance on election day.

UN PELADO

I spent that day, as I would again on election day, 1988, riding with Herminio in his 1974 Maverick. His job was to supervise balloting at 167 polling stations on Monterrey's south side. It was a cumbersome and possibly dangerous assignment, because Monterrey is more than money, modernity, and the politics of industrialists. It is Chicago's Uptown District, it is West L.A. and North Hollywood, Houston's Dowling and Wheeler streets, too. The city's hillsides are ringed by gritty industrial suburbs, settled by families from *ejidos* and towns of outlying states, in a continual diaspora whose object is jobs. The newcomers build houses from whatever they can find: cinder block, steel sheeting, even cardboard and wire. When land is not available for their makeshift homes, they occupy it anyway, in the widely held belief that the Mexican Constitution guarantees every married man the right to a homestead plot. (The Constitution does guarantee that, but only to members of groups whose status has been recognized at law.) Nuevo León's government has in recent years set aside more than fifty tracts for the newcomers, sites called Fomereyes, but it still must play a game of patronage and pork barrel with new arrivals. If electric lines aren't ready, the *colonos,* or settlers, tap them illegally. When sewer lines haven't been laid, they simply point their drains away from their houses and go on with the business of daily life; in their neighborhoods, long black lines of sewage snake down white caliche streets, seemingly unnoticed, until they reach gutters or the pavements below. Mexicans of settled circumstances call these squatter towns *ciudades perdidas,* or "lost cities," and refer to their inhabitants disparagingly as *pelados* or *nacos,* rednecks or riffraff. Some of these members of the urban poor are Spartan, rustic, and suspicious of the city. Others are given to brawling, gambling, and back-door games. Almost none of them takes to the discipline of industrial life. Their survival instinct propels them to acts requiring great energy, but the odds they face dull them to all but short-range hopes. Romantics of both the left and right look upon them as grains of gunpowder in a time bomb. Cynics liken them to the fireworks that are ignited on patriotic days: noisy, harmless, and cheaply bought.

I had a sense of the problems that Herminio would face on his fence-riding mission for the PAN because a few days earlier I'd made friends with one of these raw proletarians, and had assessed his despair. We'd met by chance in an unlikely place, at the headquarters of the PAN. Several American reporters were waiting in its lobby for a chance to interview Fernando Canales, the candidate, and—let's call him Rogelio—was there with the same goal in mind. Rogelio was a dark-skinned, husky man, dressed in run-down shoes, khaki pants, and a cotton shirt that was two sizes too tight. His hair was uncombed, and his face was unshaved. A Rastafarian at a benefit for George Bush couldn't have looked more out of place. Taking advantage

96

of Rogelio's incongruency, one of the reporters asked him why he supported the PAN. "Because the government that we have," Rogelio declaimed in a voice that was too loud, "is a government that stinks." He didn't say that the government was malodorous, as Canales would have, and he didn't say that it smelled, as Herminio might have. He said *apesta*, it stinks. The reporter penciled Rogelio's name and the quote into a notepad, and the two continued their interview. Rogelio, who said that he was a neighborhood leader, five years a member of the PAN, railed at corruption and unemployment, rigged elections, and the rest. He said that he and his neighbors didn't want to resort to arms, as their grandfathers had in the Revolution of 1910, but that with the upcoming election, they were giving the PRI its last chance: There would be a clean election or bloody unrest. The hour was late, and the reporters soon drifted away. Canales wasn't taking any additional visitors, so Rogelio and I went downtown to eat.

I paid the check, of course: Supper in even an ordinary restaurant can cost a workingman four days' pay. While we were dining, Rogelio told me what had led him to the offices of the PAN. There's an old custom in Mexico that says that public officials must attend to all citizens who ask for their aid. They don't have to grant the favors asked, but by tradition they can't deny an audience to anyone. During Rogelio's youth, when his family had been in dire straits, he and his mother had spent thirteen days waiting in the anteroom of the governor of Nuevo León. When she was at last received, she had asked for a loan. The governor had offered a public-works job instead. Rogelio's mother had scored; at thirteen, her son had become an employee of the state. Rogelio was in his late thirties on the night we dined, and the public-works job was long behind him. He was unemployed again, though he'd had a job as a welder during the boom. He'd decided that the only place he could appeal for help was to the governor, as his mother had done. But in Mexico governors can't succeed themselves, and it was election time. Rogelio told me that he might visit the incumbent, if all else were to fail, but first, he had planned to appeal to Canales. He'd picked Canales not because he thought the PANista would win—in the minds of Mexican commoners, elections aren't contests, they are conspiracy plays—but because Canales was an industrialist, who signed payrolls every week. With Canales's help, Rogelio could go to work without waiting for a change of regime. "When I get to see him," he told me, "the least he can do is send me for an appointment at his personnel office." Rogelio had been waiting for Canales for two days, and he planned to return when morning came.

Early the next day, Canales sent word that he wouldn't be dropping by the campaign office until late afternoon. So I accompanied Rogelio, aboard a bus, to his habitual post of the past few months, a park where construction workers wait for contractors to pass. Some twenty-five men were gathered in the park in groups of four and five, ironworkers here, masons there, electricians on the side. We joined a group of carpenters and waited for two hours; only one contractor stopped, to load three painters into his pickup. We boarded another bus, this time headed toward the house of a friend who had a plumbing part that Rogelio needed at home. The bus stopped in the middle of a long, streetside market where foodstuffs were sold. We trudged through the market and up a hill, and as we progressed, I noticed that the political scenery had changed.

Election times in Mexico are times of great display. Almost every exterior wall in the nation becomes a canvas for slogans; even the walls of houses aren't immune to *pintas*, or announcements. Most *pintas* are professional work, done with a sense of style and a steady hand. The PAN's *pintas* are blue on white, the PRI's *pintas* are in the colors of the national flag, red, white, and green. The PRI's *pintas* are everywhere, for reasons that most Mexicans take for granted. I once asked a Mexico City PRIista *pinta*-painter how his wages were calculated. "I'm paid a salary, what do you think?" he told me. "I work for the Department of Parks." But there was none of this in the neighborhood I entered with Rogelio. The walls were painted with murals showing the likes of Emiliano Zapata and Che. It dawned on me that we were inside the Campamento Tierra y Libertad, or Land and Liberty Encampment, a squatter settlement of some fifty thousand residents, founded in the mid-seventies by Mexican disciples of Marx. Tierra y Libertad had a reputation as a tough and independent turf. In 1976, seven of its inhabitants had been killed in a gun battle with police. Students with guns patrolled its streets during its early years and usually kept the police from entering, partly because political fugitives took shelter there. Taxis wouldn't go in, for reasons I never knew, and though journalists were usually admitted, they were not guaranteed a time of return. Residents kept them until they felt that their grievances had been fully explained. Though the settlement had outlived its armed and revolutionary phase, its leaders were still full of spunk. One of them had declared himself as an independent candidate for governor, in opposition to the PRI and PAN.

"What do you think of the leadership of this neighborhood?" I asked Rogelio, my guide. "Ah, they're a bunch of loud-mouthed communists who want to fight the PRI," he said. His answer lacked the ring of PANismo. "Don't you think that some of the demands of Tierra y Libertad were just?" I said. "Well, it helped them get land and water lines, I guess, but now that the houses are built, I don't see what they gain," he said. His second answer, like the first, didn't sound as if it came from a militant of the anticommunist right.

Rogelio's friend was not at home. We returned to the bus line, this time headed for Rogelio's house, in a rough-edged working-class neighborhood farther west in the hills. As we walked down his street, I noticed PANista stickers on a neighbor's window. "Yeah, that old bat, she thinks she's boss around here," Rogelio complained. "She and these other PAN-istas think that they're going to take over, just like the PRI." It was then that he confessed that he'd never registered to vote, let alone militated in the PAN.

We entered his house, a two-room, whitewashed, cinder-block place, with a patio and bathroom out back. His wife, a chubby light-skinned woman in her mid-twenties, was sitting at a Formica dining table that stood adjacent to the kitchen. She was watching a black-and-white television set with a hazy screen. "This is the Texan I told you about, fix us some beef," Rogelio ordered her. She folded her pudgy hands and looked upward at him in incredulity. In most Mexican homes, red meat is a luxury of the past. "Well, fix him some meat," Rogelio insisted. "But you know there's not any," she muttered, while

99

I protested that suppertime was hours away. Flustered, Rogelio left the house, saying he was bound for the butcher shop.

His wife and I began to converse. She had spent three years working in an air-conditioner factory in Fort Worth, she said, and though she hadn't liked the work, she'd liked the pay. She and a girlfriend had split the expenses of a room in a private home, and she had hoarded her earnings until her return to Monterrey. That was two years before, in 1983. She'd spent her savings to marry Rogelio, and then had borne him a son. Now that her pregnancy was past and Rogelio was out of work, she'd convinced him to accompany her on another sojourn to the north. The infant was old enough to travel, and the only problem in view was crossing the border. Her connections were burned: She had crossed with her father and his friends, by cover of night, she hadn't known where. Her father hated Rogelio and wouldn't give him advice, but a friend like me, she was sure, would know how to proceed.

Americans who are in contact with the lower ranks of Mexican society face similar situations all the time. Working-class Mexicans want to buy dollars at bankers' rates, or enter the United States on the sly, or purchase tools, tennis shoes, and tape recorders on which taxes haven't been paid. Because I am indifferent to immigration laws, I gave her my best advice, and as soon as Rogelio entered the door—a package of meat in hand—I begged my way out, into the street and gone. I wasn't shocked at the couple's desire to go north, but I had been shocked by Rogelio's designs on the PAN. I was convinced that for a week's pay, he—and probably dozens of others in his neighborhood—would rent themselves as goons or ballot-stuffers on election day. I had known revolutionaries, and Rogelio clearly wasn't one. He was a classic character of the treacherous *lumpenproletariat*, straight out of the scathing pages of Engels's *Condition of the Working Class in England*.

I was glad when Sunday came. It meant that I'd be back on official turf. The risks of making casual or unofficial inquiries into affairs that touch on Mexican politics are unpredictable. Authorities usually take a stern view of foreign probing, and they don't necessarily distinguish between background reporting—what I was doing by following Rogelio home—and spying. Had I discovered a nest of ballot-stuffers, for example, I could easily have vanished, forever: During the mid-seventies, hundreds of skeptical Mexicans were "disappeared" by government agents, and one American reporter, whose photographs of an assault on demonstrators would have shamed the government, was stripped of her film, blindfolded, and kidnapped by soldiers. But the risks of keeping company with Herminio, I figured, would fall within the framework of written law. He and I might be accused of interfering with officials, or possibly with intimidating voters, but even if we were jailed on such baseless charges, I felt assured that others would know our whereabouts, and that the protections granted other prisoners would be extended to us. There have been periods in Mexican history when reporting was treated as treason, but those days have largely passed.

The most serious challenge Herminio and I faced on Sunday was that of not getting lost. Monterrey's polling places are located mostly in homes, and residential street numbers in Mexico defy all patterns. The car doors slammed throughout the day as one PANista after another sat down in the Maverick to act as guide. Even the guides were lost when we discovered, fully a dozen times, that polling places had established substations that weren't recorded on any lists. "Have you checked *bis* number one?" a sympathizer at a poll would ask, *bis* being the designation for an auxiliary or branch. At *bis* one Herminio would learn of the existence of *bis* two, and at *bis* two, he'd be given the location of *bis* three. We traveled a never-ending and byzantine path down alleyways and residential streets, like cops looking for speakeasys during the era of Al Capone.

We spent early morning in neighborhoods of rough-and-tumble, hours marked mainly by bickering over the placement of ballot boxes. The law plainly says that boxes are to be placed in public view, but several officials balked. They'd put their boxes beneath schoolhouse tables, or in the bedrooms of their homes. "The vote is supposed to be secret!" they'd shout at Herminio. "Yes, but its deposit is not," he'd tell them, smiling

101

with magnanimity. His and the PAN's concern was to expose the use of *"tacos,"* premarked ballots, as they were stuffed in wads into the boxes.

Some of the polling places we visited were on genteel streets, well marked and clean. Election day at those spots was like a neighborhood brunch. Refreshments were served on driveways and lawns to guests who came to vote. The electoral code requires voters' thumbs to be dyed, and at those polling places, not only was the law observed, but lotion was provided to remove the ink. Poll captains understood their duties, and regarded Herminio more as a Mr. Manners consultant than as an irregularities-inspection snoop: "I've set up the tables and boxes on the patio, but don't you think it would be nice if I asked people to come inside?" one matron asked. Most of the people in these neighborhoods were rock-ribbed supporters of the PAN, and the spattering of government executives among them kept a light and conciliatory mood: "Herminio, if the PAN wins this election, will you hold open a job for me?" a neighbor jibed. More than one family man asked Herminio to tout the insurance policies he sells. But on this day, Herminio demurred, with a stare that was a little suspect.

About noon at a substation in one of the roughhouse districts, Herminio ran into a more menacing obstacle. A tall, brawny, curly-haired man was standing in the doorway of a polling place, the living room of a turquoise-painted cinder-block shack. The big man wouldn't let Herminio through the door, and he didn't care what the election laws required. He denied that his door-blocking had a political purpose. "I'm going to keep you out," he said, "because I'm a friend of the family that lives here." Then he crossed his arms and planted his feet in opposite corners of the doorsill.

Herminio's appeals fell on the deaf ears of a half-dozen soldiers and police whom he collared as they were passing by. A carload of plainclothes agents from Gobernación was on hand, but they were interested least of all: They had come to keep an eye on Herminio and the foreigner at his side. Herminio sent a sympathizer to telephone the offices of the PAN, so that a complaint could be registered with the state electoral commission—and so that he'd have reliable witnesses in case he was kidnapped. A reporter from *El Norte* showed up, and not far behind came two cars carrying female members of the PAN. The whole group of us milled around for about an hour, waiting for the man at the door to move. He let voters from the neighborhood pass, but didn't budge for the PAN. I thought his attitude showed typical Mexican localism. The voting box served people in the neighborhood, not people from the other side of town. Why, then, were strangers to be given a look inside? The man and his neighbors knew whom they could trust. None of them complained. Herminio was the suspicious figure, because he expressed an interest in procedures that, the usual Mexican understanding says, were of no legitimate concern to him. All outsiders become misfeasors when they leave the neighborhoods where they belong.

An elderly man from a house nearby approached. He introduced himself to Herminio as a minor official, the analogue of an American justice of the peace. "I kind of feel like you do, that everything is not being run exactly right," he told Herminio.

"That's what I'm trying to tell these people," Herminio said.

"But you're making a mistake," the JP said. "The man you've been criticizing for standing in the door, he's a good fellow; he's not doing it to affect the vote, he's trying to keep the house from getting too crowded."

"It doesn't matter, it doesn't matter," Herminio said, as if he distrusted the old man's amiability.

The JP, a short, wrinkled man with gray whiskers, sighed a little at Herminio's inflexibility, then tried to explain to him the realities of neighborhood life. "Listen," he said, half-exasperated. "Nobody here cares about the PRI. We know they're going to steal the election, no matter what. What we care about is our homes and the services we have." He gestured at the ground, to show that there were no black trails of sewage snaking into the street. "You see, we have a drainage system, and the government didn't put it in. We did, the people who live here. We did it at our own expense because the government kept putting us off, the way it always

103

does. And the man you're looking at in the doorway, he was important to our work. He showed us how to do it, and he did a lot of the work himself."

Herminio failed to see the connection between sewer lines and electoral procedure. "We clash! My friend, we clash again!" he exclaimed. "I beg to differ with you, sir, even if the man in the doorway is the pope. Even the pope can't stand in the doorway, that's what the law says!"

I was was watching to see if Herminio would pull a copy of the Constitution or the electoral code from his pockets, when the JP moved first. Apparently, the idea that ordinary mortals could frame a law to compel a pontiff grated on his sense of propriety. He wheeled and walked away without excusing himself or saying good-bye.

As he was leaving, I heard a woman waiting in the line on the porch say to a companion, "Hah, you can tell that those PANistas aren't from this neighborhood. Just look at how light-skinned they are." She was right. Herminio was the bronzest of the lot.

The woman, potbellied and in her late thirties and clad in a slinky synthetic dress, hollered to Herminio, "Why don't you all go home? We're all Mexicans here, *la gente de patas rajadas*, and we support the PRI." *La gente de patas rajadas* is a rural idiom meaning roughly "the people with scuffed feet," a reference to the barefoot and impoverished condition of the peasantry.

"But ladies, that's just where you're mistaken," Herminio said, nearly bowing in his attempt to exude charm. "Why should we have scuffed feet? If Mexico were run the right way, we could all wear shoes."

"Hah!" the woman spat. "I'm Mexican. The poorer one is, the more Mexican one is, no?" She and her companions laughed heartily and slapped one another on the back.

Herminio looked down at the dust and shook his head from side to side, as if he couldn't believe his ears. "What am I to do?" he said to me in a weak voice, shrugging and turning his palms outward. "Some of my people love their chains. Some of my people, they *love* their chains."

Herminio did not catch the PRI red-handed in fraud during

104

the whole course of the day. The tactic of inspecting the polls from the outside is not appropriate to that task; infiltration is what you need. But Herminio's spirits rose near sunset when a group of boys at a schoolhouse polling station brought him a wad of discarded *"tacos;"* apparently, a ballot-stuffer had lost his nerve, chunked his *"tacos"* in the trash, and gone home. Herminio gathered a group of PANistas and marched into the school chanting "Thieves! Thieves!" as the officials protested and cowered. The little march and demonstration were staged in part for the benefit of those whom Herminio and his flock took to be the press; a group of men in suits had been standing around, and one of them was filming on videotape. When the PANistas emerged from the schoolhouse, Herminio asked the men to identify themselves. "We're not from a television station," one of them said, "we're from Gobernación." Unfazed, Herminio launched into a speech intended for consumption by the political police, in which he urged foreign bankers not to extend new loans to Mexico. "Any money our government gets, it will only steal," he preached.

Herminio already knew, as we all did, that the PRI had carried the day. When the ballots were tallied, to no one's real surprise the PRI came out the winner, by a margin of more than six to four. In an honest election, it might have won anyway, though by a much narrower margin. But the PRI had stolen votes; of that there was no doubt. Several people later confessed that they'd been paid about ten cents per ballot for stuffing *"tacos"* into voting boxes. A few boxes had been stolen for stuffing; photographers caught the ballot-nappers in the act. Tally sheets were altered or made from whole cloth; in one case, they were prepared two nights before the election was held. The PAN was shorted in the numerical scheme by which minority seats in Congress are calculated, and opposition parties in the government's pay came out long.

As the crowd was listening to Herminio lecture absent bankers and the cops from Gobernación, a friend stopped by. His name was Adolfo Gonzales, thirty-four, better-known as "Popo." He is a light-skinned man of humble origins, who owns a business that repairs hydraulic lifts. He was one of the little capitalists, entrepreneurs, and shopkeepers whom Her-

105

minio has recruited to the PAN. Popo had come to the school-house to tell us that a spontaneous rally for the candidate Canales was forming on the Macroplaza. He thought that Herminio should abandon his poll-watching to attend the demonstration downtown. I got into the cab of Popo's pickup, and as we were pulling away, Herminio leaped into its bed, behind. As we headed downtown, a mile or two later we passed a lighted storefront in the descending darkness. Herminio jumped to his feet in the moving pickup, gesticulating and rapping on its rear windshield. "Popo! Popo!" he cried. "Did you check out that polling place we just passed? Let's stop to see it now, before it's too late."

Popo glanced at his leader from the side window of the cab, then waved his hand as if to brush off a fly. *"Eso ya pasó de honda,"* he said to me, "That stuff has already gone out of style." *"¡El PRI nos chingó, y puf!"* "The PRI screwed us, and that's it!" The readiness with which Popo conceded defeat brought me to ask, "Well, what do you think the PAN can do now?" Popo leaned toward me as if to tell a secret. With a sadness that struck me as entirely sincere, he said, "I guess we'll have to forget."

Popo's instantaneous resignation dismayed me. From what I'd seen that day, I had concluded that credible elections couldn't be held in Mexico, at least not in hotly contested races: If fraud didn't discredit the outcome, simple disorganization would. I expected men like Popo to be crying, "To arms! To arms!" even if they might repent of it the next day. But I had underestimated Mexican fatalism and Mexican persistence, too. In the next three years, oppositionists would stage 588 demonstrations, block 151 highways, and take over 255 buildings in protests of electoral fraud. They would force the government, at each turn, to make new promises of electoral honesty, even if, at each turn, those promises were betrayed. The oppositionists kept up the pressure because they believed that the times were on their side, and that if they didn't relax, a breakthrough would surely come. The fall of Ferdinand Marcos inspired them, and gave some of them hope that Uncle Sam would step in. Mexico's economic crisis deepened, opening new wounds of dissent. By the fall of 1987, both the PRI's defenders and foes saw clear signs that the Mexican political system was wearing out. Defenders of the system worried that Mexico itself was coming apart.

LA REVOLUCIÓN

There is an important sense in which modern Mexico and the Partido Revolucionario Institucional are the same. The party was a product of the Revolution of 1910–17. The Revolution left the country confused, exhausted, and in economic ruin, with more leaders than any people needs, most of them under arms. A force, any force, was needed to put the country back on track, any track. The PRI arose from the embers of Mexico and made the trains run, if not on time, on their assigned routes anyway. More than any other force, the PRI decided how modern Mexico would operate, and who would rule.

The PRI, the government, the Revolution, and politics since 1917 are so thoroughly intertwined that one cannot understand any of them without knowing them all. They are more akin than the members of a family, because their roles, and even their names, are interchangeable. If, for example, a contemporary Mexican politician wants to legitimize a new policy—say, that of selling State-owned enterprises to businessmen—he will say that the step is necessary to preserve, continue, or advance the Revolution. He will describe the sale of an enterprise as "Revolutionary." But if he buys an enterprise instead of selling, he will describe the nationalization as "Revolutionary," too. He will speak of himself as commander of the Revolution, he will say that his party represents the "Revolutionary alternative," etc. The Mexican Revolution was a historical act, but in the popular mythology it knows no limits, either in policy or time. The concept of the Revolution is so broad that the editors of the gastronomic page of Monterrey's *El Norte* have referred to *gorditas*, a traditional corn-based dish with pre-Hispanic origins, as "Revolutionary" fare. Anything can be called "Revolutionary," any day.

Given the omnipresent character of what is called the Revolution, discerning its actual, temporal history is important. The Revolution must be fathomed, not only in terms of its slogans or goals—the usual or textbook understanding—but also in regard to its military history. The picture that emerges is one in which the Revolution, insofar as it represented social forces, was defeated both militarily and in back rooms and halls of politics.

In 1910, Mexico was ruled by General Porfirio Díaz, an aging hero of the mid-nineteenth-century civil war that had put an end to a brief but tragic period of French colonialism in Mexico. Díaz had continually occupied the presidency for a generation, since 1884. His goal, other than remaining in office, had been to industrialize Mexico, a task that even the experience of the Soviets shows is usually accomplished at the expense of the masses. In the United States during the days when Díaz ruled, an industrial machine was being forged on the backs of hungry immigrants, freedmen, and children, the labor force of a robber-baron age. Díaz and his advisers saw no reason to believe that industrialism in Mexico could advance by more humane means. Their gritty sense of realism was widely perceived as a haughty sense of cynicism, and the regime developed a reputation as a friend of exploiters.

The Porfiriato also had a racial aspect. Though Don Porfirio was a brown-skinned man, his regime was dominated by whites. Historian T. R. Fehrenbach relates that:

> In the apogee of the Porfiriato, the European population came closer than it ever had to emerging as a true aristocracy. With independence, the most energetic military men and politicians had usually been *mestizo*. In the order of the Porfiriato, when economics prevailed above all else and property assumed greater political importance, the European propertied classes reasserted themselves. . . . Many of this class consciously bore "the white man's burden." They would privately if never publicly agree that Mexico *was* barbarous and that the whip was the only language understood by the barbarians. The Díaz regime fitted in with the British Raj in India, the French colonial empire, and other custodianships, and it was widely admired abroad. . . . It was believed that the Porfiriato was achieving something the

108

Spaniards had not quite accomplished, the civilizing of Indian Mexico.

The racial bias of the Díaz regime translated itself as opposition to everything Indian, from communal forms of land ownership to elements of architectural design. To prepare for the centennial of the Mexican independence movement, for example, Don Porfirio's administrators built dozens of new buildings and monuments in Mexico City's central district. They hired Italian architects and French sculptors to design these works, which were cast in the European vogue. Don Porfirio's plan was to stage a spectacular celebration in a city where Continental nobles and notables he had invited could feel at home.

Díaz and his administrators courted foreign investors, subsidized infrastructure impresarios, and outlawed the fledgling labor movement. In 1910, three quarters of Mexico's industrial wealth—mainly mines, oil fields, textile plants, and banks—belonged to foreigners. Porfirio and his advisers regarded traditional Mexican agriculture as backward, and they encouraged planters to appropriate Indian lands. By the end of the Porfiriato, though tillers accounted for 80 percent of the workforce, only 10 percent of them owned plots of land. Statisticians estimate that living standards fell by 75 percent in the last decade of Don Porfirio's reign. In Mexico City alone, nearly 20 percent of the population was sleeping in the streets. Don Porfirio, like Cortés, gave modernization a bad name.

But Díaz was not, as postrevolutionary commentators usually assume, opposed to the kinds of measures that in the years since have become synonymous with both the words "Revolution" and "Mexico." The government's first nationalization, of the railway lines, was an act of the Porfiriato, in 1908. When Díaz left office, of the 23 percent of Mexico's industrial wealth that did not belong to foreign firms, some 60 percent belonged to the government, and only 40 percent to Mexico's private sector. To protect national sovereignty, Díaz renegotiated Mexico's stifling external debt, and made payments on time. The latter years of his administration, though marked by misery, are among the brief and rare periods in Mexican history when government operations yielded a surplus. The general's very

Mexican anti-Americanism survives in a phrase that is usually quoted without attribution. Mexico's chief problem, the Francophile dictator said, was that it "is too close to the United States, and too far from God."

Many historians refer to the Porfiriato simply as the Dictatorship, but it preserved its outwardly democratic forms. As the election of 1910 drew near, the general spoke of the need to have a loyal opposition, and a multiparty distribution of power. But in 1910, rather than retiring as Mexico expected him to do, Díaz once again placed his name on the ballot. He was eighty-six years old. Five opposition parties arose that year, but four of them endorsed the dictator's new presidential bid. Opposition came only from the Anti-Reelectionist party, whose candidate was Francisco I. Madero, thirty-seven, a northerner with a landed background and theosophic propensities, who had been educated in France and in the United States. Madero's rallying cry was "Effective Suffrage! No Reelection!" slogans that have become the traditional closings for letters written by Mexican officialdom. But the elections of July 10, like those that had sustained the Díaz regime, were fraudulent. When results were announced on September 16, Mexico's credulity snapped: Madero was credited with only 196 votes. He fled to San Antonio, and on November 20, 1910, called Mexico to arms. His political program, the Plan de San Luis Potosí, now called not only for removing Díaz, but for a critical social reform. Madero advocated the restitution of wrongfully appropriated lands.

Much of the history of the turmoil that followed is told in the fates of Mexico's presidents. In 1911, Madero replaced Díaz, who died in exile in France. Madero was executed in 1913 by General Victoriano Huerta, who was forced to resign in 1914 by General Venustiano Carranza; Huerta died in the United States. Carranza was president in 1920 when he was murdered on the orders of General Álvaro Obregón, who was elected to the presidency some six months afterward. Obregón survived his first term of office, 1920–24, but was assassinated shortly after winning election to a second term, in 1928. General Plutarco Elías Calles, the incumbent at the time of Obregón's death, brought a halt to fratricide in what was called "the revolutionary family" by founding the PRI. Though he was exiled to Texas

110

from 1936 to 1942, Calles lived for seventeen years after leaving office, and died in Mexico of natural causes.

Few Mexicans are familiar with Calles's name, and not many can recall the names of the Revolution's other presidents. The Revolution is instead remembered as a series of legends about Emiliano Zapata, whose peasant followers went to war under the banner LAND TO THE TILLERS! and Pancho Villa, who commanded the Army of the North. Zapata was plainspoken, sedate, cautious, and upright, but Villa took seventeen maidens as his brides, invaded the United States, and lynched Mexico's Chinese. He is folk religion's patron saint of revenge. The byzantine turns of the Revolution, which made allies of men as dissimilar as these, are deservedly the topics of whole encyclopedias of Mexican history. But a short look at the rebellion's rise provides insight into the most important forces at play.

Some men were hungry for adventure. Madero's appeal for a November 20 uprising produced only a four-hour gunfight in Puebla, and the insurgents lost. His first real strength came in the northern state of Chihuahua, where one family dominated ranching. Two men, Pascual Orozco and Pancho Villa, were organizing a rural revolt. Both claimed to have been inspired by Madero's call for land reform, but they were not men like Madero. They were cut from rougher cloth. Orozco had been a pack-team driver, and Villa, under his given name, Doroteo Arango, was notorious as a cattle thief. In early 1911, Orozco and Villa proposed to Madero that they assault Juárez, an important border town. Madero, who was already negotiating for the retirement of Díaz and who wanted to risk no trouble with the United States, told them to wait. Disobeying Madero's orders, they launched their attack in early May. They took control of Juárez on May 20, giving a stunned Madero his first military win.

Some men were hungry for land. Emiliano Zapata, then thirty years old, had taken up arms before Madero fled to the United States. Zapata was the leader of a community in the southern state of Morelos that had asked its governor to restore communal lands that a planter had appropriated. The governor's office delayed. After six months, in September 1910, Zapata and a band of eighty armed peasants occupied the contested

111

Emiliano Zapata

lands. The successful land seizure set off a chain reaction in Morelos, and Zapata became a hero. He declared support for the Plan de San Luis Potosí, and began organizing a network of armed peasant clans. On May 20, ten days after the seizure of Juárez, Zapata and his ragtag army occupied Cuernavaca, a town at the national capital's gates.

Some men were hungry for democracy. The day after the Zapatistas captured Cuernavaca, rather than extend the budding revolt, Madero signed a settlement with representatives of Porfirio Díaz. They promised that the dictator would resign in favor of an interim president, pledged to holding new national elections. Madero agreed to cease advocating land reform. Díaz left the country within a week. Madero handily won the October special election, and when he took office in November, he ordered the Zapatistas to disarm. They were not interested in Constitutionalism or in electoral campaigns. They had revolted, a document of theirs explained, not "to conquer illusory political rights that give nothing to eat, but to procure the piece of land that would provide food and liberty." They wanted to divide the sugar plantations that had taken over the Morelos countryside. They answered Madero with the Plan de Ayala, which resurrected the demand for land reform, and called for a revolution to oust "the traitor president." The Revolution was irredeemably split. Land seizures continued. Combat resumed. Pancho Villa, who had been made an honorary general in the federal army, was jailed on charges of "insubordination." General Victoriano Huerta ordered him shot, but President Madero intervened to save his life. In a Mexico City prison, Pancho Villa learned to read.

Some men were hungry for power. Reportedly because he believed that the president was too weak-willed to suppress the rebels, in February 1913 General Huerta took over the government and executed Madero, who had been in office just sixteen months. Shocked by Huerta's disregard for legality, several northern governors and generals declared themselves in rebellion. Pancho Villa, who had escaped from prison to the United States about two months earlier, returned to Chihuahua to raise a revolutionary army of his own. Pascual Orozco, instead of joining his old comrade-in-arms, joined the Huerta camp. Wanting to avoid a war on two fronts, Orozco sent his own father to Zapata with a proposal for peace. Zapata answered by having the messenger shot, thereby winning the approval of Villa, and living up to the nickname that the Morelian gentry had given him, "Attila of the South."

During Madero's presidency, the Revolution had fragmented into two factions. Now, there were three. The first was the government itself, the Huertistas or Federalists, they were called. Its base area was Mexico City, its strength was its firepower and payroll. Politically, the Federalists were Porfiristas at worst, and disillusioned Maderistas at best. Members of the second faction called themselves Constitutionalists. Their leaders were landed and legalist, much in the Madero mode. Their base areas were the northern states of the Pacific and Gulf. Their soldiers were uniformed, disciplined, and trained; whole units had come over from the Federalist side. The third faction was that of the Liberation Army of the South, Zapata's network of peasant leagues. The Zapatistas were landless and lawless, anarchist, populist, even socialist in an agrarian way. They were poorly armed, loosely organized, and likely to retreat at planting and harvest time. Their home base was the state of Morelos, but they spread beyond, into Guerrero, Oaxaca, and Michoacán. Villa and his men constituted an essentially uncommitted or free faction, with no clear program. Villa was formally allied to the Constitutionalists, militarily allied with Zapata, and beholden to no one. "Villa's real pattern of 'social reform,' " historian T. R. Fehrenbach says, "was to seize haciendas and drive off their livestock, which he sold in Texas to pay for arms and ammunition. . . . He was an elemental force, loosed on Mexico." Villa's cowboy and tradesmen troops were not timid and province-bound, like Zapata's peasants in the south. They were mounted, footloose, and wild.

The Constitutionalists and Villa's forces fought their way southward, toward the capital, in the first half of 1914. Villa's army had won the allegiance of railroad men; it moved fastest, because it moved by train. To prevent Villa from taking the capital, the Constitutionalists cut off his coal supply. Constitutionalist troops commanded by Álvaro Obregón entered Mexico City in August 1914, and installed Venustiano Carranza as president. A unity convention met for weeks, but when its delegates adopted Zapata's Plan de Ayala as a program, Carranza led a Constitutionalist walkout. Unity negotiations failed, too. In December, Villa and Zapata led their armies into the capital, sending President Carranza to Veracruz in flight. The populist or peasant wing of the Revolution had reached its peak strength.

The Revolution had derailed commerce and the industrial economy, but this bothered Zapata and Villa very little. Ever since the Conquest, Mexico's economy had been built of two tiers. At its base, peasants farmed corn and beans to subsist. On its higher level, men built large enterprises dedicated to profit, mines, plantations, texile factories, and oil mills. By December 1914, in both Chihuahua and Morelos, peasants had repartitioned big estates. They were prospering, according to the standards they recognized. Their leaders did not understand the needs of the business or industrial class. The Constitutionalists did. They had always been pragmatic men, and when the two radicals took the capital, they became cynical and desperate. They did an about-face. On January 6, in Veracruz, Carranza issued an agrarian-reform program copied from Zapata's Plan de Ayala. Villa was pleased. "No matter who publishes such laws, the people will benefit," the former cattle thief said. In the belief that the goals of *their* revolution had now been won, Villa and Zapata packed up their troops and headed home. Carranza's leading general, future president Álvaro Obregón, marched on the capital. He occupied the city in late January 1915. To rally the enthusiasm of the city's organized working class, within days Carranza—despite having said that labor unions were "atheistic and hostile to the fatherland"— dictated a labor code granting fundamental union demands. His army replenished by tiller and toiler recruits, including redshirted unionists, Obregón marched off in pursuit of the "counterrevolutionary" Pancho Villa. Carranza returned to the presidential palace, and began laying plans for the Constitutional Convention of 1917.

The history of the decline of the Revolution is told in Zapata's

115

and Villa's fates. Zapata was betrayed and murdered by Constitutionalist troops in 1919, having never surrendered his arms. After several military defeats, Villa had been pacified by a grant of a ranch in Chihuahua, plus salaries and land for his most trusted men. But he was nevertheless killed in a 1923 ambush. (Three years later, his corpse was exhumed and decapitated, a contemporary convention of historians has decided, by members of Yale's Skull and Bones Society. The society and its leading alumnus, George Bush, say it ain't so.) Because both Villa and Zapata were at odds with the Revolutionary government in 1917, neither of them participated in writing the Constitution. Nor did either of them live to witness the founding of the PRI.

Nor was the Revolution's prophet on hand for either event. In 1906, an anarcho-syndicalist labor agitator, Ricardo Flores Magón, had authored a political program for the Mexican union movement that he headed from exile in St. Louis. His program demanded effective suffrage and no reelection, four years before Madero made slogans of those words. It called for land reform, too. It also demanded the abolition of child labor, mandatory public education, an eight-hour workday, a six-day work week, a federal minimum wage, and union rights—provisions Carranza adopted for his labor decree and later incorporated into the Constitution of 1917. Flores Magón was the intellectual author of the liberal Mexican state. But he never returned home. In 1922, he died in the federal prison at Leavenworth, Kansas, while completing a term for an American political offense, advocating resistance to the military draft. His contemporaries knew him through the newspapers he published from exile, but few Mexicans today have ever heard his name.

So convulsed and tortured was its course that disbelief in the worthiness of the Revolution has always been widespread in Mexico, especially in the northlands held by Villa and the Constitutionalists. In reminiscences, most survivors of the era told of the theft of livestock and poultry by marauding bands, or of taking shelter during hostilities, or of the sacking of warehouses and the despoliation of crops—acts with no inherent political meanings. The American journalist John Reed, in his masterwork, *Insurgent Mexico*, written during the heat of the Revo-

116

lution, reports the following conversation with a band of warriors:

> "Why do you fight?" I asked.
> Juan Sánchez, the flag bearer, looked at me curiously:
> "Why, because it's good to fight. You don't have to work in the mines!
> "We're fighting to put Francisco I. Madero back in the Presidency. . . ." [Madero had been dead for about two years at the time when the conversation with Reed took place.]
> "We are fighting," said Isidro Amayo, "for *libertad*."
> "What do you mean by *libertad*?"
> "*Libertad* is when I can *do what I want*! . . ."
> But, just to be square, I'll have to report Juan Sánchez' remark:
> "Is there war in the United States now?" he asked.
> "No," I said untruthfully.
> "No war at all?" He meditated for a moment. "How do you pass the time, then? . . ."

Herminio Gómez relates the following account of his disillusionment with the revolutionaries of 1910:

"On a November 20, the anniversary day of the Revolution, in 1979, I believe, I went down to Monterrey's monument to revolutionary veterans, for a celebration. We do it every year. Two veterans of the Revolution were present that day, an old man and an old woman. After the speeches were made, I introduced myself to them. I said to the man, 'Oh, it is an honor to meet one of those who fought for effective suffrage. But tell me, what do you think has happened since? We've had the same government ever since the Revolution ended.' The old man looked at me kind of slyly, and he said, '*Joven, ¿acaso tu crees que peleé por principios?*'—'Young man, do you believe that I fought for principles? I went with Villa, and do you know why? Because in those days, there were armed groups riding around, and when they came to your house, you either joined them or they killed you on the spot. I went with Villa because the Villistas came to my house first.' Well, I could hardly accept what he was saying, so I asked the woman, 'And you, *señora*?' She said, 'Well, I was only thirteen at the time. But some Villistas came to the house, and one of them, he was a colonel, dismounted from his horse and said, "You're going to be my woman." I could see that if I didn't agree to be his woman, they were going to make me the woman of them all. So I went with him, but the truth is, I was taken by force.' "

Official histories say that the Revolution ended on February 5, 1917, because the Constitution was adopted by a special congress on that date. Other historians favor July 28, 1920, because that's the date when Villa agreed to lay down his arms. The years between 1917 and 1920 mark a watershed, because during them the man who would define the Mexican political system, General Plutarco Elías Calles, consolidated his hold on the Revolutionary leadership. But if the Revolution ended in 1917 or 1920, it was followed by a series of civil wars that Revolutionary historians generally ignore. Even a casual reading of the events of that era demonstrates that violence wasn't laid to rest until a decade later, after both the Cristero rebels of 1925–30, Catholic guerrillas, and the Revolution's own dissident elements ran out of steam. Here, for example, is the report of a compendium of Mexican history for the events of 1927:

Apart from the Cristero War, there were only attempts or beginnings of insurrection, thunderously quelled with executions. The principal of these were of the two anti-reelectionist candidates who confronted Obregón: the General Francisco R. Serrano, who prepared a barracks uprising, and the general Arnulfo R. Gómez, who had to revolt to save his life. Serrano, by an order of Calles written to general Fox, was killed along with thirteen of his co-conspirators at kilometer 47 of the Cuernavaca highway (Oct. 3, 1927); Gómez, in the cemetery at Coatepec, Veracruz (Nov. 5), along with the colonel Gómez Vizcarra. These killings were preceeded, simultaneous with or followed by others: colonel Anzaldo (Jan. 5, 1926), general Agapito Lastra, colonel Aurelio Manzano and all the officers of the sixteenth batallion (Torreón, Oct. 3, 1927), general Arturo Lasso de la Vega (Pachuca, Oct. 4), generals Alfredo Rodríguez and Norberto C. Olvera (Zacatecas, Oct. 4), Luis T. Vidal, governor of Chiapas (Oct. 4), general Alfredo Rueda Quijano (Mexico City, Oct. 5), general Oscar Aguilar (Monterrey, Nov. 18), generals Bertani and Lucero (Minatitlán, Veracruz, Dec. 3 and 4.). . . . Obregón was unhurt in a dynamite attempt (Mexico City, Nov. 13) by the engineer Luis Segura Vilchis. . . . With great publicity, but without any trial, Segura Vilchis and his collaborator Antonio Tirado were shot in the company of Humberto Pro and of his brother, Father Miguel A. Pro, S.J., who had nothing to do with the attempt (Mexico City, Nov. 23). Toral was tortured in prison so that he would "sing," and after a long trial, shot (Mexico City, Feb. 9, 1929).

The death toll for political conflict in the ostensibly post-revolutionary year of 1927 included ten generals, a governor, thirteen "co-conspirators," "all the officers of the Sixteenth Batallion," and a priest subsequently beatified as a Christian martyr—some thirty to fifty men, not counting the foot soldiers who died in their defense. Also uncounted are casualties of the Cristero War, in which some thirty thousand people died over the course of five years. Precise figures do not exist, but it is generally believed that about a million people, some 6 percent of the total population, perished in the Revolution and its civil wars, about three times as many as in the American War Between the States. Another quarter million took refuge in the United States, and most of them stayed.

THE PRI

The PRI was initially nothing more than a network of generals, with Plutarco Elías Calles in command. Its purpose was to name candidates for elective office, and to see that they were installed. Similar conspiracies had existed everywhere in Mexico since the fall of Díaz. The secrecy of these groups and the limited resources at their command had merely encouraged opposing cabals, creating the spiral of bloodshed that gave the Revolution its name. But Calles had visited Europe during the early twenties, and had returned with three concepts—frontism, centralism, and presidentialism—that with Mexican adaptations would bring an enduring and flexible regime to birth.

The Europe that Calles saw was a caldron where totalitarian

119

P. E. Calles

ideologies boiled. The right was convinced that amoral, cosmopolitan capitalism had created the First World War and its defeats; the left was convinced that unrestrained nationalist capitalism had been responsible instead. Even centrists believed that the fundamental institutions of Western society would need reconstruction at their bases. Because almost no one in politics had limited goals—art, religion, family life, and pro-ductive activity would all have to be reformed—political parties extended their reach across the whole of life. They did this through two types of organizations, party fronts and popular fronts.

A popular front is any independent movement or organi-zation that a political party establishes or enters for the purpose of advancing its particular interests. Pop fronts, as they are called in activist slang, can be dedicated to any purpose what-soever: electing a candidate, reviving a language, even staging a swimming meet. In recent American history, the Right-to-Life movement provides an example of a (Republican) pop front, even though all participants in the movement might pro-test the charge. In successful pop-front campaigns, party lead-ers rise to leadership or otherwise acquire the capacity to influence organizational decisions, and they recruit members of the group to the party itself. But because parties do not directly or fully control pop fronts, agitation inside them can be politically hazardous. Party operatives can be exposed or expelled, or can collide with the pop-front agents of opposing political groups. On a grand scale, the Mexican Revolution had been nothing more than a pop front founded by Madero in 1910 for the purpose of restoring electoral honesty. As with the European pop fronts of the twenties, conflicts between mem-bers of opposing cabals had destroyed its ability to function and had darkened the vague vision from which it arose.

When the pop front went out of European vogue, the party front came in. Especially in Germany, Italy, Spain, and France, workers joined anarchist, Social Democratic, Communist, or Fascist unions, dedicated to earthshaking ends. Youth, wom-en's, sports, and farmers' organizations were grouped by party loyalty, too. These organizations were founded for the declared purpose of extending party ideology and power. Though the recruitment of nonparty members was a primary goal—party members were required to join the fronts—nonparty recruits were usually ineligible for positions of leadership. Decision making rested, not in local chapters of the fronts, but in the centralized party agency that administered them. The potential of party fronts would not be demonstrated to most Europeans

121

until Mussolini, Hitler, and Franco had established their states, but the astute Calles saw unique and immediate possibilities for frontism at home.

The chief factor that retarded the success of party fronts in Europe was the contending position of all political parties. Party fronts were attempts to acquire power from the bottom up. Calles did not face this problem in Mexico. There, the critical question was not seizing the reins of government, but of holding on to power against new mutinies and revolts. Calles and his cronies did not have a permanent political organization. If they had a centralized party, he reasoned, fronts could be easily established from the top down. And fronts could orchestrate electoral turnouts and victories.

His accomplishment, if it may be called that, wasn't that he copied or imported ideas from Europe. He didn't do that. Instead, he adapted European frontism, a mere form, to Mexico's circumstances, and to his own lust for power. The Revolutionary generals were no longer oppositionists, as most European frontists were. Unlike European leaders, members of the "Revolutionary family" had no use for class-struggle doctrines, internationalisms, or other varieties of ideology: The generals were armed and powerful; programs and promises were excess baggage for them. The PRI declared allegiance to neither capitalism nor socialism, but to the eclectic, irreconcilable, and already betrayed "ideals of the Mexican Revolution." It practiced an allegiance to monopoly power and social peace. Because no ideology could measure its success, the PRI could not fail. In the sixty years following its formation, the PRI kept for itself the presidency, all governorships, and all Senate seats, as well 80 percent of the seats in the Chamber of Deputies. The PRI has been in power longer than any contemporary political organization, except for the Soviet Bolsheviks. As in the Soviet state, the PRI, the government, and the front organizations constitute an all-embracing corporate state.

Largely for management reasons, the PRI parceled Mexico into three sectors, each under the guidance of its own umbrella front: the Confederación Nacional Campesina or CNC, the peasant front; the Confederación de Trabajadores Mexicanos or CTM, the workers' front; and the Confederación

Nacional de Organizaciones Populares or CNOP, an amalgam of "peoples' organizations," mainly representing small businessmen. Each of the fronts gave birth to subsidiaries, and over time new fronts developed, independent of the Big Three but always pledged to the ruling party. Today, there are some two hundred national fronts and tens of thousands of locally affiliated groups. The national fronts include at least two sets of soundalike workers' organizations: (set A) the National Confederation of Workers and Peasants, the National Confederation of Revolutionary Workers and Peasants, and the Revolutionary Confederation of Workers and Peasants; (set B) the Unionist Confederation of the State, the Mexican Unitary Unionist Confederation, and the Unitary Confederation of Workers. The number of subsidiary groups is infinite. The CNC alone claims "32 leagues of agrarian communities, two thousand regional and municipal committees, 17 national producers unions, 14 national affiliates that group professionals, technicians and public servants connected with the countryside, 52 councils of indigenous peoples, and three thousand womens' and youth leagues."

The fronts became Mexico's lobby groups. Like lobbies, they blur the lines between private interests, party interests, and the interests of the State. For example, the CNC, or peasant front, recently convinced the Mexican customs service that high duties on imported models had created a shortage of pickups in the countryside. The customs service agreed to allow CNC members in one state to import some two thousand pickups duty-free. The import permits became an object of political pressure and graft, and when the program reached its end, the organization's leaders complained that only six hundred of the permits had actually gone to agriculturalists; one of the "peasants" who imported a pickup under the plan, for example, was the owner of a hot-sheets motel.

After Calles consolidated the PRI, leadership ceased to arise from independent or regional bases. Important provincial leaders—governors, senators, and metropolitan mayors—in the party that Calles founded are selected by a circuitous route that inevitably passes through Mexico City. As young men finishing college, they typically accept minor bureaucratic appointments in their hometowns. There they join the PRI and the appropriate party front, and seek the favor of those who can authorize their transfer and promotion to Mexico City posts. In the capital, they join a circle of rising frontists or agency executives, united by allegiance to a leader; regional ties, at this point in the game, are fetters to be discarded. If their Mexico City clique wins favor with those at the apex of the PRI, they are then tapped to go home—after an absence that has usually lengthened to twenty or thirty years—to govern or represent the locales that they left behind. Local party conventions are called not to initiate their nominations, but to confirm them.

The most notorious and grandiose concept that Calles taught the PRI, however, is not frontism or centralism, but adoration of the head of state. Mexican presidentialism takes a thousand forms, some as formal as law, others as funky as celebrity fetishism. Editorial cartoonists observe an unwritten rule banning unflattering caricatures of the chief of state. Public servants caught with their hands in the till are routinely accused of "disloyalty to the office, the Constitution, and the President of the Republic." The president is pictured, without fail, in every nationally televised newscast, and on half the front pages of the daily press, every day of the week. In the first or second breath of all public speeches, elected officials give thanks and pledge allegiance to him. By tradition, no one can refuse a direct request from a head of state, nor an invitation to reason with him.

Once in office, the president is invested with visible powers and declared honors that are shared by few elected heads of state. The president names candidates for Mexico's thirty-one governorships, and its sixty-four Senate seats. Ninety-five percent of the legislation passed by the Mexican Congress comes from the office of the presidency; neither vetoes nor overrides are factors in Mexican politics. Seven national holidays are set aside to honor each president, one on his inaugural day, and one each year on the day he presents his annual State of the Union message. Mexican presidents need not fear public nonacceptance, because they cannot Constitutionally return to office. Nor need they worry about the posturings and maneuverings of ambitious vice-presidents, because the Constitution does not provide for one. Of all the powers exercised by the Mexican president, the most important one is naming his own successor. Mexicans quip that each six years, the nation elects not a president, but a PRIista king. PRIista presidential candidates are named by *dedazo*, or fingering, by the incumbents, who explain their choices to no one.

Innumerable theories, mostly with a conspiratorial cast, have evolved about presidential genesis. The most widely held theory is that the Mexican presidency is auctioned or sold to the highest bidder much as other jobs are. (Schoolteachers, for example, often must pay a kickback to the principals who hire them.) Common logic assumes that the presidency is traded in the same way. According to this widespread belief, the president's favorites—presumably bankers and industrialists, as well as politicians—go to their backers, requesting funds. After polling their supporters, the favorites present their bids to the president. As plausible as this may seem—the theory would explain, for example, Mexico's exemplary role in paying its external debt (Who could outbid the candidate of the International Monetary fund, after all?)—no shred of evidence has turned up to support it, or any selection theory.

The president is the model for all subordinates. It's almost fair to say, for example, that on days when the president's picture isn't on the front page of a Mexican provincial newspaper, the governor's picture is. Senators and governors give the *dedazos* to federal and state posts, and leaders of front organizations operate as governors and presidents do. If a municipal labor leader makes a speech, its first two or three paragraphs will be dedicated to praising those whom he must revere, the president, the governor, and the chief of his front. Only inside the secrecy of a cabal do subordinates openly criticize their bosses. The accepted means of showing displeasure with one's superiors is to be brief when mentioning their names. It's a dangerous practice in terms of career advancement, but inferiors do get a chance to send messages of discontent upstairs at election time. It is their job to turn out the vote. If abstention is great, leaders understand that there is resentment below. Elections in Mexico are a commentary on politics. They approve, or disapprove of, policies and leaders the people can't change.

BIRTH OF THE OPPOSITION

The hierarchy that Calles and his cronies established gave Mexico stability of rule. Its political miracle was matched by economic progress, too. During the forties, Mexican industrialization advanced under what might be called a negative impetus. American manufacturers, wedded to war production, no longer provided competition to their Mexican counterparts, and in the breathing spell Mexico's industry moved forward on its own, developing both internal markets and satisfying some American import demands. The Mexican currency was stable from 1952 to 1976, and during the two decades that ended in 1970, the country's rate of economic growth averaged about 6 percent, nearly twice the rate of population growth. Statistically, living standards doubled in the span of a generation.

But the "Mexican Miracle," as American news magazines called it, was unevenly spread. The nation's rural population, more than half of the total, continued in its ancestral folkways and poverty, and rumors began reaching the cities that the peasants were arming, as they had during the Revolution. Following a spectacular and bitter railroad strike in 1957, Mexico's intellectuals turned left again; by 1960, several of the country's leading lights would be in jail on charges of "social disillusionment," Marxist heresy. The PAN, though clearly a minority voice, continued its antiliberal and antitotalitarian ravings, sometimes winning a mayoral or legislative race. But on the broad national scene, the opposition, both left and right, was unrepresented. Mexico's prosperous and ostensibly democratic development benefited urban residents and the PRI, but almost no one else.

Leaders of the PRI were embarrassed by the party's unrivaled success. The government that they had built resembled Europe's one-party, fascist republics as much as it resembled any parliamentary state. The PRIista majority had little to lose by showing magnanimity, and in 1963, it took its basic step toward what would later be sloganized as "The Democratic Aperture." Under President Adolfo López Mateos, Mexico enacted the principle of proportional representation. The Constitutional changes that created proportional representation would renew Mexico's democratic facade for fully twenty-five years, until 1988, when Mexico would again explode in scandal over "Effective Suffrage!"

Proportional representation is almost unknown in the United States. Our political system is essentially one of strict majority rule. If, for example, we are to elect a legislature of one hundred seats, and one political party wins 51 percent of the ballots cast for each seat, it wins them all, even if a second party polls 49 percent of the votes cast in each locale. In a system based purely on proportional representation, fifty-one seats would be granted to the majority party, and forty-nine to its competitor. At the level of theory, proportional representation is more democratic because the profile of the citizenry's political preferences is preserved in the assignment of legislative seats.

The chief difficulty with schemes of proportional representation is that for practical purposes they require an electoral system of two tiers, one direct, the other indirect. In the first tier, voters cast ballots for known candidates. In the second tier, after election results have been tabulated, an agency *other than* the electorate decides which candidates will take office. The problem is inescapable since, for instance, in the example cited, when the result are tabulated, there will be one hundred winning candidates, only fifty-one of whom can take office, and one hundred losing candidates, forty-nine of whom will take office.

This difficulty is complicated by the custom, common to both the United States and Mexico, of tying elections to local boundaries. In the hypothetical example, if the U.S. Senate were the legislative body involved, each state, presumably, could be granted one majority-party senator, with one senator, presumably of the majority, left over. All states except one could be granted a minority-party senator. But which state would be denied its minority spokesman? And whose local interests would the supernumerary majority senator represent? The contending parties could resolve these conundrums only by negotiations and trades involving factors outside of the electoral process.

When the Mexican measure was proposed, all seats in the Chamber of Deputies, a body roughly equivalent to the U.S. House of Representatives, by an agreement inside the PRI were assigned under quota to spokesmen for the fronts. None of the fronts wanted to sacrifice seats to the opposition, and therefore a system creating an expandable Chamber was designed. The Chamber was to be composed of a fixed number of seats, elected by direct majority, and an open-ended number of minority seats, assigned to those parties that polled less than a majority but more than 2.5 percent of the national vote. The mixed system, in part a strict majority system, in part a proportional system, satisfied the internal requirements of the PRI, but in practice it produced insufficient results. The proportion of opposition deputies in the Chamber never exceeded one sixth. The PRI could, of course, have rigged the election of oppositionists—some people say that it did—but its jealous lower ranks would never have understood why.

The Mexicans grappled with the perplexities of proportional representation by making Constitutional changes under four presidents until they hit upon a workable formula for the elections of 1988. The Constitution, as then amended, called for the election of three hundred Chamber deputies by uninominal, or majority, vote. Two hundred additional seats were to be divided among those parties, including the majority party, that had received a minimum of 1.5 percent of the national vote, with one condition: No party, regardless of its strength, was to be granted more than 350 seats. To preserve a semblance of local representation, plurinominal, or minority, deputies were to be selected not from a national pool, but from five regional lists provided by the contending parties. The plan was exceedingly complex—almost nobody understood it—but for the opposition it held out hope: No matter what, parties other than the PRI were guaranteed 30 percent of the Chamber's seats. The measure didn't guarantee democracy for Mexico, but it seemed to be a significant gesture of good faith. Either that, or

128

as some pundits said, the PRI in its self-confidence had over-stepped its strength.

1988

The 1988 campaign year began in August 1987 with a series of breakfasts hosted by the PRI in Mexico City. Over the course of two weeks, in alphabetical order, six leading party figures addressed the party and the nation. These six men, the press was given to understand, were the *precandidatos* or *tapados*, "hooded ones," the likely corps from which a presidential pick would be made. They included five Cabinet-level officers of the government and Mexico City's mayor. The breakfast introductions were a new tactic; never before had *tapados* been presented to the public. The PRI hadn't given in to demands that it nominate its leading candidate in an open convention; but for the first time, it had presented the president's favorites to the public.

The Mexican press began discerning signs and reporting rumors, as it always does during *tapado* time. Matt Moffett, *The Wall Street Journal*'s Mexico City correspondent, observed:

> The analysts considered it notable, for example, that the pugnacious budget secretary, Carlos Salinas de Gortari, jabbed his finger into the air 39 times during his address: that the youthful energy secretary, Alfredo del Mazo, made 16 references to "modernization," six to "renovation" and three to "transformation"; that the wily head of electoral and security affairs, Manuel Bartlett Díaz, used the word "political" 25 times. . . . The morning of Mr. Bartlett's address, five carloads of reporters followed him from his home to the party assembly. . . . They analyzed every page and every word of his speech and then reported the number of pages (22) and words (3,930). . . . Such trivia must substitute for information of more substance that the press can't obtain. There wasn't any opportunity for the assembled officials to question the *precandidatos* and Mr. Bartlett wouldn't answer questions from the reporters dogging him.

On the morning of October 4, energy secretary del Mazo summoned reporters who were waiting outside his house. He told them that the president had made his decision, in favor of another of the *tapados*, the attorney general Sergio García Ramirez. Del Mazo further informed them that he was on his way to deliver congratulations to the García home. But about two hours later, Jorge de la Vega Domínguez, the PRI's chairman, called a press conference to announce that the choice had been made in favor of Carlos Salinas de Gortari, the budget minister. Del Mazo's announcement had been only a ruse, a prank played on a press that PRIistas regard as overly curious about the party's internal affairs.

The populist wing of the PRI groaned at the choice of Salinas, and its most important leader, eighty-seven-year-old labor chieftain Fidel Velázquez, walked out of the official announcement ceremony in a show of protest. For the fourth time in a row, the party had hitched itself to a *tecnócrata*, or administrator, instead of a candidate who could be billed as a man of the people. Salinas, forty-three, a small, balding man with prominent ears, had been born and raised in Mexico City as the son of a career PRIista who was then serving as a senator, representing the state of Nuevo León. As budget secretary, the young candidate had a pinch-penny or conservative reputation, and his speaking style, while superior to that of *tecnócrata* President de la Madrid, still left much to be desired. Further, he had liabilities from a nationalist point of view. Salinas holds a doctorate and two masters' degrees from Harvard. During the 1982 campaign, PRIista press managers had repeatedly asked reporters to tone down the Harvard connection for alumnus Miguel de la Madrid. But most discouraging of all, Salinas was not a politician. He had never held an elective office. He was, the old-timers whispered, merely a bright young *"junior,"* or Yuppie, moving up fast with sponsorship from the top. The perceptions and fears of the PRIista Old Guard were accurate indeed. "Carlos Salinas was selected," an American analyst noted, "because of President Miguel de la Madrid's conviction that the cronyism of Mexico's older generation of politicos is responsible for the nation's present predicament."

PRIista doubters were comforted only by the PAN's choice of a millionaire. In open convention in November, it named a

Sinaloa businessman, portly, white-bearded Manuel Clouthier, to head its campaign. Clouthier, fifty-nine, a grower and exporter of tomatoes and cucumbers, had graduated from high school in California. As a college student at Monterrey's Universidad Tecnológica, Mexico's MIT, he had played American football, not soccer. During a prior campaign for the governorship of Sinaloa, his home state, peasants had occupied parts of Clouthier's farms, calling for their repartition under agrarian-reform laws: He had thereby acquired a reputation as a *latifundista*. His critics also found it significant that Clouthier had been a member of the PAN for only five years, and though he denied past membership in the PRI, he had journeyed to China with PRIista President Luis Echeverría, and had been considered—and passed over—as a PRIista candidate for mayor of Culiacán.

Clouthier's analogue on the left, nominated in a September inner-party primary, was Mexico's most prominent socialist, Heberto Castillo, fifty-nine. A former engineer, mathematics professor, and political prisoner, Castillo had made a name for himself during the seventies with a unique and lonely critique of the oil boom. The PAN's predictable attempt to persuade the nation to sell its oil monopoly to private interests had attracted little attention, but Castillo's critique, perhaps because of its prophetic quality, had created a growing following. As early as 1976, Castillo had argued that it was foolhardy to "put the nation in hock" to develop its oil fields. PRIista and Pemex officials, he'd predicted, would mismanage and steal borrowed funds, and Mexico would wind up in debt for generations. His leave-it-in-the-ground urgings were a novel heresy, and the nation had watched him with amusement and increasing respect. But everyone knew that Castillo and his Partido Mexicano Socialista, or PMS, didn't stand a chance of influencing the elections. Socialist ideas have a natural or historical appeal in Mexico, but only when cast in an agrarian form. For military reasons, probably no form of socialism has a future in Mexico, and for ideological reasons, Mexico cannot accept orthodox Marxism, whose fundamental values are European, urban, and industrialist. European-style socialism declared its hostility for Mexico in 1848, when Frederick Engels, commenting on Mex-

131

ican coups and the country's invasion by the United States, wrote:

> In *America* we have witnessed the conquest of Mexico and have rejoiced at it. It is also an advance when a country which has hitherto been exclusively wrapped up in its own affairs, perpetually rent with civil wars, and completely hindered in its development, a country whose best prospect has been to become industrially subject to Britain—when such a country is forcibly drawn into the historical process. It is to the interest of its own development that Mexico will in the future be placed under the tutelage of the United States.

The Partido Mexicano Socialista of Heberto Castillo does not profess Marxist orthodoxy. But many of its members do. The PMS is the child of a prior socialist coalition, the Partido Socialista Unido de Mexico, or PSUM, which is itself descended from the Mexican Communist party, founded in 1919. Despite the relative permanence of a socialist movement in Mexico, the PSUM polled only 3.4 percent of the vote in 1982. Socialism in Mexico, unlike the Maoist movement of prerevolutionary China, for example, has not been able to take a national form.

In 1982, the PRI had been credited with 68 percent of the vote, the PAN with 16 percent; a slew of minority parties had shared the remaining 16 percent. Most observers were expecting that the 1988 elections would be a rerun of those of 1982, with one important caveat.

In late October, the Calles dynasty had suffered a hemorrhage. A group of dissidents who had for two years been calling themselves the Democratic Current of the PRI had bolted the party in the wake of the Salinas nomination. Two party leaders were among them. The first was Porfirio Muñoz Ledo, a former labor secretary, party chairman, and Mexican ambassador to the United Nations. The other was Cuauhtémoc Cárdenas Solorzano, who declared that he was running for president.

Cárdenas had been governor of the state of Michoacán, where his administration had made a name for itself by closing down whorehouses and prohibiting the sale of alcoholic beverages on weekends. But the candidate's record counted for nothing; his name counted for everything. The original Cuauh-témoc was the Aztec prince who led his people's last stand against the Conquest. Almost everybody knew Cuauhtémoc's name and legend, which are taught in school and on the streets of daily life as well: Cuauhtémoc's name and image are on the fifty-thousand-peso note, a bill worth about twenty dollars.

More important than that, Cuauhtémoc Cárdenas is the son of General "Tata" Lázaro Cárdenas, the man whose image appears on the humble ten-thousand-peso note, and the only president whom most Mexicans ever really liked. As anybody with a ten-thousand-peso note can tell, Cuauhtémoc also looks like his father, slender and long-faced, with high, prominent cheekbones and tiny, delicate eyes. Had the presidency not slipped into the *tecnócrata* camp, Mexican-educated Cárdenas might easily have been the PRI's 1988 presidential candidate, because Mexico is a festival- and commemoration-conscious country, and 1988 was a year of celebrations of the fiftieth anniversary of the petroleum nationalization. When Cuauh-témoc Cárdenas vowed to return the nation "to the goals of the Mexican Revolution," millions hoped that he was his father reincarnate. As an American analyst noted, he became "a symbol of revolutionary nostalgia to disaffected PRIistas, radical chic to university students, and land redistribution to the peasantry." His announcement as a candidate also produced an immediate shift in policy analysis.

During the heady seventies, the Mexican government had bought and founded businesses at a breathtaking rate. It became an operator of smelters, sugar refineries, grocery stores, even hotels, shampoo factories, bottleries, and a bicycle plant. In 1975, 14 percent of the workforce had been employed by the government. By 1985, the figure had risen to 22 percent. In 1975, the government had been responsible for 30 percent of the nation's payroll. By 1985, it paid 40 percent. Liberals in Mexico tended to find in this circumstance the fruition of Tata Lázaro's vision. But most of the government's holdings weren't money-makers, and a good number of them had been losers before the state stepped in; nationalization had become an alternative to bankruptcy in the circles of PRIista businessmen. When the oil bust came, Mexico's bankers at the International

Monetary Fund began questioning the government's portfolio and bureaucratic girth. Sales and closures began, along with reductions in ministry staffs. During the *sexenio,* or six-year reign, of Miguel de la Madrid, some 60 percent of the government's business holdings were liquidated or reprivatized. Conservatives complained that the government's divestitures accounted for only 3 percent of the income derived from state-owned enterprises. The Cardenistas complained that the divestitures aggravated unemployment; in 1985 alone, some 265,000 public employees had lost their jobs. Cuauhtémoc Cárdenas accused the regime of insensitivity, and called for renegotiating the external debt. During the *tecnócrata* era, he said, the PRI had gone from the politics of center-left to those of center-right.

Leading PRIistas had anticipated the attack, even wished for it. They used it to expound, in a self-defensive tone, a program for reforming the PRI, and all of Mexico. Past governments, President de la Madrid said, had been unwise and inept. The private economy had relied on subsidies and trade protections, rather than developing its competitive power. Labor unions had featherbedded, universities had lost sight of the basics, leaders had not led. What Mexico needed, they proclaimed, was a period of "modernization" of both its economic plans and its concept of leadership. He also said that Mexico needed "plupartyism," or opposition parties, and he promised that the upcoming elections would be spotlessly clean. PANista cynics said that PRIista leaders were advocating perestroika and glasnost.

During this debate, workers at Aeronaves de México, one of two state-owned airlines, went on strike. The government, rather than conceding to union demands, put the airline out of business. Aereonaves had been notoriously lax; its soccer team was salaried and its pilots spent only thirty hours a month in the air, less than half the time of their American counterparts. Liberals and the left howled. Rosario Ibarra de Piedra, a Trotskyist presidential candidate, said that by allowing American lines to pick up some of the international routes that Aeronaves had flown, de la Madrid had ceded "the sovereignty of Mexico's airspace."

Candidate Salinas used the opportunity to scathe enemies and to win allies as well. In a speech to Monterrey industrialists, he promised to lower import barriers, to ease restrictions on foreign partnerships, to establish a program of investment tax credits—and to continue dispossessing the government of its business holdings. His Thatcher-like economic program so surprised Mexico that Manuel Clouthier was moved to remark, "The PRI has stolen my economic platform." The PRI had done just that. Before long, it was sloganizing the Salinas message as "A Smaller Government Is a Stronger Government." The candidate surrounded himself not with old-line politicians from the fronts, but with recent Ivy League graduates like himself.

Salinas also cut into opposition from the left by adopting the Cárdenas call for tying debt payments to economic growth. His promise wasn't empty rhetoric, either. Sources inside the government said that negotiations had been under way for months, and that Mexico's lenders had already agreed in principle to payment reductions for 1989. They'd been able to win at the negotiating table, they said, because during his term President de la Madrid, by budget-cutting and business-selling, had made Mexico an exemplary debtor nation. To talk of unilaterally reducing debt payments, as Cárdenas sometimes did, was "demagogic and irresponsible," candidate Salinas said. Populism, he told the nation, is "a nostalgia for the past."

The debate, however, passed over the heads of most Mexicans, who didn't have fixed opinions about the government's economic role, anyhow. They were less interested in knowing what politicians promised than in knowing whom they could trust. The issue of public confidence was paramount.

Almost everyone in Mexico expected the PRI to win, by hook or by crook. People paid close attention anyway. In a country where fraud is the usual order of things, electoral activity takes on a new meaning. It is a measure of determination—of the government's determination to stay in power, and of the opposition's determination to christen a new era. It is also a measure of strength, style, and finesse. Fraud is not automatic. It must be wrought, and strong, united parties are more capable of faking an election than are parties in decline. Experienced observers watched the Mexican elections of 1988 with several

135

questions in mind: How much fraud would be necessary to ensure a PRIista victory? What tactics would the party use to steal the vote, those of desperation or those of planning? How far would the party go to defend a dirty victory? Could it still hijack an election and avoid social unrest? If it stole the elections, could it nevertheless placate, or even co-opt, the opposition? Shrewd Mexicans watched the campaign like trainers watching an up-and-coming young boxer. They didn't expect the challengers to win, but they wanted to see if any of them showed championship class.

Cuauhtémoc Cárdenas probably had an edge on all the candidates on the instinctive level at which most voting decisions are made. But in polls conducted between December and May, he was rated third, behind the candidates of the PRI and PAN. A great number of voters hadn't made up their minds, and they were withholding their faith. The mood of the times was captured by a *Newsweek* correspondent who eavesdropped on an old man named Estrada at a Cárdenas rally in Querétaro: " 'You're a Cardenista?' asked one of the organizers. 'Yes—of the father,' Estrada said. The organizer: 'And of the son as well?' Estrada: 'We'll see.' "

Cárdenas was suspect in the circles of educated Mexico, both for his PRIista past and for the affiliations he made upon leaving the party. In Mexico most political parties are standing organizations, maintained by internal funds, and by government subsidies as well. Subsidies are allocated not as matching funds, as in the United States, but on the basis of the percentage of the total vote that each party polled in previous elections. The subsidy pool for 1988 came to some $126 million, $88 million, or 70 percent, of which went to the PRI. The PRI's subsidy paid only a small part of its estimated total campaign expenses of some $260 million, more than the amount spent by either the Republican or Democratic parties in the American presidential elections of 1988. The PAN received no government subsidy: Until late 1988, it refused such funds. The balance of the Mexican electoral subsidy fund, some $38 million, was destined for six minor parties, three of which declared support for Cárdenas. Minority parties, unlike the PRI, derive most of the funds for their national operations from the government's subsidy payments.

A change in the law by which subsidies were granted gave some minority parties special reason to worry about their strength in the elections of 1988. Previously, subsidies had been granted to all parties that polled 1.5 percent of the total vote or more. But for 1988, a new standard had been enacted. To maintain their subsidies, parties had to win at least 2.5 percent of the vote. The three parties that declared support for Cárdenas were ideologically heterogenous; what they had in common was that their subsidies would be lost if they didn't make improved showings in 1988. The first of them to declare support for Cárdenas was the Partido Auténtico de la Revolución Mexicana, the Authentic Party of the Mexican Revolution, or PARM, a group formed in 1954 by generals who had conservative views. In 1982, the PARM had polled only one percent of the vote. Cárdenas also won endorsement from the Partido Popular Socialista, the Peoples' Socialist party, or PPS, an ostensibly Marxist group dating to 1948. In 1982, the PPS had received 1.5 percent of the vote. Both the PARM and the PPS had legitimate followings in regional pockets of Mexico, the PARM in the northern state of Tamaulipas, and the PPS in peasant communities scattered across the south. But in prior presidential elections, both had also at times endorsed the candidate of the PRI.

Cárdenas persuaded an imperiled third party, the Partido Socialista de los Trabajadores, the Socialist Workers Party or PST, to change its name to El Frente Cardenista de Reconstrución Nacional, or Cardenista National Reconstruction Front. The party adopted a new logo, showing the figure of Lázaro Cárdenas, not Cuauhtémoc. It had no base. Formed in 1973, it had engaged in operations that most of the leftists who were its potential supporters viewed as suspect. But in 1982, it had polled 1.4 percent of the vote, more than the PARM and nearly as much as the PPS. On the streets, the parties that had declared support for Cárdenas were regarded as *paleros*, or shovelers, a reference to the servile status of hod carriers. They were parties whose purpose, able critics said, had been to provide a pluralistic facade for PRIista rule.

137

In living rooms and coffee shops, Mexicans on the left and right speculated about the honesty of candidate Cárdenas. He was raised in the PRI: Maybe he was loyal to it yet. He balked at criticizing PRIistas who took office before 1982: Maybe he was representing former presidents Echeverría and López Portillo, whose populism Salinas abhorred. He was receiving support from Joaquín "La Quina" Hernández Galicia, the Jimmy Hoffa of Mexican unionism: Maybe he was the candidate of the PRI's most corrupt elements. A new and expanded system of proportional representation was going into effect: Maybe he was the PRI's insurance policy, a guarantor that change wouldn't get out of hand. The national debt was being renegotiated: Maybe he and Salinas were partners in a debtors' version of the Mutt and Jeff game. Maybe, in a word, Cuauhtémoc Cárdenas was an undercover agent for Carlos Salinas. From the PANista right came a slogan, "A Vote for Cárdenas Is a Vote for Salinas!" The slogan was echoed on the left.

TACTICS, TRIVIAL AND OTHERWISE

Mexican elections, like those in the United States, are times when trivial charges are thrown into the air, and sometimes unethical tactics are used. They are also times of rampant bad taste, as in the United States. Early in the election, the Mexico City daily *Excelsior* in an eight-column headline reported that cultural figures had accused the administration of Miguel de la Madrid of having "deformed" Mexican opera. In Monterrey, *El Norte* reported allegations that the PRI had abandoned support for the game of chess. Both stories reflected the belief, nearly traditional in Mexico, that the president is the guarantor of almost every facet of life.

Two half-brothers who claimed to be illegitimate sons of "Tata" Lázaro were presented on the nation's leading telecast and in various newspapers. The two had come forward, they said, to bring the nation a message: that daddy would turn in his grave if he knew of Cuauhtémoc's defection from the PRI. Their appearance, I suppose, gave testimony to the importance of brothers, even half-brothers, to presidential politics: Jimmy

Carter and Mother Rose were lucky in comparison to Cuauh-témoc Cárdenas. Neither of the two bastards mentioned their mothers' pasts, and no comment came from Tata's widow, who was busy helping her son campaign.

Unions ordered workers to attend Salinas rallies, and exacted fines—usually of one or two days' pay—from those members who failed to sign a roster at the site where he spoke. Government agencies rewarded their employees with a day's holiday, following the day of rally attendance. Reporters at one Salinas rally asked well-wishers why they'd come. Forty percent of them admitted that their attendance had been compelled by union or job superiors. Apparently, the PRIista thinking was that huge rally turnouts produce—or justify—huge electoral margins. In order to rally a quarter-million people in Mexico City for the close of the Salinas campaign, the PRI bused supporters from locales as far as five hundred miles away.

Some of the PRI's attempts to orchestrate support produced sour notes. At a February rally in Coahuila, candidate Salinas was forced to abandon the podium when ostensibly supportive peasants broke into his speech chanting "¡Cárdenas! ¡Cárdenas!" At a gathering sponsored by the PRI's Mexico City think tank, an artist cast aside a prepared welcoming address to tell the candidate, among other things, that he should dispense with the "ass-kissers" who surround him. In a May Mexico City meeting with unionized municipal employees, whistling workers—whistling is the equivalent of booing in the United States—halted Salinas after he'd spoken only 239 words of his speech—and then they walked out of the meeting hall.

The PAN complained that Televisa, Mexico's private network, slandered and ignored the opposition. Its charges were especially aimed at Jacobo Zabludovsky, Mexico's Walter Cronkite. Ninety percent of the airtime devoted to the campaign by 24 Horas, Zabludovsky's program, consisted of reports on the activities of Carlos Salinas, the PAN alleged. A Televisa special program about the opposition superimposed footage of Mussolini and Clouthier, and another report by the same network associated Cuauhtémoc Cárdenas with images of Castro, Khrushchev, and Salvador Allende.

Most of the media were partial to Salinas, because publishers had to protect their advertising profiles and reporters needed *embutes* to survive. PRIista candidates for the presidency and the newsmen who cover their speeches fly from city to city on Mexican military aircraft whose seating is free, and are booked at party headquarters. Hotel accommodations, restaurant meals, and spaces on the campaign's tour buses are arranged by the *partido*, too. Newsmen on tour are shepherded by press managers whose chief tools are local party contacts and an evaluation, flown in daily from headquarters, of stories published about the campaign. The PRI uses its information about the press to calculate the *embutes* that are discreetly paid to reporters each night, and after the presidential campaign, to lobby with publishers regarding the selection of reporters for presidential and Cabinet-level beats. To get a fat *embute* today and to land a lucrative and important beat tomorrow, Mexican reporters have to stay in good with the PRIista managers of the press. If they don't, they may get beaten over the head with a stick.

Not many reporters have seen the PRI wield its stick, but I saw it in 1982, with the de la Madrid campaign. I had arranged to join the tour in the state of Baja California, and for several days, I was the only American aboard the PRI's bus. Two others, both from a San Diego daily, joined the tour at Tijuana, and I naturally struck up a quick friendship with them. They weren't with us for long. On the second afternoon of their journey, as they tried to board the bus, Mexican reporters blocked its doorway. When the two tried to pry their way inside, they were hurled to the ground. Failing on the press bus, they tried to board the bus for photographers, and were again thrown into the dust. Because I'd been keeping company with the two Californians, my ascent was blocked, too. The two Californians, it seems, had written a report that was critical of the PRIista governor of the state of Baja California, and he had made his influence felt through the national campaign apparatus. Only after I negotiated with the tour's press officials and made clear that I wasn't a Californian was I permitted to re-board. A couple of my Mexican press companions apologized to me for the error of mistaken identity. They had acted as goons, they told me, to win favor with the PRI, and they were truly sorry, they said, to have obstructed me, a neutral to the conflict. Nothing they said indicated that their first loyalty was to the press rather than to the PRI.

In an attempt to publicize itself without depending on the usual media, the PAN resurrected a technique from the 1986 campaign of Francisco Barrio in Chihuahua. After Barrio was denied the governorship, PANistas had used rubber stamps to mark bills of currency with slogans like "Mexico Demands Democracy." The bills and the sensation they created gave a limited national circulation to the party's protest, despite a virtual blackout of coverage by the national television media. The government had responded by ordering its banks to withdraw marked bills from circulation, but in the north the order had little effect: The truth was, many of the bills were being marked by PANista tellers inside the banks. Early in the 1988 campaign, bills bearing the slogan "I Am Free, I Don't Want Repression" began appearing. The Treasury responded, this time by declaring that marked bills would be refused by banks as worthless. The opposition did not unite. Even the socialist Castillo defended the Treasury edict. The marked bills were refused, and the PAN lost a tactic.

At several points during the campaign, the opposition had to face—or had to ignore—an unethical voice in the press, that of the anonymous advertisement. In May, for example, a half-page ad appeared in several national newspapers, showing, on its left side, an American postage stamp. The stamp bore the image of John Paul Jones, and a quote, "I have not yet begun to fight." On the ad's right side, a drawing depicted a PAN rally beneath a banner saying, in Spanish, "We Have Not Yet Begun to Fight." The ad's text read, "Plagiarism or a pro–United States mentality? The PAN in its political propaganda uses a phrase of North American origins." The ad was testimony, among other things, to the persistence of xenophobia in literate Mexican society.

Propaganda forgery was also part of the game. The PAN denounced the appearance of blue-and-white brochures, ersatz party literature, whose text included paragraphs like: "Maquío is an agronomist. Before, he studied in Military Academies in the U.S.; he pledged loyalty to the North American flag and

141

has taken various courses in counterinsurgency with *gringo* advisers." Faked bulletins bearing the seal of the PPS declared, "For the dictatorship of the proletariat! This 6 of July vote for Cuauhtémoc Cárdenas to throw out the exploitative bourgeoisie." In Mexico City, telephone and electric-company crews were dispatched in company vehicles to paint the words "Communist" and "Marxist Leninist" over *pintas* that bore the image of candidate Cárdenas.

But all these were mere pranks, having little influence on the outcome of the election. The opposition didn't expect a completely clean campaign; it did hope for fair elections. During the campaign, dozens of worrisome signs appeared, omens for July 6:

• In Mexico City, oppositionists who scrutinized a voting roll found seventy-two people registered at the same residence—that of the PRIista mayor, whose home occupies half a block. To conceal the registrations, thirty-one voters were registered at one entrance, twenty-six at an entrance on a second street, and fifteen at a third.
• A PARMista candidate for the Chamber of Deputies in Monterrey resigned after inspecting the voting rolls for his district. The rolls, he said, included the names of two thousand dead voters, and more than ten thousand false addresses.
• A candidate of the Mexican Socialist party in Juchitán, Oaxaca, brought criminal charges because his examination of voting rolls showed that 40 percent of the registrants had been given more than one voter's card, and that 20 percent of them had more than three cards, usually issued to different addresses.
• In Cadereyta, Nuevo León, a passerby recovered seventeen of some eight hundred voter's cards that, he said, had fallen from a window of the town's city hall. Mexican law requires that cards be mailed to voters by federal authorities.
• In June, Cardenistas raided a Mexico City printshop and carried away ballots being printed there, ostensibly for use in a Sonora legislative election. The Cardenistas claimed that private printing of election ballots is illegal under federal law, and alleged that the ballots were being printed for use as *tacos*.

142

Federal and Sorona officials denied the charge. Both sides swore criminal complaints, but no one was prosecuted.

• The leader of an urban settlers' group in Monterrey turned over to PANistas a packet of 161 registration cards that he said had been given to him by the PRI, in preparation for July 6 fraud. He said that he had been asked to recruit settlers to cast second votes for the PRI, using the cards. PANistas investigated the names and addresses on seventy-seven of the cards, and found that about half belonged to voters who had registered but had never received their cards; another half of the fake cards belonged to people whose names were unknown at the addresses listed.

• At a funeral in Morelia, Michoacán, on July 5 Cuauhtémoc Cárdenas showed members of the press fifty-seven ballots marked in favor of the PRI. He said that the ballots had been brought to his local campaign offices by a sympathizer. The ballots bore the seal of the district electoral commission, the body responsible for assuring the authenticity of election reports.

• During the first week of July, American newspapers disappeared from the stands in Mexico City. Vendors were unable to explain why their copies of *The New York Times*, *The Wall Street Journal*, the *Los Angeles Times*, and other dailies no longer arrived.

• The national voting list was itself suspect. It showed that some 38 million Mexicans had registered to vote, more than 90 percent of the voting-age population. Private polls indicated that only 70 percent of the population reported having registered.

THE POLLS

Independent polls of public opinion were plentiful during the 1988 campaign, for the first time in Mexican history. Essentially, what the polls showed was that Cárdenas was gaining strength at the expense of the PRI. Initial polls, in December, had shown the PAN with between 15 and 20 percent support, a figure that did not change in subsequent soundings. But the PRI's early strength, in excess of 50 percent, dropped about ten points by June, while support for Cárdenas increased from about 15 percent to nearly 25 percent of sample populations. Details from a June poll showed that big businessmen were divided: 35 percent favored the PRI, 33 percent the PAN, and 26 percent the Cardenista candidacy. Government employees by a margin of 63 percent to 11 percent picked the PRI over the PAN, with 18 percent favoring the Cardenista option. Workers preferred Cárdenas by 41 percent to 37 percent for the PRI; only 14 percent admitted support for the PAN. In the countryside, the PRI led the Cardenistas 48 percent to 35 percent, and the PAN trailed badly with only 10 percent support. In general, older voters preferred the PRI, and younger voters Cárdenas; only in Yucatán and the northern states did the PAN show widespread support among poor and working-class Mexicans. Had the election been held on June 1, its result would have been taken for granted.

But on June 5, a Cardenista surge began. On that day, the Partido Mexicano Socialista and its candidate, Heberto Castillo, endorsed the Cárdenas campaign. In addition to giving Cárdenas its electoral support, 5 to 10 percent of the vote, the endorsement more than doubled his organizational strength. Cárdenas got the benefit of what was arguably Mexico's most dedicated corps of supporters, and also a gain of public-relations importance: If Castillo supports Cárdenas, the left-wing intellectual community concluded, then Cárdenas is sincerely opposed to the PRI.

Any remaining doubts were expunged on July 4, when the press reported an event that was to be the most electrifying news of the campaign. On the night of July 2, forty-one-year-old Francisco Xavier Ovando, a Cárdenas aide, was murdered in Mexico City. Ovando had been the chairman of the PRI in the state of Michoacán during the Cárdenas tenancy as govenor. He had also been a federal deputy under the sponsorship of Cárdenas. He had worked in the Federal Electoral Commission, the agency responsible for reporting election returns, and on the night of July 2, he'd been working in the offices of the Democratic Current, the Cárdenas faction within the PRI, preparing a computer simulation for use in detecting fraud. About

10:30 that night, he'd left the Current's office in his metallic-gray Atlantic, accompanied by two assistants, Román Gil and Jorge Fernández. Ovando was bound for his sister-in-law's house in Iztacalco, a neighborhood on Mexico City's south side. Fernández got out of the car at a subway stop along the route. Ovando and Gil continued, but neither of them reached home. About 11:30 P.M., the police received a telephone call telling them the location of a gray Atlantic, in an industrial district on the south side of town. Two dead men were in the car's backseat, the anonymous caller said.

Both Ovando and Gil had been shot at close range. Police found an unspent .380-caliber-pistol round on the rear floorboard of the Atlantic, and concluded that at least two assailants had been involved in the killing; Ovando and Gil had died of .22 caliber wounds. Neither had been robbed; Ovando's Rolex watch was still on his wrist when officers reached the body, though it would later disappear. A briefcase and papers Ovando had been carrying also vanished, though in the confusion of investigations, no one came forth to say whether his killers or the police had taken them. There was no apparent motive for the crime, which remains unsolved. But almost everyone in Mexico was sure that politics were at base of the two deaths. Candidate Cárdenas blamed the PRI, and his followers equated a vote for him as a vote against gangsterism in public life.

WITH HERMINIO

As the news of the Ovando killings was breaking, I was on my way north. I reached Monterrey on election eve. Herminio woke me about sunrise on election day, far too early for my pleasure. While I drank coffee downstairs, he and Tencha hovered around the telephone, answering calls and making them, rousting PANistas to their duties and giving last-minute instructions on details of the electoral code. Tencha left for the poll she was to supervise, Herminio's son assumed a vigil at the telephone, and a newspaper reporter came. He, Herminio, and I loaded into the Maverick and began our rounds.

145

We spent the first part of the morning in the immediate neighborhood, driving paved streets all the way. A survey by the newspaper *El Norte*—which fielded three hundred representatives to keep watch on the city's some sixteen hundred polls—found that 46 percent of them opened on time. All of those we visited were in operation when we arrived.

The most vexing problem that we found was that several voting places had moved their locations without leaving a sign saying where they'd gone. With electoral code in hand, Herminio browbeat the voting-station officials until they promised to place signs at the announced locations—and after an hour or so, we'd return, to see that they had complied. The other problem was that many polling-station officials had not read their instructions. The state electoral commission had included in its kit of materials a *mampara*, or divider, intended to give voters privacy when marking their ballots. The dividers stood about two feet tall. They were made of plywood, covered with white wrapping paper. On their sides were bumper stickers reading NUEVO LÉON ELECTORAL PROCESS 88 About half the polling officials took these dividers to be signs. They placed them outside the doors of their homes. After a couple of tries, Herminio gave up attempting to explain that the *mamparas* were supposed to be inside the voting area, not outside. The use of the dividers as signs seemed to be an improvement, anyway.

According to *El Norte*'s survey, 75 percent of the polling stations, when they armed their voting boxes, failed to insert in them a little tin sheet whose purpose was to prevent the insertion of wads of ballots, or *tacos*. People told me that they didn't know what the tin sheets were, or that inserting them required a manual dexterity beyond their capabilities. Herminio did not check on their use because it was too late: Ballots had been cast by the time we arrived. My impression of the voting process, in those first hours in a lower-middle-class district, was that the government indeed was trying to keep its pledge to electoral honesty. The problem I saw were those of inevitable Mexican disorganization, not malice.

All sorts of things were happening in other parts of town. We stayed in touch through PANista and *El Norte* poll-watchers, and by telephone calls to the PAN's headquarters. In the suburb of

Garza García, taxi drivers were ferrying voters to the polls for the PRI. Between runs, they congregated at a bar that a reporter from *El Norte* briefly entered. Inside he saw plastic bags bearing the PRI logo, filled with bottles of cooking oil, sacks of flour, cartons of toothpaste, and other grocery items. He also saw men drinking beer; dispensing alcoholic beverages is illegal on election days. The taxi drivers at the bar noticed the reporter's camera and tape recorder, and tried to take them away. He scuffled out of the grasp of the goons, and scrambled off.

On days when multiple elections are held in Mexico, voters are given a separate ballot for each office being contested. On this election day in Nuevo León, each voter was issued a ballot for marking a presidential choice, one for a choice of two senators, by party affiliation—splitting the ticket wasn't allowed —a ballot for choosing a uninominal Chamber deputy, and one for the state's legislative elections. Each polling station also had four voting boxes, one for each race. At Substation 1 of Box 126 in Monterrey's third federal district, voters were issued Senate ballots for the election being held in the state of Veracruz. The ballots bore the same national party labels as in Nuevo León, but the names of the candidates did not of course correspond. A voter mentioned this bizarre circumstance to the PANista poll-watcher on duty—who said that he'd challenge the results of the box only if the PAN lost the race.

In the Santa Catarina area, some twenty men filtered into a polling station, each wearing a loose-fitting shirt. On each shirt was pinned a gold-colored button. One by one, the men took their turns to vote. Two female PANista voters saw one of them stuffing a wad of *tacos* in the box for presidential ballots, and alerted the polling-station officials. As the man attempted to stuff *tacos* into the box for legislative representatives, the polling officials halted him. He was arrested, and the officials decided to close the polling place. They were opposed by a delegation of some twenty men who showed identification from the electoral commission. But the polling-station officials closed anyway; the ID cards the men showed had been signed by a traffic cop, not by electoral authorities.

About noon, Herminio, the reporter, and I passed by Herminio's house. Some fifty little white boxes were sitting on its

147

patio. They contained sandwiches and fruit, intended for PAN-ista poll-watchers. The boxes were apparently a spontaneous donation of a restaurant in the area. No one had expected their arrival, nor had preparations been made to distribute them. Herminio and the reporter packed the boxes for delivery. To make room in the backseat, and to give my fever a rest, I went inside the house and upstairs to bed again.

Low-grade fevers are, I suppose, as much a blessing as a curse. If they don't incapacitate you, after a day or two you accustom yourself to benefit from the promptings of a fevered state of mind. As I lay in my bed upstairs in Herminio's house, fever brought back with clarity the once-lost memory of elections in the small Texas town where, fifteen years earlier, I'd learned the reporter's trade. The town used paper ballots back then, as Mexicans do. The Texas ballots were printed on legal-sized sheets of white paper, one ballot for all the offices being challenged; Mexican ballots come with four-color printing designs, to help illiterates identify party symbols. But the chief difference, I recalled, was that Texas ballots bore numbered tabs. Each of them was separately registered. Poll officials could not work backward from the voting list to the numbered ballot issued a voter. Secrecy was not imperiled, but ballot-stuffing was thereby discouraged. Any *tacos* admitted to a box would have to bear numbers within the series issued to a box.

In the Mexican election of 1988, thousands of men and women like Herminio were cruising the nation's polling stations, hoping to see someone come into the polls from outside carrying a wad of ballots identical to those issued at that station—identical because Mexican ballots are unnumbered. A good part of Mexico's electoral fraud, I realized, was due to the mere absence of numbered ballots. I was stunned: All this hassle over nothing, I thought. During the years that I'd followed Mexican elections, I'd never read or heard of any official or opposition leader who had demanded numbered ballots. The elections seemed merely a game whose chief rule was: I'll let you fake the election results, as long as I can survive by hollering "Fraud!" By not demanding numbered ballots, under the threat of an electoral boycott, the opposition had given the government and the PRI the chance to ensure election victories.

148

The system, with its flaws, gave power to some men, and gave others an excuse for having none.

When Herminio and the reporter returned, I joined them in the Maverick again. They had decided that Herminio would hunt for fraud in a district outside of his own, where he had no poll-inspector's credentials but could nevertheless look in as a citizen, as we'd done in 1985. We were to go to the Fomerreyes and the rough districts again. Herminio and the reporter were excited by the prospect of the hunt. But it was hot, I was feverish, and now out of sorts with the Mexicans. If they would only number their ballots, I told myself, none of us would have to take this ride.

As soon as we were rolling and the air conditioner had cooled us a bit, I asked Herminio what he knew about demands for numbering the ballots. He didn't know of any such demand, nor did he understand why it should be made. When I explained to him the virtues of numbered ballots, he merely brushed me aside. "Oh, yes, well that may have been a good idea in other elections. But what we're hearing is that this time, the PRI is going to perpetrate its fraud on the regional level." I couldn't imagine what fraud on a "regional level" might mean, and I was too disgusted to ask. I leaned back in the seat and watched out of the side window as the city passed by.

We passed through what seemed to be a residential district with a big building on one block. The building, as I recall, was two or three stories high and was the headquarters of the Confederación de Trabajadores Mexicanos or CTM, a PRIista union front. Though election days are holidays, buses and vans were parked at curbside, all around, for a distance of some three blocks. Men in working clothes were gathered in clumps, five here, a dozen there, twenty-two more on the corner. "This is Fraud Central," Herminio told me. "This is where the *tacos* are distributed."

The charge, or something very much like it, was probably true. That July 6, reporter Francisco Betancourt of *El Norte* gained the confidence of a member of the Confederación Revolucionaria de Obreros y Campesinos, or CROC, the Revolutionary Confederation of Workers and Peasants, a rival PRIista labor front. Posing as a unionist and with his friend's

149

connivance, Betancourt secured admission to the CROC's head-quarters, where he and some eighty legitimate unionists pre-pared for *taquero* work. His CROquista superiors provided him with a credential that, under a false name, identified him as a poll inspector for the PRI. They also gave him a gold-colored metallic button that, they said, he should show to soldiers or police in case of arrest; the button, they said, would guarantee his release and immunity from legal harm. With a half-dozen others, Betancourt was driven to a polling station and given about one hundred ballots to stuff, half of them marked in favor of Carlos Salinas, the other half marked for the PRI's senatorial candidate. Betancourt managed to call his editors, then stalled at the polling station for hours, while observers and photog-raphers from *El Norte* filtered in. Late in the afternoon, with his CROquista co-*taqueros* impatiently waiting for him to do his job, Betancourt left the polling station, saying that he was going to buy some chewing gum. He instead went to the offices of *El Norte*, which, with his report and documenting photos, told the story the next day.

It was an afternoon for confessions, I suppose. As we drove in the Maverick from the headquarters of the CTM toward Fomerrey up in the hills, our reporter began reminiscing. In 1985, he said, he'd been a university student and a member of an athletic team. His coach had recruited him and a half-dozen others to work as *taqueros*. While Herminio and I had been cruising the polls in that election, our reporter friend had voted at six polling stations, stuffing about fifty ballots each time. Herminio was charmed by the story, but I wasn't at all amused. In Mexico, I believe, there will always be more *taqueros* than confessors, unless—I now doubted that it would ever be true —the ruling party steps in on the side of electoral honesty.

We spent the rest of the day and all of that evening cruising from spot to spot. At one voting station, an adobe hut no more than twelve feet by twelve feet big, we arrived as a fist fight was breaking up. Someone had tried to stop a *taquero* from stuffing a wad. A melee had ensued, *taqueros*—three or four were in the tiny hut at the time—against PANista and Car-denista poll-watchers; nobody was sure whether the election officials had fought to break up the partisans, or had joined the *taquero* side. The contents of the little house were in disarray, but by some miracle, the fragile election boxes had survived. Voting resumed almost as soon as the *taqueros* made their exit.

About eight-thirty that night, we came to a polling place in a neighborhood where no one had expected a fuss. It was on the second floor of a two-story brick house on a paved street. Iron gratings with locks kept us from entering its driveway. We were told that party representatives, including one from the PAN, were in the lighted room upstairs, tabulating the day's vote. But a crowd had been gathered on the street below since midafternoon, when those inside the polling station had refused to admit voting inspectors, despite the credentials they showed. Something was amiss at that voting box, everyone was sure. Herminio decided that we should wait.

Several members of the MCM were on hand, and in the crowded street I met two young men, dressed in jeans and American T-shirts, who told me that they'd been standing guard all day, since the hour when the polling station opened its doors. They weren't registered poll-watchers, either with the government or any political group. They were the sons of PANista parents, who'd asked them, and various brothers and sisters, to keep watch as mere witnesses in case incidents of violence occurred. I thought they were Miracle Boys, kids who took time to perform what was, after all, a public service, merely to satisfy a parental sense of civic concern.

Three other young men from the neighborhood had come to the gathering, boom boxes in hand; fortunately, they took turns at serenading the neighborhood with their tapes of rock music. Since the crowd was a large one, motorists were avoiding the street. The absence of cars made the pavement an ideal playground for tykes on tricycles; parents stood by to cheer them as they rode. A corner grocery and a café on the block were supplying the onlookers' needs. Young couples walked the street, arm in arm, as if in a city park at festival time. I leaned back against a parked car and traded stories with neighborhood people who wanted to tell me about trips they'd made to the United States.

Not until nearly midnight did the people in the lighted room come out onto the upstairs porch. As the law requires, they posted a sign stating the tally they'd made, and then they quickly bustled out, refusing all comment. With Herminio, I walked up to the fence of the home's front yard and looked up at the sign the voting officials had made. The PRI had won at that box, but that wasn't what concerned me. I was stunned by the disparity between vote totals for the four races that had been contested that day. In the presidential race, 355 people had cast ballots, but 401 had voted for Senate seats. In the federal Chamber contest, 339 ballots were tallied, but only 292 in the legislative race. The disparity between the number of votes cast in the different races was 109, or 27 percent, yet every voter, one presumed, had been given four ballots to mark. Why had it taken more than three hours to tally 1,387 ballots, when other polls counted five and six times as many in a couple of hours? Was the tally the result of fraud, or merely of slipshod organization? Had I viewed the tally in a sound frame of mind, I'd have sworn that I could have concocted its numbers only in a feverish dream.

THE VOTE COUNT

Earlier on election day, an issue of the magazine *Impacto* had gone on sale, carrying the news that Carlos Salinas had polled 20 million votes, handily winning the election. Other prominent Mexican publications waited until the next day to make that kind of claim. CARLOS SALINAS DE GORTARI TRIUMPHED IN CLEAN VOTE, headlined the national daily *El Heraldo* of Mexico City. MEXICO GAVE THE VICTORY TO SALINAS DE GORTARI, *El Día* echoed. Morning newspapers carried a description of the Nuevo León elections, doubtless purchased by the office of the state's governor. Its lead paragraph said, "Governor Jorge Treviño informs us that in the state of Nuevo León elections were carried out in an atmosphere of total tranquillity, without difficulties and without incidents of any kind. . . . The state's chief officer . . . eulogized the participation and maturity that Nuevo León citizens displayed in this electoral contest. 'Pluralism,

freedom of suffrage and social participation have been fundamental elements in this day of elections,' he summarized."

Nevertheless, for the next two weeks conscientious newspapers were crammed with reports of fraud, in locales across
the nation. Many of the denunciations concerned the "regional
fraud" to which Herminio had alluded in his election-day conversation with me. In Mexico, ballots are tallied at the polling
station, and are then sent, along with a tally sheet, to one of
the country's three hundred electoral-commission offices. The
regional or district office prepares a tally of returns for its territory, and sends the ballots, along with both the polling station
and district paper work, to Mexico City, where a national count
is tabulated. Documentary fraud, called "alchemy" in Mexican
electoral slang, is practiced at every level along the way.

For example, the polling station in the village of Tlacualoyan,
in the state of Tlaxcala, in east-central Mexico, tallied 103 votes
for Cuauhtémoc Cárdenas and only 55 for Carlos Salinas, the
PRI's nominee. But four days later, the district electoral office
in Apizaco announced a different result, 103 votes for Cárdenas,
155 for Salinas: Somebody in the district office had added a "1"
in front of the Salinas tally. A voting station in the village of
Cebollas, Durango, reported a tally of 200 votes for the PAN,
0 for the PRI; the PAN, and not the PRI, contested the count.
"This is for Ripley, because the person who did the alchemy
in Cebollas made a mistake and put the result they wanted into
the column of the PAN instead of the PRI," a PANista official
explained.

In the state of Guerrero, 100 votes cast for Salinas in one
precinct became 580 in the district tally, twice the number of
total ballots cast. At another box, 8 votes cast for Salinas were
reported by the district office as 308. *Newsweek*'s international
issue reported that "In La Felicidad, part of Coyuca township,
50 registered voters managed to cast 550 votes for Salinas—an
especially remarkable feat since, according to sworn statements
gathered by Cardenistas, no ballot boxes ever arrived there."

Probably with satiric intent, the Mexico City daily *La Jornada*
on July 7 headlined its electoral roundup story ELECTION DAY
PASSES IN NORMALITY IN MOST OF THE NATION. It reported that:

153

• In Juárez, Chihuahua, PANista sources claimed to have found eighty-one of the city's four hundred voting boxes already stuffed with ballots when the polls opened.

• In Moreno, Jalisco, hundreds of voters vainly waited for two polling places to open. "After several hours," the newspaper said, "they decided to take the voting boxes and burn them. They later discovered that these polls were phantom polling places and were not legally registered."

• In the state of Oaxaca, spokesmen for the Cardenistas claimed that the authorities in two mountain villages had prepared ballots and tally sheets giving Carlos Salinas 80 percent of the suffrage—two days before the election was held.

• "There was, in the middle of the incidents," *La Jornada* decried, "the case of the clergyman who got permission to vote. It treats of the priest Pablo Ortega Farías, who presented himself dressed in sport clothes at poll 59, in the Industrial Aviación neighborhood of the first district of San Luis Potosí. The polling representatives recognized him as a clergyman, and even so they agreed to give him permission to vote." *La Jornada* did not reveal whether or not the priest consummated his civic lust by actually casting a ballot—a crime for priests in Mexico.

In Michoacán and Jalisco, thefts of voting boxes were reported; a demonstration of PANistas waited at a Jalisco district electoral-commission office until some one hundred of the missing boxes were delivered, more than twenty-four hours after they had been surrendered by polling stations. In Michoacán, as in Nuevo León, "traveling" ballots were used: Some Michoacán voters were given ballots from the states of Jalisco and Oaxaca. In rural Nuevo León, turnout heavily favored the PRI. At one box, ballots were cast for 116 percent of the number of registered voters; at another 101 percent voted, and at two others 104 percent. A national survey performed after the election showed that Salinas had won 12 percent of his support from boxes in which he was credited with margins of 99 to 100 percent of the vote, and that nearly half of the votes credited to him came from the 28 percent of voting boxes at which no oppositionists were present as poll-watchers. Altogether, opposition parties recorded irregularities at 52 percent of the polls.

The best story of alchemy may have come from Monterrey, when oppositionists, representing both the PAN and the Cardenista movement, tried to inspect a poll in the Seventh Federal District. Voting-station officials grabbed the voting boxes and ran when the oppositionist delegation arrived. When the PANistas and Cardenistas gave chase, the officials and their thugs, called *"porros"* or cheerleaders, broke open the boxes, spilling their ballots on the ground. The oppositionists gathered them up, and sat down at a table to do an unofficial vote count. The polling officials tried to drive them away by, among other things, hurling soft-drink bottles at them. When the oppositionists realized that they couldn't hold out, they ripped the ballots to shreds and fled. The entire incident was recorded by a photographer who entered his series in *El Norte*'s contest for election-fraud photo coverage. Despite the destruction of the ballots and the scandal, the electoral commission reported a result for the poll: Salinas, 633; Clouthier, 25; Cárdenas, 0. "How is it possible, if we did everything but dance the *jarabe tapatío* on those ballots?" asked Javier Livas, a PARMista candidate and observer who took part in the fracas. No arrests were made in connection with the dispute at the box.

LEGITIMIZING THE RESULTS

The week following July 6 was one of the longest in modern Mexican history, as an uneasy people waited tensely, and probably unnecessarily, for the Comisión Federal Electoral or CFE to announce national results. Vote tabulation has traditionally gone slowly in Mexico, because the Mexico City CFE headquarters can't begin work until electoral packets arrive from its three hundred far-flung district offices. But the CFE had been given a new image and new equipment for 1988. A minority of opposition-party representatives were seated on the commission, to give the look of fairness, and telephone connections were established with the district offices, to give the look of modernity. Furthermore, the CFE's chairman and secretary of Gobernación, Manuel Bartlett, had ordered the installation of computers, which, he promised, would collate district reports instantly, providing projections and other assessments of an advisory nature. According to the plan, the three hundred district offices were to report their results unofficially by telephone on Wednesday night, July 6, within hours after the polls closed. Their reports, listed poll by poll, would be fed into the CFE's computer system, which would begin producing figures before midnight. By midday Thursday, an unofficial but total result would be available. Official results would not be announced until about a week after election day, following examination of the electoral packets by the CFE in Mexico City.

On the night of July 6, the CFE announced that its computer system had failed. High voter turnout was the initial reason given for the breakdown; in the days that followed, overloaded telephone circuits would also be blamed, and in a press conference, Bartlett said that "atmospheric conditions" had been responsible. Copies of telephone reports from the districts were passed on to CFE members only after great delay, and not fully: On Sunday, July 10, the courtesy was halted. The CFE had received electoral packets from all districts, and to provide CFE members with copies of both telephone and written reports would be superfluous, Bartlett said. He didn't point out that there was an important difference in the reports. The telephone reports included poll-by-poll tallies. The district reports that the CFE would use for its work were mere summaries. The result of the change was that neither the members of the CFE nor the press would ever see poll-by-poll results for twenty-five thousand of Mexico's fifty-four thousand voting stations.

Manuel Bartlett at first announced that despite the computer breakdown, he'd make preliminary results available on Friday, July 8. This promise was later fudged to Sunday, July 10, and then was forgotten altogether. While these moves were being made, as might be expected, the opposition was charging that the delays covered fraud, and the press was finding evidence, always from off-the-record sources, that the charges were accurate. ". . . Officials inside both the Government and the PRI . . . are saying the leftist opposition candidate, Cuauhtémoc Cárdenas, was the winner of Wednesday's elections," *The New York Times* reported.

Reporters also found evidence of an unprecedented split in

the PRI. In many informal conversations and in a few stories, they mentioned "dinosaurs" and "modernizers" within the PRI. According to the perceptions of the press, the PRI's strong labor factions, which wanted to resist economic change, were exercising their muscle against the technocrats or "modernizers" aligned with Salinas and de la Madrid. But nobody agreed about who was falsifying election returns, or why. "Salinas now is desperately trying to preserve his hold on the party's electoral machinery so it will manipulate the tally in his favor," the *Houston Chronicle* reported. "Mr. Salinas was said by political experts to be trying to prevent disgruntled members of the party's old guard from manipulating tallies to improve his showing. . . ." said *The New York Times.*

While their government writhed, Mexicans were drawing conclusions of their own. Belief in a Cárdenas victory was widespread, sustained by rumors from a thousand sources. Exit polls could not speak to the subject, because in Mexico exit polls are considered to be illegal "infringements on the secrecy of the vote." But the country's leading university, La Universidad Nacional Autónoma de México, or UNAM, published a hasty study based on projections from actual but incomplete poll results. The UNAM study showed Cárdenas as the election's winner, with 39 percent of the vote, Salinas as its runner-up, with 34 percent, and Clouthier as its also-ran, with 22 percent. The UNAM study and the rumor mill produced a contagion that touched even American observers. A few weeks after the election, columnist Pete Hamill, for example, would pen a version of the Cárdenas myth from his home in New York:

> When Cuauhtémoc Cárdenas announced that he would run against the candidate of the PRI, virtually nobody gave him a chance. He had no money. He had no grass-roots organization. During the campaign, he seemed even more like another version of Don Quixote. The newspapers opposed him, or ignored him, filling their pages with the paid-up products of *embutismo*. Television, as usual, disgraced itself.
>
> And yet Cárdenas won.

If Cárdenas didn't win, Hamill and the Mexicans believed, it could only be because of fraud.

157

On the night of July 13, a week after the elections, the CFE announced the results of its canvass of the presidential vote: 50.36 percent for Salinas, 31.12 percent for Cárdenas, 17.07 percent for Maquío Clouthier, candidate of the PAN. It reported a total turnout of 19 million voters, or 52 percent of those registered, a light turnout by Mexican standards. The CFE figures granted Salinas the slimmest majority of any PRIista presidential candidate in history, and made a mockery of the party's June prediction that it would win by 60 percent of the vote, with a total of 20 million votes for its own candidate. Cuauhtémoc Cárdenas had said that a Salinas victory would be tantamount to a coup d'état, and Maquío Clouthier called the elections "the most barbaric in the history of Mexico." Both men vowed that they'd refuse to accept the Salinas victory as legitimate, and would prevent his installation as president by any legal means available. Cárdenas rallied a quarter-million protestors in Mexico City, and PANistas shut down highways and bridges in six cities. For a few weeks, pundits worried that civil disorder was at hand.

Thousands of Mexicans were ready to resort to arms. Officials in the Cárdenas camp made calls for restraint, and daily sent home with admonishments peasant and student representatives who came to campaign headquarters offering to rise in revolt. The campaign offices received more than seventy thousand letters from peasants, most of whom pledged "ultimate" or "mortal" loyalty, and offered to rise on call from Cuauhtémoc. Typical of these peasant missives was a letter that said:

"Your *papá* was our *tata* and we still consider him as such because he hasn't died, he sends you to see how we his children are living, so that you can see if the mandate he made as President is being honored. . . .

"He ordered land to the peasants with respective credits. We don't have land, much less credits. He expropriated petroleum for the benefit of the Mexican people and it is the *gringos* who are now taking advantage, and we are paying a price for gasoline as if it were brought here from Europe. . . .

"We want you to know that . . . we are supporting you, not with tears and prayers, but physically and morally, as we offer you the little that we have materially. If it should become necessary to take up arms, we will wield them as we do the plow."

But there was no upheaval, in part because the results divided Mexico in a characteristic way: The common people took one view, the leadership elite another. Most ordinary Mexicans saw no cause for hope. The PRI had won, as always, and details of its victory didn't matter. "What the government wants is to minimize its defeat . . . and to use the opposition to continue legitimizing itself," a daily in isolated Yucatán explained.

Intellectuals and the national and international press took a different view. They saw victory shimmering beneath clouded electoral returns. MEXICAN POLITICS SEEMS FOREVER TRANSFORMED BY CLOSE 3-WAY VOTE, said a headline of the usually staid *Wall Street Journal*. "The secret and free vote of Mexicans," wrote poet Octavio Paz, "in one day finished the one-party system." "This is a new country," enthused Carlos Monsiváis, Mexico's leading leftist writer.

The ecstatic mood of Mexico's elite was based largely on a projection drawn from the presidential count by those who understood the system of proportional representation. If the percentages of the CFE presidential count were matched in balloting for the Chamber of Deputies, the thinking went, no more than 255 PRIistas would sit in the new Chamber, and no less than 245 oppositionists. The projection was important for two reasons. First, it promised jobs on the federal payroll to 245 opposition leaders and their aides, a benefit only a handful had enjoyed before. But more important, the Chamber of Deputies sits as Mexico's Electoral College, with final authority over presidential elections. Though Cardenistas and PANistas did not share similar views on anything else, they all agreed that the elections had been fraudulent, and they pacted to vote for nullification or revision of the results. They hoped to be joined—and to form a majority with—a dozen PRIista delegates, mainly candidates of the oil workers' union, who had either sworn neutrality in the presidential race or had endorsed Cárdenas outright. The opposition hoped to block the confirmation of Salinas as president.

Two additional promises beckoned to the opposition from

159

within the briar patch of the Constitution. First it offered the opposition a chance to alter the Chamber's ultimate party composition. Second, it offered a chance to precipitate what was called "a Constitutional crisis," or to benefit from threatening to create one. The first opportunity arose from the tiered structure of Mexican electoral supervision. The CFE's job is to name ostensible senators and ostensible uninominal delegates to the Chamber of Deputies, as well as an ostensible president. In cases where the CFE doubts the election returns it has examined, its only power is to fail to name an ostensible winner, leaving final selection to the Congress. A second body, the Tricoel or Tribunal de lo Contencioso Electoral, roughly, Tribunal of Contested Elections, plays a similar but negative role: It can impugn an outcome in its recommendations to Congress, i.e., name ostensible losers. The Congress as Electoral College determines its own composition. After ostensible senators take their seats, they examine the conduct of their elections, and confirm or deny the outcomes. Uninominal delegates to the Chamber of Deputies review their own elections, then select the Chamber's two hundred plurinominal representatives, and then, as a full Chamber of five hundred, review the results of the presidential vote. Both the Senate and Chamber have the authority to name new winners in elections whose outcomes they overturn. Though the oppositionists who would be seated in the Chamber during its own confirmation—uninominal delegates—would not have the strength to win any vote against the overwhelming PRIista majority, their leaders believed that they would have bargaining power. The Chamber was not slated to begin certifying itself until August 15, and the Constitution required it to finish the job by September 1, the date mandated for the president's annual *informe*, or State of the Union message. The opposition believed that by merely creating delays, it could jeopardize the Constitutional schedule of government. It hoped to use the threat of delay as a means of forcing the PRI to concede those seats that the CFE or Tricoel impugned.

The opposition fought skirmishes on three fronts: in the CFE, at the Tricoel, and in the Chamber. In the CFE, it raised demands that electoral packets be opened so that polling station tallies could be compared to district summaries. It also demanded that the CFE make public the telephone tallies that Bartlett refused to divulge. Had either of these demands been granted, "regional" fraud would have been exposed. But of course the PRIista majority ignored the demands, and the CFE oppositionists walked out—but only for a day. The CFE majority tried to mollify the oppositionists by "freezing" thirteen deputy seats, i.e., by failing to name ostensible winners in those races. The opposition was not satisfied, and on August 12, Cuauhtémoc Cárdenas took a largely symbolic step to dramatize his displeasure. He filed a criminal complaint against Manuel Bartlett and the CFE's technical officer, Fernando Elías Calles, a descendant of the PRI's founder. The complaint against Elías Calles was viewed by PRIistas as proof that the "Revolutionary family" had devolved into lamentable and perhaps irremediable fratricide.

The opposition's second skirmishing ground was the Tricoel or Tribunal. But the odds they faced there were overwhelming, too. The Tricoel's evidentiary rules require that before a challenge can be accepted regarding any of the nation's three hundred electoral districts, accusers must present presumptive proof of fraud regarding 20 percent of the district's polling places. Presumptive proof, in turn, requires, among other things, testimony by a notary or judge. In Mexico notaries are powerful men, more important than attorneys, less important than judges. Like judges, by tradition they all go into hiding on election days! Proving fraud before these officials is difficult, even when they can be found, one opposition speaker noted, "since notaries get their licenses from the governors, and judges are appointed by the president, and everyone knows that the governors and the president are the agents of fraud to begin with."

The Tricoel's evidentiary rules created other conundrums, too. For example, PANistas challenged any results that might be posted in a Sonora election district, on grounds that the CFE had never received the tally sheets certifying the vote. "The complaint was rejected," an American correspondent reported, "in part because the party failed to submit sufficient evidence —namely, the tally sheets the PAN was trying to obtain." Further, despite a requirement that challenges be posted in a timely fashion, the Tricoel required that all challenges be delivered to its offices by mail. At least two were delayed past their deadlines by the slow and careless Mexican postal service. Despite these hurdles, the opposition presented challenges in fifty-eight districts, and a half-dozen cases were cited by the Tricoel for scrutiny in the Chamber.

Before the seating skirmish could begin in the Chamber, Mexico's attention was again distracted by murder. During the early hours of July 24, in the border city of Juárez, Manuel Gómez had headed home in a white Chrysler New Yorker, a car with smoked windshields. Gómez is a former editor of the newspaper *Diario de Juárez* who in 1986 had been press secretary to PANista gubernatorial candidate Francisco Barrio. With Gómez on the morning of the twenty-fourth were his pregnant wife, a television anchorwoman, his mother, who had been celebrating a birthday earlier that evening, and a family friend. An unmarked car came alongside the New Yorker, signaling it to stop. The unmarked car's occupants identified themselves as policemen. But Gómez, who had only hours earlier been paid some fifteen thousand dollars for publicizing a circus tour, refused to stop, fearing robbery. The men in the unmarked car ultimately ran him to a halt, and then, without asking questions, opened fire with automatic weapons. Everyone in the New Yorker except Gómez was killed. Early stories of the incident pointed to political motives: Friends said that Gómez was writing a book about the electoral campaign.

In the days that followed, the incident was clarified. A few hours before the Gómez shootings, federal policemen had battled with dope runners who had escaped in a white Chrysler New Yorker with smoked windshields; a car of that description was later found, its trunk loaded with cocaine. The Gómez killings were a case of mistaken identity, Juárez authorities explained. They also admitted that the Gómez killers were not real cops, but *madrinas* or free-lance cops, men with no official certification whose services were sometimes rewarded after they'd brought suspects into custody. A wife, a mother, and a friend had been killed, in effect, by bounty hunters. The case

162

had no direct political relevance, but it reminded Mexicans of the need for reform.

Censorship also came into the news during Mexico's mid-summer irritation with quasi-politics. *Senda de Gloria,* a dramatic history of the rise of the modern Mexican state, had been making an encore on the privately owned Televisa network. Its sponsorship was secure—the Mexican social-security system was paying the bill—and its ratings were high. Even foreigners liked *Senda;* both the Soviets and the Italians purchased overseas exhibition rights. Though *Senda* was in its second showing, censors at Gobernación began taking a newly critical view of the film. At the end of May, one of them wrote a stiff letter to both Televisa and the program's sponsor. Making reference to episodes describing actions of General Calles during the Cristero War, the censor said, "In different circumstances, these scenes could, contextualized, have a place in a *telenovela.* But from another points of view, if the opinion is that of a State project to favor our historic knowledge and pride in the institutions and constructors of modern Mexico, then the problems mentioned in these scenes demerit their purpose. I realize the technical problems that you will have to face in the cases mentioned. However, in honor to the obligation I assumed, I cannot fail to mention that I consider it totally inconvenient that the referenced scenes be included." The censor also sent a copy of his letter to Gobernación subsecretary Fernando Elías Calles, grandson of the PRI's founder. On July 30, Televisa halted *Senda*'s encore. Included in the cut footage was part of the career of Calles—and all of that of President Lázaro Cárdenas. The event was interpreted as a tiff between the descendants of Calles and Cárdenas, and between living Cardenismo and the PRI. A week later, when the Mexico City home of socialist leader and former presidential candidate Heberto Castillo was fired upon by a group of men armed with nine-millimeter weapons, people began to wonder just how long Cardenismo might live. No perpetrators of the attack were named, but investigators from the federal justice department theorized that the shots had been fired from the neighboring home of Victor Manzanilla Shaffer, PRIista governor of Yucatán.

Opposition sympathizers were additionally distracted, and PRIistas were overjoyed, by the congratulations that began to arrive. Chiefs of state from around the globe, including U.S. president Ronald Reagan, sent telegrams congratulating Carlos Salinas on his election victory, a victory that, under Mexican law, was still in doubt. The establishment media and PRIista leaders bandied these messages about as proof that cooler, foreign heads saw no reason to impugn the Salinas triumph. PANistas who attended the GOP convention as observers protested the Reagan telegram, but neither end of the ideological spectrum was spared embarrassment. Leftists blushed when they read that Fidel Castro's telegram greeted Salinas as "Your Excellency."

Newspaper readers were settling in to follow the Chamber jousts when, on August 21, murder interrupted again. This time Mexico City was the site. Four young men of college age had been cruising in a Volkswagen Beetle when surrounded by two vehicles, one a gray van with a rotating red light on its roof, the other a cream-colored Dart with a radio antenna on its rear bumper. The occupants of one of the interloping vehicles ordered the boys to stop, but they paid no heed. The two pursuing vehicles began ramming the Beetle. When it halted, eyewitnesses saw men in civilian clothes herd three of the boys into the van. Another man in street clothes took the wheel of the Beetle, with the fourth young man inside. All three vehicles, the Beetle, the Dart, and the van, left together for an unknown destination. Later that night, the four boys were found in the backseat of the Beetle, parked at a curb. All four had been shot to death. The car's interior was littered with Cardenista propaganda. Its owner, father to one of the boys, is a former Chamber candidate and a computer expert for a minor Trotskyist party that had recently entered into a postelectoral coalition with Cárdenas; the Beetle had been used only hours earlier as the sound truck for a Cardenista postelectoral protest. At a funeral for one of the boys, Cuauhtémoc Cárdenas said that the killings were "political assassinations intended to intimidate the nation's youth," and that the crime's intellectual authors were "people at very high levels of government."

164

DISORDER IN THE CHAMBER

By the time of the Volkswagen murders, the Chamber of Deputies had become a bedlam for reasons of its own. The PRIista majority had turned deaf ears to opposition demands that electoral packets be opened, and evidence had turned up indicating that perhaps there was no point in pursuing the dispute. The packets had been trucked from the CFE's warehouse to the basement of the Congress, where oppositionists were denied even the opportunity to set eyes on them. But in archival records, they'd found that the packets were now a mess. The number of packets received for the state of Nuevo León, for example, did not correspond to the number of the state's polling places, as it should have. The cause of the confusion was that Nuevo León's packets had been mixed with those of Chihuahua, Tamaulipas, and Sinaloa in the north, and with those of far-off Yucatán in the south—i.e., with the packets of those other states in which PANistas were rumored to have a legitimate majority. Next to his entry for receipt of the Nuevo León packets, the Congress's archivist had written, "all mixed up."

The PRIista's essential argument for not opening the packets was that doing so would violate the Constitutional separation of powers! "It is unjust to reduce the whole matter to electoral packets," one of the Partido's defenders argued, "when the moment to open them came at the level of the district committees, and by a principle of judicial integrity it cannot be presumed that the Electoral College [should] hold a new election to supplant the one held at the voting places and in the district committees. That would be tragic for a system with a division of powers."

Disorderly European parliaments would have looked in shock on the proceedings of the Chamber. As in Europe, its deputies took ideological seating positions, the PAN to the right of the speaker, the Cardenistas to the left, the PRI in the safe center section. The debates were so histrionic that a new word entered unnoticed into daily use: *mayoritear*, to "majoritize," or wield majority power like a club. At one session, Cardenistas in the galleries showered the Chamber with baskets of charred

165

"negative *tacos*," salvaged from an incinerator; the green carpets below were powdered in ash. (For those readers keenly
interested in the technical refinements of Mexican elections,
there are two kinds of *tacos*, positive and negative. A positive
taco is a ballot marked for the party of one's preference and
illegally inserted into a ballot box or electoral packet. But to
produce a credible ballot-box total, it is is sometimes necessary
not only to stuff ballots for one's own party, but also to discard
ballots cast for opposing parties. The discarded ballots, or negative *tacos*, must be destroyed, for they are evidence of fraud.
Most of the ballots brought to the Chamber were negatives,
marked in favor of the opposition parties.) Television stations
did not exhibit scenes of the Chamber's disorder, but Héctor
Moreno, a reporter from *El Norte*, captured a typical scene in
three paragraphs on August 20:

"In the galleries the PRIistas, and beneath them, the presumptive legislators of the same party, whistled, shut up with
applause and insulted Manuel Marcué Pardiñas for a speech
in which he accused them of being 'loafers' and 'thieves.'

"The PRIistas, violating a parliamentary agreement, took refuge in singing the national anthem to quiet the accusations that
were being made from the podium.

"PANistas and Cardenistas demanded that the chairman of
the debate, Juan José Osorio Palacios, throw them out for scan-
dalousness and lack of respect for the national anthem."

So unruly was the Chamber that in its first week of sessions,
it confirmed fewer than fifty seats. To insure that the Congress
would be installed by August 31, the PRI proposed that the
Chamber go into "permanent" or twenty-four-hour session. Its
interest was patent: The PRIistas had to clear the way for President de la Madrid's State of the Union message. But the opposition voted for the measure, too, because a trade had been
negotiated. In exchange for opposition support of the new work
schedule, the PRI promised to cede nine of the thirteen seats
that had been "frozen" by the CFE. Cardenistas and PANistas
congratulated themselves in the belief that their strategy was
working.

In a university speech on August 24, Cuauhtémoc Cárdenas

said, "We have obligated the government to exhibit itself time after time. It has discredited itself even more. We have obligated it to give the results for twenty-five thousand polling stations, and they say that they're going to review the tallies. And all of this is not a concession, it's an achievement." It was a Pyrrhic boast. Promises may have been made, but they were not completed. Presidential results from the twenty-five thousand polls were never revealed, nor were the electoral packets opened.

On the same night that Cárdenas gave his speech, the PRI began its counteroffensive. To provoke the opposition, it voted to expel spectators from the Chamber galleries. In a show of support for the banned public, opposition deputies walked out. During their absence, between the hours of 1:00 A.M. and 4:00 A.M. on the morning of August 25, the PRIistas approved the seating of twenty-five deputies, one of whom had been elected in a contest impugned by the Tricoel. Twenty of the deputies who won sunup approval were from the PRI.

But when the oppositionists returned, delays began again. By August 27, only 167 deputies had been permanently seated. An agreement was made regarding 83 of the 133 remaining uninominal posts, and in these second-round negotiations the PRI reduced its concessions concerning the thirteen "frozen cases": It now offered only seven posts to the opposition. The process of seating the Chamber would go all the way to the deadline, and to accomplish its task, the PRI would have to unquestionably show its face, the face that lay beneath election-year speeches about pluralism and electoral honesty. But the circumstance did not wholly disadvantage the PRI: Irregularities would be visible only to those few who had penetrated the mathematics of proportional representation. The PRI had designed an electoral apparatus that was truly *chingón*, one in which ultimate proof of wrongdoing was passed from the CFE to the Chamber, and from the Tricoel to the Chamber, and in the Chamber—it was lost in a mountain of math.

On August 30, a committee of the Chamber introduced a document whose purpose was to lay to rest all remaining questions about uninominal seats, and to establish the proportions by which parties, including the PRI, would divide the body's two hundred plurinominal seats. No opposition representative voted for its passage, but because the PRIistas had a majority, it passed into law.

The purpose of the document was to allow the PRI to recoup in plurinominal seats the strength it had lost, or had conceded, as a result of CFE and Chamber debate. It did so in an unconscionable way. According to the Constitution, plurinominal seating is to be based on the total national vote for uninominal Chamber seats, once the strength of parties polling less than 1.5 percent of the vote has been discarded. This calculation had assigned to the PRI 51.93 percent of the Chamber vote, or 260 of the Chamber's total seats—but that was before any concessions or disqualifications had been made. To preserve a 260-seat majority, the PRI needed to preserve its ill-gotten uninominal votes for the purposes of calculating plurinominal entitlements. For example, in the most innocent case, Enrique Resendez, a PRIista deputy elected in the border town of Nuevo Laredo, had been disqualified after it was shown that he had been born on the north side of the Rio Grande. Because other irregularities were alleged and because his election had been frozen by the CFE, the PRI conceded his seat to the campaign's runner-up, a Cardenista from the PARM. But for the purposes of plurinominal calculations, in its August 30 dictum the PRI insisted on preserving votes cast for Resendez as plurinominal votes for the PRI. Had it not done so, its total share of the Chamber vote would have fallen to 51.89 percent of the vote, and it would have lost the right to a plurinominal seat. In another case, a deputy elected in Tabasco to represent the PRI declared that he was a Cardenista after reaching Mexico City. The Chamber seated him as a uninominal representative of a Cardenista party—but the PRI in its dictum, for plurinominal purposes, claimed the votes he'd won as votes for the PRI. The Tricoel had recommended the annulment of the votes from thirteen boxes in a Guanajuato district that had given a victory to a deputy from the PAN. During the mid-August negotiations, the PRI had agreed not to annul these boxes. But to discount the PAN's dubious votes for plurinominal calculations, in its dictum the PRI annulled the vote from box 53, a polling place not mentioned in the Tricoel's recommendation.

For plurinominal purposes, the annulment of box 53 reduced the PAN's Guanajuato margins from thousands to a mere 153.

Though opposition deputies refused to vote for the PRIista dictum, as the Guanajuato example shows, it is unlikely that all of its terms took them by surprise. During the Chamber's weeks of negotiations, members of all parties had done what they'd promised never to do: They'd played games with the PRI. The opposition deputies hadn't profited, as they'd expected to. The PRI wound up with 260 Chamber seats, 233 uninominal and 27 plurinominal. The Cardenista parties, in addition to four seats on the Senate side, would have 139 Chamber seats, 29 uninominal and 110 plurinominal seats, divided between four political parties. The third-force PAN was assigned 38 uninominal and 63 plurinominal seats, a total of 101. Since the total opposition strength was 240, the PRI had a 20-seat margin for any measure it might propose, and since the opposition was ideologically divided, the PRI could bloc with the left or right, depending on the measure involved, and establish margins of 72 percent or more—enough to pass Constitutional amendments, which require a two-thirds majority. The 1988 congressional elections had been nasty from election day until the last confirmation vote, but they'd given the PRI what its leaders had wanted since the 1963 Constitutional reforms: a pluralistic Chamber of Deputies whose decisions the PRI could control.

A NEW PRESIDENT IS NAMED

On the morning of September 1, the day of President de la Madrid's *Informe* or State of the Union message, an aging jurist named Emilio Krieger resigned from the job he'd held for several years as a member of the Tricoel. He wrote a letter of resignation that, I believe, spoke for millions of Mexicans. His letter was directed to the speaker of the Chamber of Deputies in protest of the Chamber's failure to heed the Tricoel's recommendations regarding fraud. The letter said, in part:

"It is evident that the whole system of electoral legality is founded on a legal hypothesis, that the Electoral Colleges, as

169

last resort, in accord with Article 60 of the Constitution, will admit, examine and evaluate the proofs offered to them. When the Colleges refused to open the electoral packets and to examine, analyze and evaluate the proofs contained in them, the whole system of legality collapsed. No political party, no citizen can now trust in the legality of the decisions of qualifying organs that, from the first, shoved aside the proofs at their disposal . . . and based themselves on the arrogant argument of decision by majority.

"I must confess that . . . when those entities refused to open said packets . . . I felt that all the effort made in the Tribunal de lo Contencioso Electoral to give a legal value to the election of July 6 had fallen to the ground; I confirmed my worry that all of the commitment to give a frame of legality to the electoral process had been converted into a hypocritical legal varnish that neither legitimized anything nor contributed anything to the process of democratizing Mexico."

When Miguel de la Madrid walked to the podium of the Chamber of Deputies, the PRI and the government knew that he would be facing a hostile audience. Thousands of soldiers and policemen—nobody could count them all—had swarmed on the Congress of the Union. Thousands more lined the streets between the Congress building and the national palace, to which the president would retreat after giving his speech. Preparations had been so carefully made that television reporters were excluded: All filming would be done by in-house crewmen from Gobernación, and all commentary would come from newscasters hand-picked by the censoring ministry. Because presidents give their *Informes* on that date, September 1 is a legal holiday in Mexico. Because this was Miguel de la Madrid's last September in office, newsmen and dignitaries had been flown to Mexico City from across the globe.

Wearing a navy-blue suit and his red, white, and green sash of office, he walked to the podium of the Chamber of Deputies, lightly stroked a graying temple with his left hand, and looked out over the audience. He began his speech: "Honorable Congress of the Union, Mexicans . . ." but he didn't complete its salutation. A Cardenista deputy had risen and was wildly flail-

170

ing his arms and demanding in a loud voice that he be recognized by the chairman. The speaker of the Chamber
admonished him: "Just a moment, Mr. Deputy. A moment,
Mr. President. With all respect, this is a session of the Congress
that meets specifically for the purpose for which it was con-
voked: to declare the Congress installed and to hear the *Informe*
from the president. This is the only purpose of the meeting."

The interrupting deputy, Jesús Luján of the Partido Mexicano
Socialista, didn't stop yelling, and because of the racket, the
president couldn't continue the speech.

Miguel Montes, the Chamber's chairman, continued his
pleading.

"I urge you, with all respect, Mr. Deputy Luján, that only
in sessions of the Chamber may deputies make comments and
not in the Congress, the same as the senators; there you can
comment as you wish. I also beg, attentively, of all the legislators, that for whatever reason you direct yourself, I repeat,
with all attentiveness I beg you"—Montes was having trouble
making himself heard—"to the president of the Congress. Go
ahead, Mr. President, with the reading of your *Informe*."

De la Madrid was able to utter only a couple of words before
Luján interrupted again. This time he was seconded by deputies
shouting, "*¡Y duro, Jesús!*" "Sock it to him, Jesús!" Again
Montes began explaining the purpose of the session, and again
he was interrupted, this time by PRIista deputies who had
adopted a chant of their own, "*¡México! ¡México! ¡México!*"
When calm returned, de la Madrid continued his speech, but
he knew that he was in a minefield now.

The speech the president had prepared was eighty-three
typewritten pages in length. Advance copies had been distributed to PRIista senators and deputies, but not to congressmen
from the opposition. Somehow, they had obtained photocopies
anyway. They had marked the passages where interruptions
were merited, and they were acting on cue. On page 14 of his
Informe, de la Madrid intoned, "An essential aspect of political
renovation was the elections of the past July." His voiced was
drowned by the Cardenista chant, "*¡Repudio total al fraude electoral!*" "Total repudiation of the electoral fraud!" and at this
point, the PANista deputies, who considered shouting as be-

171

neath the dignity of the event, rose in a phalanx, each of them holding a *taco* from Guanajuato above his head. They stood for about five minutes, and the Chamber remained in disorder until they sat down.

De la Madrid went swiftly through his *Informe*, ducking and stopping when interruptions exploded in the wake of his words. He omitted phrases that he thought might ignite, and though no Mexican president had ever faced such disrespect, he did not come unglued: While Montes tried to calm one turbulent eruption, de la Madrid calmly sipped from a glass of water. The protests from the aisles degenerated from the level of political slogans to that of mere catcalls. "Oh, everything is perfect, no?" a Cardenista deputy hollered while the president was reviewing the state of Mexico's railroads. "It's not so!" another bellowed when de la Madrid cited a statistic about Pemex. When the president reached page 72 of the *Informe*, deputy Celia Torres rose to her feet, shouting and waving her topknot to attract his eyes. De la Madrid ignored her, but before he had finished reading the page, Satan himself took the floor.

Satan, in PRIista eyes, is not Cuauhtémoc Cárdenas, whose disappointment at missing a PRI presidential nomination is a matter of empathy. Instead, Satan is Porfirio Muñoz Ledo, the number-two man in the Cárdenas crusade. The PRI's *tecnócratas* dislike him because he was party chairman and labor secretary during the *sexenio* of free-spending Luis Echeverría, and he doesn't disown the legacy. They see him as a demagogue and as an architect of the problems that now beset them. Mainstream PRIistas regard him as a coward and snitch, as one who could have stomached party discipline, as they have done, but sought opportunistic advancement instead. At 1:55 in the afternoon, nearly two hours into the de la Madrid speech, Senator Muñoz challenged the chair. "Citizen President!" he roared in a voice loud enough for de la Madrid to hear. The president looked to his left and stared, as if to say, *"Et tu, Brute?"* The assembled PRIistas could not restrain themselves. Shouts of "Traitor" and "Judas" rang across the Chamber.

Miguel Montes ordered an aide to read a congressional rule providing for expulsion of deputies. The aide began reading a rule that provides for the removal of rowdies from the galleries of the Chamber, not from its legislative seats. "But we're the people's representatives!" Cardenistas shouted back. The aide had read the wrong ordinance: Finding his place in the rule-book, he then read the appropriate regulation. When he'd finished, PRIistas cheered, "*¡México! ¡México! ¡México!*"

But of course Muñoz Ledo and the Cardenistas had expected as much. "If the president refuses to hear us, we'll abandon the hall!" Muñoz Ledo threatened on cue. As he turned to lead the Cardenista delegation in its walkout, three assailants went into action. Miguel Angel Barberena, governor of the state of Aguascalientes, grabbed Muñoz by the neck. Miguel Borge Martín, governor of Quintana Roo, threw torso blows. Xico-téncatl Leyva Mortera, governor of Baja California, punched at a target he thought was Muñoz Ledo but turned out to be a newspaper reporter instead. The Cardenista honcho freed himself from his attackers, but as he and his followers bolted from the hall, the loudest chants of the day echoed in his wake: "Traitor! Traitor! Traitor!"

Thousands of Mexicans were watching the *Informe* on television. But they did not see the brouhaha. When Muñoz Ledo rose to speak, the cameras closed in on *el Presidente*. No one at home saw the walkout, either. Nor did announcers mention it during the two hours of commentary that followed the address. Viewers were aware of most of the shouting, however, though the broadcast volume decreased during outbreaks, and in the quiet that followed, de la Madrid made allusion to it himself. "For me," he said near the close of his *Informe*, "it has been a pleasure to serve Mexico in difficult times." That line made his mother, up in her opera box, break out in tears. Then he urged his countrymen to "prop up liberty, to care for democracy, and to be tolerant even in the face of the insults of our adversaries." That line made some of his PRIista allies think he'd lost his mind.

When the president finished his speech, he was ushered outside—the Cardenistas had by then gone to a downtown demonstration—was given a twenty-one-gun salute, and was escorted to a white, roofless Volkswagen van for a fifteen-min-ute ride to the national palace. Earlier in the day, Mexico's governors had been told that they were expected to walk behind the van on its route to the palace, but the order had been canceled, apparently to speed the president's arrival. Under the new plan, his security men would have to run at a trot to stay even with the van. The guards were nevertheless joined by two governors, Absalón Castellanos of Chiapas and Xicoténcatl Leyva, the frustrated pugilist. Neither of them had caught the cancelation order, and both dutifully ran in the president's trail.

The following day, dozens of editorialists excoriated the Cardenistas for having offended *el Presidente*. The government daily, *El Nacional*, quoted scoldings from sixteen governors, a dozen senators, executives of four national chambers of commerce and the U.S.–Mexico Chamber of Commerce. Even the left-liberal *La Jornada* upbraided the Cardenista lack of decorum. But one sector of usual political debate was silent, the men from the PAN. The PANistas did not walk out with their opposition brethren. They'd tried it before, in 1982, when José López Portillo gave his final address, and the year before, with Miguel de la Madrid. Some of them had lately grown tired of spectacular protests. They'd resigned themselves to fulfilling their contracts as members of the decorous opposition.

On the afternoon that the president spoke, the PRI gained a deputy from the PARM, one of the parties in the Cardenista clan. Salvador Miranda Polanco, representative of Baja California, said that he was crossing party lines because the Cardenista antics at the *Informe* offended him. A more credible story came from a second defector, Raul Placencia Arellano, a peasant leader from Veracruz. He told the Chamber that he was quitting the Cardenista Front for practical reasons. Since the *Frente* hadn't won the presidency or a legislative majority, he didn't think that it could help procure land for the peasants in his constituency. The PRI, on the other hand, had offered to give him some $130,000 to make the switch. Placencia told the Chamber that he planned to divide the money with the landless. To make sure that he would have enough, Cardenista topknot-waver Ceila Torres hurled a handful of hundred-peso coins upon his desk. Both defectors would be at the PRI's side in the final skirmish of the electoral year, the confirmation of Carlos Salinas.

. . . AND CONFIRMED

The move to confirm Salinas began on Thursday, September 8, when the PRI introduced a dictum whose purpose was to finalize election returns. Because the results of twenty-one polling places had been nullified during the weeks of CFE, Tricoel, and Chamber bartering, the document showed a total presidential vote of 19,091,843, a number that should have fallen beneath the original CFE count by 63,169 votes. But it didn't. The figures didn't match: The PRIista dictum showed 4,839 votes too many. The error was a mere oversight, having no legal effect, but it gave yet another testimony to the carelessness with which the election had been managed. With the results of the twenty-one annulled polls cast aside, slightly new percentages for the Big Three presidential candidates emerged: Salinas, 50.74 percent, up .38 points, Cárdenas 31.06 percent, down .06, Clouthier 16.81 percent, down .26. The new percentages showed that from their three-month struggle to rectify election returns, the opposition forces had lost—though only about a third of a point—rather than gained.

The confirmation debate began about 7:20 P.M., September 8. Cardenista deputies greeted it with a walkout. While the PANistas dawdled, trying to decide what to do, the Chamber's speaker ordered a roll call. There were 323 deputies present, 72 more than were needed for a majority of 251. Then the PANistas walked out, too. A new roll call was answered by 253 deputies, all of the PRI. By a slim margin, the ruling party had achieved a quorum. It declared the Chamber in permanent or twenty-four-hour session, and reading of the dictum began. Having lost their attempt to prevent the session from opening, the opposition deputies faced certain defeat. The Cardenistas decided to return to the Chamber to disrupt. Their plan was to take over the podium. *Excelsior* described what happened in these words:

"The first to mount the podium were Francisco Ortiz Mendoza, Jesús Luján and Pliego Aldana, but they encountered resistance from the secretary of the Chamber of Deputies, Ismael Orozco Loreto, who, adopting the role of an American football player, tried to block access to the dais.

175

"In this moment the pulling, the verbal and physical aggressions began. On one side, José Murat tried to shield the dictum, but it was snatched away from him and partially destroyed by the Frentista deputy Octavio Moreno Toscano. Taking advantage of the confusion, Rafael Aguilar Talamantes grabbed the microphones to give them to Ortiz Mendoza.

"Upon seeing this situation, Miguel Montes decreed a recess, while on every side groups about to come to blows could be seen.

"The verbal confrontation persisted for a while, until the sergeant-at-arms of the Chamber, Sergio Guerrero Mier, had the brilliant idea to begin serving the supper, a measure which brought about even the return of the PANistas to the legislative hall."

Despite the gentlemanly scuffles, the presidential dictum was approved on the night of September 8, but a second reading was required by law. The Chamber convened for this purpose about 10:00 P.M. on the night of September 9. Some sixty-five deputies, mostly oppositionists, signed on to speak during the debate. About 11:30 P.M., after roll call and other housekeeping details, deputies began their turns at the podium. The session was slow and acrimonious. By 3:30 A.M., fewer than a dozen speakers had been served. About 4:10, the Cardenistas rushed the podium, taking control. A brawl broke out. Later, at least one PRIista deputy, Ismael Garza of Monterrey, would have the bad taste to boast that the PRI, and not the opposition, had won the hassle, though apparently the PRI did win. ". . . A group of us deputies spread the word that 'we are going to bring them down,' " Garza wrote in a letter to El Norte. ". . . Forty or 50 PRIista deputies (about as many as the other side), without help from the Chamber personnel . . . evicted those who had been stationed there. We did it . . . only by shoving and with a few knocks on the head that we were able to land. . . . Politics is passion and we as the legal majority had to use all the resources available . . . to push democratic life down the Constitutional road."

After their rout from the podium, the legislative delegation of the Frente Cardenista de Reconstrución Nacional walked out. Twenty minutes later, the Cardenistas of the PARM followed suit. About 4:30 A.M., a dispute developed between the PAN-istas and all the remaining deputies, including those from three factions of the Cardenista movement. Only two PANistas had signed the speakers' list, but nearly a dozen had risen to speak, demanding recognition for points of privilege. The other parties tired of the PANista interruptions, and the Chamber resounded with chants of "Fascists out! Fascists out!" The debate that resumed after order was restored was so droll that about 5:30 A.M., a speaker had to admonish deputies to refrain from making paper airplanes. About 6:00 A.M. PRIista delegates received copies of an important communiqué. When they had successfully confirmed Salinas as president, the message said, they were to rise, chanting these slogans:

"¡Cuauhtémoc miente, Salinas presidente!"
(Cuauhtémoc lies, Salinas president!)

"¡Salinas ganó, Maquío enloqueció!"
(Salinas won, Maquío went crazy!)

"¡Panistas, fascistas, los tenemos en la lista!"
(PANistas, fascists, we have you on the list!)

At about eight-thirty, the Partido Socialista Popular and other remaining Cardenistas abandoned the Chamber. Only the PRI and PAN delegations were left. At 8:45 A.M., the vote on the final reading of the dictum was taken. The PRI had a full house, its original 260 deputies plus the votes of 3 defectors, including the most recent, Alfonso Escamilla, formerly of the Cardenista Frente. The PAN cast eighty-five votes in opposition. When the tally was taken, the PRIista cheers and chants began. In an all-night session, Mexico had named a new president.

Return to Macuiltianguis

Iᴛ is a cool October afternoon and I'm standing in the aisle of a city bus in Xalapa, Veracruz, riding with an old friend of mine, Ramón Pérez Alavéz, thirty, who's been living here for about a year. Ramón is an ambulatory photographer. He keeps office hours at the Juárez park from three o'clock until six o'clock on Sunday afternoons. Those are good hours to be in the park, because young women who are household maids gather to gossip there on Sunday afternoons. I've been living in Xalapa partly because I want to watch Mexico through Ramón's eyes, to see the ordinary Mexico that most foreigners don't spot. Ramón is a short, dark-skinned, stout young man whose stature and accent identify him to most Mexicans as an Indian, as he is, a native of a Zapotec village in the neighboring state of Oaxaca. I've accompanied him on his delivery rounds this afternoon not only because I want to study mundane life, but also because I've got some errands to

178

Ramón Pérez

179

run. My wife has asked me to bring home a cabbage and a can of powdered milk. Ramón and I have already made a couple of deliveries downtown, and now we're headed for a neighborhood known as La Colonia Revolución.

Xalapa is a city of some three hundred thousand inhabitants, built on the slopes of a mountaintop on the coastal or Gulf edge of the Eastern Sierra Madre mountain range, in Central Mexico. From Xalapa, Mexico City is a drive of five hours west. The city of Veracruz lies about ninety minutes to the east. Xalapan, as it was then known, was a minor Mexica settlement when the Spaniards came. They made it into a provincial capital because of its location and climate. Americans who pass through today are reminded of the climate of California's Bay Area, cool and foggy. In Xalapa the Spaniards took refuge from tropical plagues, and from its highlands they administered coastal plantations and the port of Veracruz, Mexico's gateway to Europe. Because government is big business and Xalapa is the capital of the state of Veracruz, the city is relatively prosperous, clean, and well-organized. It is home to the University of Veracruz, and is a headquarters for the region's coffee, sugar, and cattle industries. Most Mexicans know it as Jalapa, the legendary home of jalapeño peppers. Road signs in the area use both spellings indiscriminately.

Ramón and I left my place about two hours earlier. We took a bus that went downtown. We went to deliver photos that he had taken at a law-school graduation the week before. The students, it turned out, lived in lower-middle-class homes on the fringes of the commercial district, homes with televisions but without cars. But descriptions like "lower middle class" are nearly vacuous, and can be deceptive in international use. For example, one of things that "lower middle class" normally means in Mexico, and never means in the United States, is that in lower-middle-class areas neighborhood stores sell little paper bags filled with sawdust, bags about the size of a carton of cigarettes. The bags sell for about a nickel, or for about a dime if their sawdust has been soaked in diesel fuel. They are kindling, or substitute firewood, for hot-water heaters, which in Spanish are called *boileres*, a term of clearly English-language origins. To procure hot water in a lower-middle-class home, you must build a fire at the bottom of a *boiler*. Almost no one in the lower middle class has access to hot water twenty-four hours a day, nor do most people in the middle-middle class. I rent an apartment in a middle-class condominium complex— there's a parking lot out front—and where I live, *boileres* are heated with bottled gas. But nobody in the complex uses a *boiler* with a thermostat system. When we want hot water, we, too, must strike a match and wait for water to heat. If you're going to take a shower in most Mexican homes, you've got to fire the *boiler* an hour in advance.

The graduate wasn't home at the first house that Ramón and I visited. Her father, shirtless and apparently an upholsterer by trade, looked at the photos and smiled, but told us to return the next day. We walked a couple of blocks, took a turn downhill, and passed a small shop where a man and his wife were training parakeets to pick slips of paper out of boxes packed with fortune-telling scripts. Then we came to the second of the addresses we sought. A graduate's father answered the door, studied the picture that Ramón proffered, and agreed to buy it, but not for Ramón's asking price. Ramón's usual fee for photos—when he can contract with their subjects—is $1.75, about fifty cents of that paid in advance. But at graduation exercises, it's hard to corner people for discussing such details. Nothing had been paid on the photo we brought. The father offered about $1.35, or 3,000 pesos instead of 4,000. Ramón's cost in the photos is about fifty cents each. He accepted the deal. *Regateando,* or price-haggling, is still a usual fact of life on Mexico's streets, though no longer inside of its stores.

We next visited a young woman who lived across the street from an infirmary. She said that she wouldn't pay the usual $1.75 for each of the photos she'd asked Ramón to take, because other photographers had come along, taken other graduation-day pictures of her, and collected their fees. She had enough pictures already, she said, offering to pay about $5.25 for the lot of six. Ramón accepted her price, too, because there's really not much he can do to protect himself from competition: His competitors, in many cases, are members of his own union.

After collecting for those pictures, we waited at a bus stop for a graduate who'd promised to be there by five o'clock. But she didn't show, so we took the bus to La Revolución.

Mexican streets and neighborhoods usually bear the names of national heroes, like Lázaro Cárdenas, patriotic dates, like 5 de Mayo—the day of an important military victory against French occupiers—or the names of government programs, like Reforma Agraria. Street names are merely street names; La Revolución is an ordinary neighborhood, not a den of guerrillas. I lived on First of May Street in Xalapa, in the Worker-Peasant *colonia* or neighborhood, the kind of address that would be more appropriate in Cuba than in Mexico. May 1 in Mexico and in most of the world is a legal holiday that, ironically, commemorates the nineteenth-century American labor agitators who were hung after a bomb exploded during a protest demonstration, killing several Chicago cops. The Martyrs of Chicago—a reference to the agitators, not to the policemen—is also a common street and neighborhood name in Mexico. The United States, as far as I know, hasn't experimented widely with ideological street names. Who would want to live on "New Frontier" or "Great Society" or "Humanitarian Aid" Street? Yet most Americans are racists, and we've named hundreds of streets after the Reverend Dr. Martin Luther King, Jr. The point isn't whether or not one in the abstract favors such names; it is that in a perfected democracy, citizens wouldn't need to take street names, as most Mexicans do, with a grain of salt.

The bus we're taking to Revolución, like all in Xalapa, is of school-bus type, of sheet metal, inside and out, and with bench-like seats for forty passengers. But it isn't as nice as the bus we'd taken earlier in the day. The first bus was brand new, shiny blue and white on the outside, shiny cream-colored on the inside. It had three blue-green handrails affixed to its interior roof, one on each side of its aisle, one in the middle. It had been crowded, with about fifty passengers, including two standee milkmen with their galvanized cans, and two standee plumbers with hacksaws and leather shoulder bags. This second bus is old, dented, and smudged, and doubly packed. I estimate that it is carrying between seventy and eighty passengers, but the truth is, I can't see to count: I'm surrounded by

182

other standees. A fifteen-year-old youth guards the accordion-like door on the passenger or curb side of the bus, at the rear. The door is open, even when the bus is in motion. The young man leans against the rearward side of the doorway, bracing himself on the opposite side with an outstretched arm. The hand at the end of that arm rests in the empty window frame of the folded door; only God knows what happened to its glass. Passengers await on nearly every corner. The young man's job is to ensure that those who try to board the bus at the rear door have already paid for a ticket at the front. When everyone at a bus stop has boarded, he also notifies the driver that it's safe to proceed. He does that by tapping twice on the side of the bus, boom, boom.

Most Americans believe that in Mexico life is comparatively cheap, and there are grounds on which that myth is true. Bus fare to La Colonia Revolución costs only seven cents. But a Ford Taurus, for example, manufactured in Mexico and exported to the United States, costs about ten thousand dollars in the United States, and nearly thirty thousand dollars in Mexico! Mexican food prices, still subject to various subsidies, do guarantee subsistence. A pound of tortillas costs less than a dime, and a pound of dried beans can be bought for about twenty cents, two thirds to half of the American price. But beef and pork prices are nearly the same as in the United States. The structure of the Mexican economy permits an individual to survive on wages of three dollars to five dollars a day, but it does not allow carpenters, even skilled ones, to buy cars—even used cars—or eat bacon. Nor does it enable working-class families to dress well. Clothing in Mexico is about a third more expensive than in the United States, while wage scales are less than 20 percent as high. In September, when the school year opens, Mexican pawnshops exhaust their capital in loans to family heads, partly because most schools ask students to purchase a jogging suit in school colors, for wear only during parades. The suits cost about sixty dollars. Many of the household conveniences that Americans take for granted, telephone service, for example, are prohibitively expensive in Mexico; telephone installation costs about six hundred dollars, or some four months' wage earnings. Spending money on household appliances can be foolhardy, too: Most stores do not offer refunds or accept returns on merchandise. The consumer has little to spend, and when he does spend, given the poor quality of Mexican manufactured goods and after-sale service, he's often disillusioned.

HOW WORKING PEOPLE LIVE

I hate to engage in writing of the sort that might make the reader conclude that I'm beating a dead horse, but one of the reasons that Ramón and I are taking this ride to La Colonia Revolución is the failure of the Mexican Constitution. Its Title Six sets forth rights for workingmen that have never been respected. In its present form, the Constitution guarantees workers an eight-hour day, paid at rates established by federal minimum-wage decrees. As in many union contracts in the United States, overtime hours are to be compensated at double the usual hourly rates. Workers are guaranteed the right to form unions, the right to strike, and rights to inclusion in bonus profit-sharing, retirement, medical care, and housing plans. Pregnant employees are granted twelve weeks of paid maternity leave, and during lactation, mothers are guaranteed two half-hour breaks for nursing their offspring. But only government employees and members of elite unions—about a third of the Mexican workforce—routinely benefit from these Constitutional labor protections. Most Mexicans who have jobs are employed on labor's black market, at salaries beneath the minimum wage. Had the Constitution been honored, for better or worse, Ramón might still be working at an hourly wage.

He and his older brother, Rafael, had in their native village operated a woodshop, founded by their father, which produced furniture for the local market. On several sojourns to the United States as an illegal immigrant, Ramón had performed similar work, usually earning five dollars or more an hour. Because he was familiar with woodworking techniques, in Xalapa he quickly landed a job as an interior or finishing carpenter. He built a bar and did decorative work in a nightclub under construction, and afterward worked on a crew that built the interior of a mansion. The federal minimum wage for finishing carpenters was about seventy-four cents an hour, or about thirty-three dollars for the legal or forty-four-hour work week. The Constitution guarantees every Mexican a job at the minimum wage; but since unemployment insurance and the dole don't exist, the promise doesn't mean much. Ramón earned forty-four cents an hour, or $4.40 for a ten-hour day, and he worked fifty-five hours a week, with no additional compensation for overtime. Men who furnished their own power tools, as Ramón did, gained an additional eighty-eight cents a day. Paid legal holidays required by law were denied, and so were medical and other auxiliary benefits. When Ramón and a coworker brought these violations of Constitutional law to their contractor's attention, his response, Ramón says, was, "What do you think this is, a union job?" Had they gained union protections, Ramón and his cronies would have been have been exposed to income taxes—because they would have been employed on the aboveground labor market—but would have nevertheless gained about five dollars a week in take-home earnings. Even with union support, however, they'd have earned only about thirty dollars a week, hardly a wage to dignify skilled labor. Nor was there much hope for Ramón in any trade. Mexico's minimum wages—in practice, nearly maximum wages—are one third as high as those in Hong Kong and Singapore, and only half as high as those in Costa Rica and the Dominican Republic. Despite its populist rhetoric, Mexico is not a place where labor is respected with pay.

As nearly all Mexican workers do, Ramón looked for an alternative. On one of his sojourns to the United States, he'd paid $115 for a secondhand 35mm camera, and with a book his brother loaned him when he returned, he'd taught himself to use it. One Sunday afternoon he took his three-year-old daughter to a city park, and he took his camera along, too. Noticing it, other parents asked him to take pictures of them and their children. After he'd taken a half-dozen such pictures, he was approached by a professional photographer who worked in the park. The photographer told Ramón that before he could exercise the trade, he'd have to join a PRIista "union," an organization that, Ramón would learn, functions more like a consumers' cooperative than a labor organization. But the

185

union's initiation fee was cheap, about seventy-five cents. Ramón joined and thereby became immediately eligible for steep discounts on film purchases and processing fees. Within two weeks after first taking his camera to the park, and on the basis of an investment of $115.75—or about $120, if initial film costs are calculated—he was earning a doubled income. As a street photographer, he attended amateur soccer games, took pictures at dances, photographed church processions, and loitered in parks, waiting for work to come his way. In an average day, he earned about nine dollars, twice as much as he'd brought home from carpentry. Mexico lost a seasoned woodworker, and gained a mediocre shutterbug.

In statistical reports, Mexican sociologists and economists refer to unemployment and to "marginalization," the latter being the livelihood category of those like Ramón the photographer, who do not have a regular schedule of income and are outside of, or below, the standards for established commerce. Men who hawk newspapers or wash windshields, chewing-gum vendors, itinerants who sharpen knives, free-lance street sweepers, bootblacks, women who peddle tortillas or refill disposable cigarette lighters—all of these millions in Mexico are officially "marginalized." According to most studies, unemployment in Mexico has stood at about 15 percent during the oil-bust years, but unemployment plus marginalization accounts for nearly 40 percent of the workforce—i.e., about a quarter of the economically active in Mexico are "marginals." In the sociological view, marginalization is a tragedy, a symptom of economic failure. Most marginals pay no income taxes —they do not declare their incomes—and except for those within union structures, most are ineligible for social benefits. But as Ramón's experience shows, marginalization is often preferable to regular employment. It persists because it often pays well.

It is also often the only employment available. María Eugenia, or "Mary," Ramón's wife, a graduate student at the University of Veracruz, dropped out of school when Ramón was working as a carpenter. She wanted to help make ends meet, but she couldn't find a job, any job. After the couple had saved a small amount of capital, about two hundred dollars, from Ramón's earnings as a photographer, he made a trip to his home state and invested their savings in native crafts. Mary began selling these *artesanías* from sidewalks surrounding the university. On weekends, she and another former grad student peddled used clothing from a flea-market stall. Mary, too, began earning an enviable sum, about six dollars a day. Mexico's modern labor codes had failed them, but its traditional economy—the pre-Hispanic marketplace of the streets—had made a way.

The living standard that Ramón and Mary attained in their new status wasn't more comfortable than before, but it was more secure. They didn't leave their typical working-class quarters. Instead, they put away money for building a house; financing for ordinary homes hasn't been available since *la crisis* began. The family of three lived in a single room about 15' × 15' in size, illuminated with a single light bulb and a small skylight that leaked when rains came. The floor of the room was made of concrete, and the roof of Spanish tile, a material that let cold winds blow through. There was no finished surface beneath the interior of the roof, such as Americans would call a ceiling. Nor did the room have any heating facilities; few homes in Mexico do. Ramón and Mary furnished their room with three tables of unfinished lumber, one for dining, one for preparing food, and one for reading. They also bought a table-top two-burner range, fed by a bottle of butane they kept outside their doorway. Ramón built bookshelves, a pantry, and a bed in which he, his wife, and his daughter slept. There was no closet in the room. Between two walls in one corner of the room, Ramón strung a rope, on which clothes were hung. When the couple's daughter came of age to ride a tricycle, each night Ramón and Mary cleared away furniture and boxes so that she could pedal in circles around the apartment floor.

There was no plumbing in the room: 50 percent of Mexico's people do not have running water within their own living quarters. Instead, with other tenants in the *casa vecindad* or "neighborhood house" where they lived, Ramón and Mary shared a shower, a bathroom with plumbing, and an outhouse. The house in which they rented their room was a one-story affair, spread out in a fairly typical Mexican fashion, along the sides of its lot, in the form of a stunted U—with one arm or branch shorter than the other—around an open-air patio. At its entrance, facing the street, was, on the left, the bedroom of Doña Paz, the owner of the place.

Doña Paz was a somewhat stooped and wrinkled old woman in her early seventies. She had dark skin and always wore her gray hair in pigtails. I never saw her dressed in anything but cotton dresses, long cotton stockings, and black shoes. Like most of her age peers, she usually wore an apron about her dress, even when she went downtown. She was in good health, and like most Mexican widows, was both cheerful and sure of herself. Though she had come to Xalapa from a Náhuatl village, she denied speaking a native language, and her Spanish bore no accent. She was a typical Mexican grandmother.

On the right-hand side of the entrance to her house was the bedroom–living quarters of two young women, students at a tourism school located about a block away, down the unpaved street. In between these two frontal quarters was a gate of bars of steel. The gate was never locked, but late at night Doña Paz would rise from bed and put a huge rock against its inner side, so that if anyone entered, the noise of the sliding rock would wake her. Hanging in the doorway, just a few feet inside the gate, was a sign one of her sons had lettered. Fastened to its cardboard surface was a magazine illustration of the Virgin of Guadalupe, Mexico's patroness. The sign said THIS IS A CATHOLIC HOME. WE BELIEVE IN THE VIRGIN MARY. Its purpose was to discourage door-to-door evangelists from the Protestant sects.

On the far right wall of the house, behind the room where the two students lived, and offset from the room a few feet to the right, was the bathroom and its shower. The *boiler* for the house, a white cylinder of steel with a ten-gallon capacity, stood just outside. On the back side of the open space created by the offset stood twin *fregaderos*, shallow concrete sinks with ridges on their bottoms. There was one on each side of a concrete water tank, about two-and-one-half feet deep and wide, and about three feet long. A naked water pipe ran over the water tank, about a foot above its topside, and with a faucet at its end. *Fregaderos* are designed for washing clothes, and most working- and lower-middle-class Mexicans still wash that way.

The procedure that Mary and Ramón followed was to buy a small plastic bag filled with cold-water detergent. With a plastic cup, they bailed water from the tank onto the piece being washed, while adding detergent and agitating the clothing along the *fregadero*'s washboard surface. Bailing water was necessary because the water pipe ran over the tank, not over the *fregaderos*; passing the waterlines over the *fregadero* would only encourage the wasting of water. Wires were strung here and there over the sidewalks and concrete of the patio, for use as clotheslines.

A set of windows from the corner room occupied by Don Bartolo opened over the water tank. Don Bartolo was a man in his late fifties, a little paunchy and graying and bespectacled, but still with something of the air of a party animal. None of us—not Ramón or Mary, or Miriam, my wife, or I—ever learned if Don Bartolo had been married, though we assumed he had been. He was one of the sons of Doña Paz and was a cobbler, as his late father had been. A sister who lived not far away each week brought Don Bartolo several sacks full of shoe soles cut from leather by other members of the family, and sheets of leather or artificial materials, which Don Bartolo cut and stitched into a finished product. Inside his room was an electric sewing machine and a table stacked with knives—the industrial capital of his craft—a bed, a dresser with a radio on top and, standing on wooden legs in the middle of his concrete floor, a black-and-white television set on which Ramón and Mary's daughter sometimes watched westerns. Don Bartolo's walls were painted turquoise and were hung with calendar pictures of pinup girls, and also with depictions of the Virgin. His only diversion, other than jiving with the neighbors and glancing at television, was prolonged drunkenness. Once every three or four months, Don Bartolo would arise in the middle of the night and go outdoors. When he returned in the morning, he'd be staggering and smilingly drunk. He'd sleep, go away again, and return home to sleep, rarely eating. His bouts lasted for a week at a time.

Behind Don Bartolo's room was the space where Ramón and Mary lived, and behind it a similar-sized room where one of Bartolo's younger brothers lived, a man in his forties who

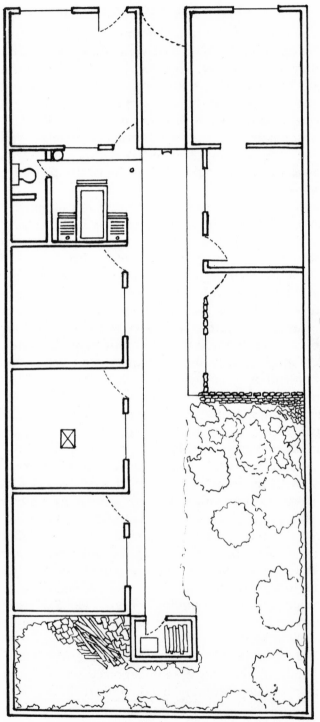

The house of Doña Paz

worked at a shoe shop downtown. Next to his room, the last on the row, was the outhouse, and behind it for more than twenty-five yards the garden that Doña Paz kept for reasons that we'd only gradually ascertain. We never walked far into the garden, because there didn't seem to be any point: We saw no vegetables or anything edible there, nor was it laid out in rows. It looked to us like an accidental convergence of little trees, shrubs, and weeds.

The most interesting spots in the house were across from Don Bartolo's shop, the doña's living room and kitchen. These were separate rooms, unconnected by a door in apparent deference to the indigenous custom that says that kitchens must be maintained in separate quarters of some kind. The doña's kitchen was typical of those of women her age: Its only cooking facility was a large earthen mound, or hearth. Her children had offered to buy her a gas-burning range, but Doña Paz saw no need for it: Most of her contemporaries still cook on hearths, even if their offspring have provided them with stoves. The walls of the doña's living room were painted a pale blue, and against one wall stood a dining table, though the room was used for meals only when guests came. The living room was primarily a shrine. Placed in one corner and spanning its walls was a three-tiered altar laden with the pictures of a half-dozen saints, each of them surrounded by vases of fresh-cut flowers from the garden at the patio's end. To save on energy costs, Doña Paz rarely touched a light switch, and she went to bed at sundown. But her saints were never in the dark, because votive candles twinkled at their feet.

LA SANTA FE, OR THE HOLY FAITH

Mexican Catholicism, as practiced by Doña Paz and most of her countrymen, is not the religion that Rome would want. It was brought to Mexico on a sword, and it faced strong competitors in some two hundred native or indigenous cults. Forced to adopt a new religion or perish, Mexico's masses adapted as best they could, sometimes by maintaining their old worship in secret ceremonies—under threat of death—and, more usu-

191

ally, by subverting new forms with old ways. Mexico became a country whose religious practices are in many ways similar to those of Haiti: a mixture of European and non-European traditions, a dash of witchcraft, a dash of herbalism, and a dash of the doctrines of the Holy See.

Drawing the line between Spanish and indigenous religious influence is always difficult, even more than lines of demarcation between the European and indigenous races. The peoples of both continents had evolved rites so similar that early Spanish missionaries mistook the legendary Toltec figure Quetzalcoátl for Saint Thomas, and today's Mormon scholars believe that the Olmec civilization was founded by Jews and later visited by Jesus. Anthropologist Eric Wolf lists the following points of coincidence between pre-Conquest religions and the Catholicism of Spain:

"Both religious traditions had a rite of baptism. In Catholicism, the child was baptized and named, thus including him among the true believers. The Mexica similarly bathed and named the child in a religious rite, and the Maya celebrated with a ceremony the first time the child was carried astride the hip. Both religious traditions had a kind of confession. The Mexica and the inhabitants of the Gulf coast confessed their sexual transgressions to a priest of the earth goddess Filth-Eater; the Zapotec had annual public confessions; and the Maya confessed themselves either to priests or to members of their families in case of illness. Both religious traditions possessed a ritual of communion. The Catholics drank wine and swallowed a wafer to symbolize their contact with the divine blood and body of Christ; the Mexica consumed images of the gods made of amaranth and liberally anointed with sacrificial blood. Both people used incense in their churches; both fasted and did penance; both went on pilgrimages to holy places; both kept houses of celibate virgins. Both believed in the existence of a supernatural mother; and both believed in virgin birth. Where Catholics held that Mary conceived immaculately through the power of the Holy Spirit, the Mexica believed that their goddess Coatlicue had given birth to Hummingbird-on-the-Left, impregnated by an obsidian knife which fell from the sky.

Both people made use of the cross. A white St. Andrew's Cross, representing the four directions of the universe, often graced the hat and shield of the Shining Serpent, and the Maya made frequent use of the symbol of the foliated cross."

The Church does not take a neutral view of efforts to corrupt its doctrine with native influences. It has historically fought back in kind, co-opting native traditions and icons as its own. The most concrete proof of the co-optive process can be found at the base of almost any colonial cathedral: Most are raised on the foundations of ancient pyramids, and built with their stones. But co-optation is a tug-of-war, and it's often difficult to tell which side has won. The best-known example of this struggle is the story of the Virgin of Guadalupe, Mexico's patroness. According to the version accepted by believers like Doña Paz, at between four and five o'clock in the morning on Saturday, December 9, 1531, a Christianized Náhuatl, or Aztec, named Juan Diego was walking toward the cathedral at Tlatelolco, today a site on the northern edge of downtown Mexico City, when an image of the Virgin appeared to him from atop a hill called Tepeyac. She told him to tell Tlatelolco's bishop to build a temple in her honor on the hill. Juan Diego secured an audience with the bishop on the following day, but the bishop wanted confirmation of the Indian's vision, and dispatched a party of credible Catholics to accompany him on his return walk home. Juan Diego lost his companions, and instead went alone to the site where he'd seen the Virgin, to ask her for material proof of her apparition, a proof he could show the religious authorities. Then he went home, where he learned that an uncle was deathly ill. Not until Tuesday, December 12, did Juan Diego return to the cathedral, carrying in his poncho a bouquet of roses that he'd picked on Tepeyac, presuming them to be the proof that he had requested. When he opened his poncho before the bishop, letting its roses fall to the floor, the bishop and other observers saw in its fabric the image that had appeared unto Juan Diego, that of a dark-skinned Mother Mary. At about the same time, the Virgin appeared to Juan's uncle, healing him of the illness that some modern scholars believe was typhoid. The purportive poncho of Juan Diego, with its image of the Virgin, today hangs in the basilica of the shrine to the Virgin of Guadalupe, at the foot of Tepeyac hill. Some 2 million people visit it every year.

It is not necessary to determine whether or not the legend of Guadalupe is true in order to understand how Mexican religion has worked. What is instead important is to know that an image of a Virgin of Guadalupe was venerated in Spain before 1531. The Mexican image was named for its similarity to the Spanish apparition, and it is that similarity that has for centuries argued against confirmation of the Virgin's appearance at Tepeyac. Further, the Virgin of Guadalupe was the patroness of Hernán Cortés, central Mexico's conqueror, whose headquarters were near Tepeyac. Aztecs had seen the Spanish image of the Virgin of Guadalupe because it appeared on the conqueror's battle flags. Spaniards who were living in Mexico at the time the cult of Guadalupe arose welcomed it as a sign that they were, after all, winning the hearts and souls of the vanquished Aztecs.

On the other hand, Tepeyac wasn't an ordinary hill when the Virgin appeared. Until the Conquest, ten years earlier, Tepeyac had been the site of worship to a goddess named Tonantzin. The church built on the hill replaced the pyramid that the Aztecs formerly had used. Whatever the original political motives behind the cult of the Virgin, if indeed there were any, over the decades she became the favorite of clerics and intellectuals who favored independence from Spain. When the country's separatist struggle first arose in arms, in 1810, its leader, Father Miguel Hidalgo, led his bands of ragtag, largely Indian troops into battle behind standards emblazoned with the image of Guadalupe. The Virgin, in those days and ours, symbolizes the belief that Mexicans, despite their indigenous heritage, are children of God, too.

The Mexican synthesis of pagan and Catholic customs is also evident in the country's commemoration of All Saints' Day, November 1, and the Day of the Dead (All Souls' Day), November 2. The conquistadores were mainly from the provinces of Andalucia and Extremadura, in southwestern Spain. At home they had marked All Souls' Day by, among other things, memorial suppers and drinking bouts in graveyards. In Mexico on November 2, the Aztecs had paid homage to the god of the hunt, Mixcóatl, by leaving miniature arrows and two tamales on the markers of plots where they had buried the ashes of their ancestors. In addition, almost all of the civilized peoples of Mexico maintained altars in their homes for the veneration of the family tree. Both the Indo-American and European cultures in those days viewed death more as a passage than as an end, and when the two cultures met, they gave birth to a notorious but happy set of customs.

Beginning in October, candy vendors offer miniature skulls of white sugar, festooned with sequins, ribbons, and slivers or chips of brightly colored foil. On its forehead, each skull carries a first name, Hilario or Juanita, for example. Purchasers choose a skull bearing the name of a deceased relative, take it home, and place it on a multitiered altar that is displayed, like a Christmas tree, in the family's living room. Images of saints, ears of corn, fresh fruits, breads in the shape of the Sacred Heart of Jesus, candy, prepared foods, soft drinks, even liquor and cigarettes, are stacked upon the altar, until its lace- or cloth-covered shelves can hold no more. An incense burner is placed on the floor, just in front of the altar, and candles are lit both atop the altar and upon the floor. The purchase of all these items creates a rush of commerce that is comparable to America's Christmas season. Whole streets are roped off to make room for seasonal vendors and their stalls.

The ancient tradition, still believed in some quarters, is that the dead return about midnight on November 1, to receive the gifts that the living have placed on the altar. In most homes, floral petals are spread from the front door to the spot where the altar stands, as a sign of welcome, like a red carpet. Shortly before midnight, a vigil begins. Doña Paz, for example, does not drink, but each year a few days before November 1, she purchases a bottle of her departed husband's favorite liquor, pours him a glass, places it on the altar, and though she does not keep late hours on any other night of the year, she waits for him in the candlelight until the wee hours of November 2. In climates warmer than Xalapa, some families keep their vigil at graveside.

Even newspapers get into the act. For them, the season is

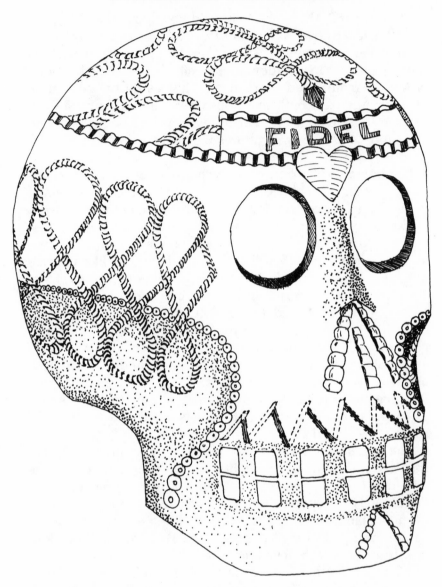

April Fools' Day. They publish special editions filled with caricatures of public figures, local and national. The dignitaries presented in these issues are always drawn as skeletons, cadavers, or ghosts. Even though most Mexican newspapers won't otherwise take the names of officials in jest—that would ordinarily be interpreted as disrespect—beneath each Day of the Dead caricature is a satirical epitaph in verse. For example, the epitaph written by Xalapa's leading daily for outgoing President de la Madrid said:

> With guile and bad faith
> The cadaver goes laughing
> At him who carries his cross.
> He didn't want to die alone
> So he carried before him
> The people of Veracruz.

As if it were New Year's Day, the newspapers also write epitaphs for the year:

> All is fear, tremors and scragginess,
> The poor, middle class and opulent,
> Everywhere creaking can be heard,
> Of unburied bones and teeth.
>
> Year of horror, in the provinces all,
> Year of opposition, a deep abyss,
> The ghost of the PRI dangling on the rope,
> The scaffolds for Clouthier and Cardenismo.

November 2 is a holiday for Mexico, as in the days of Mixcóatl. Most people grab a machete, a rake, a shovel, and a picnic lunch, and go to the graveyard for a reunion with other kin. They spend the day cleaning graves and repainting tombs. Everyone brings fresh flowers for the dead of their own clan, and for the graves of old friends and associates. Vendors of ice cream, cotton candy, and balloons post themselves at cemetery gates; children run in and out. Adults chat with the neighbors from adjoining graves. As during the holiday season in the United States, everyone makes acquaintanceships that are re-

197

newed only once a year. The atmosphere in Mexican cemeteries on the Day of the Dead is that of the annual company party or picnic. The graveyards are as congested as a football stadium, and for blocks outside, traffic is jammed. When graves have been put aright and the children have taken their runs, families go home and Thanksgiving begins: The delicacies unconsumed by the dead go up for grabs.

I had never paid much notice to Doña Paz and religious icons until after I made a visit to the fair at Huamantla, in the state of Tlaxcala. Huamantla is a center for Mexico's million surviving Náhuatl and their "deindianized" descendants, those who no longer speak the Náhuatl tongue. Each August, in homage to the town's patroness, the Virgin of Charity, the people of Huamantla and the surrounding countryside build three massive floral murals, about five by ten yards square, on the plaza of the town's principal church. These murals, depicting biblical and other religious themes, are destroyed and built anew each night for twenty-one successive nights by local craftsmen; every night about midnight, new scenes arise on the sites of yesterday's murals. Though cut flowers are the chief elements of design, one of the murals I saw included materials of a jarringly mechanical origin. In its center stood the Virgin of Charity, in her blue cape. She was surrounded by a background of blue sky and white clouds, made from colored powders, and beyond, by red, white, and yellow floral designs. Arranged around the sky and clouds in geometric patterns were auto-timing chains, valve springs, and empty brass cartridges from deer rifles: Those romantics and critics who assume that Mexico's indigenous cultures are static would have stuttered had they been called to explain.

Huamantla's floral murals are showcase pieces, even museum relics, some critics would say. A century ago, the townspeople laid floral carpets on the streets surrounding their cathedral so that at the festival's height their image of the Virgin of Charity could be carried in her litter on a walk around town. Other Náhautl towns still build floral carpets on their streets. But in Huamantla, longer ago than even its eldest citizens recall, hardware stores began selling chemical dyes that crafty locals combined with sawdust from the region's lumber mills to produce colored materials nearly as pretty, and not nearly so dear, as flowers. Today, the streets of Huamantla—more than three miles of them, anyway—are laid with sawdust carpets on the night of the Virgin's outing. From what I saw, Huamantla's most festive night compares admirably with the far more commercial Rose Bowl and Mardi Gras celebrations in the United States.

Preparations begin a year in advance, as with any successful civic blowout. On each block along the parade route, a meeting is held to select a *mayordomo,* or foreman, for the coming year's celebration. Dues are assessed and plans are made. Someone must be put in charge of obtaining sawdust and dyes, someone must take charge of refreshments, someone must volunteer to design the lighting—each block erects a system of lights for the big night—and several people must volunteer to submit designs. The patterns painted in sawdust are different on every block, and prizes are given for the most pleasing designs. Floral and religious motifs predominate, but geometric patterns are common, too. The block meetings in which festival business is conducted are theoretically run by majority vote, but in practice, voting is rarely a resort. A consensus system that looks to seniority and skill is usually achieved. Nobody would consider giving street-painting responsibility to a neighbor who had never served refreshments or swept the streets. Nor would anyone dare challenge a prize-winning designer's desire to try for a second win: The designers of the floral murals at the cathedral are selected from the best craftsmen in sawdust.

About nine o'clock on festival night, street-sweeping begins. Doors open at the homes where refreshments are served: Any passerby is welcome to step in. Light-rigging starts, using the head-high poles that are kept in storage except on this day. Neighbors begin marking the streets in chalk, and dusting begins. Most murals are built upon a base color that is applied by shaking sawdust-filled boxes made of wooden slats and window-screening materials. Once a base has been laid, big stencils, about 12' × 15' in size, go into use. Dusters stand over the stencils, applying color through their apertures. Behind the stencil-workers come the most skilled men and women on the block, those who will add finishing touches and fine lines by sprinkling sawdust of different colors with their fingertips. Highlights and shadows and special features—the red lips of a Virgin, for example—are applied in this way. While this work is being done, anybody with a minute to spare is walking nearby streets, inspecting the work of other block-dwellers, or having a drink with old friends. About midnight, the Virgin's bearers bring her out of the cathedral, and the procession begins. The carpets become colorful swirls of dust under the trampling of feet and the bending of knees: On each block, a rosary is said for the unforseen events of the coming year. It is nearly sunup when the Virgin is returned to her pedestal, and by then most people in Huamantla are dazed from drink and lack of sleep, and the town's streets are a mess.

Several times on my visit to Huamantla I had to remind myself that no matter what I saw, I wasn't hallucinating. I wandered into the city's indoor market, merely to have a look around, and at its very center I came upon an altar taller than I am. Inside a glass box sat a baby boy doll, dressed in a white medical smock, white pants, and white lace-up shoes. The doll was seated in a chrome chair with padded crimson armrests and a padded crimson backrest. A black leather bag, like doctors in my childhood used for house calls, was sitting on the floor of the glass box, next to the baby doll's chair. Affixed to the bag and tied by ribbons here and there outside the glass box were trinkets of the kind Mexicans call *milagros* or *promesas*.

Promesas are trinkets that may symbolize a discredited practice from Mexico's past. Believers pray to a favorite saint or image, as in Spain or anywhere else, asking for a cure for heartbreak, a leg ailment, eye troubles and the like, even for a bountiful harvest. In their prayers, they promise, or make a *promesa*, that if the miracle or *milagro* they ask is granted, they'll gift the saint's image with a token in the form of the organ or person healed, or in the case of harvest prayers, in the shape of an ear of corn. *Milagros* or *promesas* are usually made of brass and are sold outside almost every church in Mexico. But priests don't approve of them. At the shrine to the Virgin of Guadalupe, for example, every afternoon a priest makes rounds with a pair of scissors, cutting *milagros* and their ribbons from the gratings that protect saintly images. "Most *milagros* are made in the shape of body parts," a priest told me. "They remind us of the pre-Hispanic custom of human sacrifice."

A merchant lady passed by as I was beholding the glass box in the marketplace. "Tell me, who is this in the altar?" I asked, fearing that I'd be scorned. "Why, that's the Doctor Boy Jesus," she said. A small throng gathered while she told me of the miracles that he'd worked, right there in the marketplace where we stood. "Yeah, well what's the black bag for?" I asked with an American's usual cynicism. "Well, maybe it's to tell you that you don't have to come here to see Jesus," she hectored. "He'll come to your home." I felt beset and I fled the marketplace. But on my way out of town, I purchased a small image of the Doctor Boy, in a gilded plastic frame. I placed its magnetic base on the dashboard of my car, and left it sitting there, to await whatever strange apparition Mexico had in store next.

About a week later, I peeked into the doña's living room for the first time. At the center of her altar stood a huge 17" × 21" print of the Doctor Boy Jesus. I went to her with new questions to ask. For one thing, I wanted to know about the origins and image of the cult of Dr. Boy. But Doña Paz couldn't inform me. All she knew was that several years earlier, when neither she nor six doctors could cure an ailment she'd had, a friend had given her the picture of Dr. Boy, and with her prayers she'd gotten well again. "My motto today," Doña Paz enthused to me, "is, 'First to Jesus and Then to the Doctors Downtown,'" and of course she assured me that despite her advanced age, she'd enjoyed good health ever since Dr. Boy had come into her home. "Well, there's something else I'd like to know," I said, refusing to pass comment. I pointed to the letters that appear to be stitched on Dr. Boy's smock, the letters *H.H.J.J.* I asked what they could mean. "I couldn't tell you," Doña Paz confessed, "because, you see, I've never learned to read."

As much to satisfy my own curiosity as to please Doña Paz, I went on the trail of the Dr. Boy cult. I tracked the original Dr. Boy image to a church in the little Náhuatl town of Tepeaca, about twenty miles southeast of Puebla. In 1961, a local historian told me, a Tepeaca nun belonging to the Sisters of Josephine won an image of the baby Jesus in a raffle. She dressed

The Boy Jesus

it in medical garb and placed it in the hospital where she worked; *H.H.J.J.* is a form of abbreviation for Sisters of Josephine. Believers who prayed before the image claimed miraculous healings, and pilgrims began coming to the hospital. When the hospital went out of existence, the image was moved to its present site, the St. Francis of Assisi Church. Ever since, Tepeaca's biggest celebration has been not the annual festival that marks the town's founding, but the festival of Dr. Boy. The ten-day fiesta opens on April 30, the date that in secular Mexico is designated Day of the Child. Like other children in Mexico, on April 30 Dr. Boy receives a new set of clothes; his are prepared by the faithful at the church. When I saw the image, it was dressed in a white clerical robe with blue trim, and with blue seat cushions. But the medical bag never leaves Dr. Boy's side. Intellectuals scorn the healing claims made in Dr. Boy's name, but his cult is a testimony to the unconquered creativity of Mexico's native religionists.

Whenever Mary complained of an ailment, or her child, Haydeé, was bothered by a cold, Doña Paz went into the garden and picked the leaves of an appropriate herb. She ordinarily brewed teas from these herbs, and some of them had the desired effects. Her treatments could halt diarrhea, abdominal pains, and sometimes headache. But occasionally her *curanderismo* went too far. Once, to cure a fever that bothered Mary, she skinned the leaves of a fleshy plant and stuck them to her patient's temples, saying that the leaves would "draw out" the body's excess heat. Another time she rubbed ammonia into Mary's neck until her skin burned. When Haydeé had the flu, Doña Paz pulled on the skin of the child's back until it snapped, as if ripped from its subcutaneous moorings. Ramón never spoke of his health in the doña's presence, because he couldn't abide the prayers that she administered with her nostrums.

One afternoon I passed a truly terrible clipping to Ramón. It told of a young woman in Monterrey who had been reading her Bible, to help her husband find a job in America, the clipping said. While she was reading, their child wandered onto the patio of her house. The child fell into a bucket of water and drowned. I didn't believe that the tale spoke well of the Bible's protective powers, so when I handed it to Ramón, I told him, quite in jest, "Why don't you show this to Doña Paz?" Later that day, at his house, I saw him hand the clipping to her. We heard Don Bartolo reading it aloud in the next room. A few minutes after he'd finished, the doña was knocking at Ramón's door. She returned the clipping to him. "I guess that the Lord was punishing that woman for having joined the Protestants," she said. "You know, they're the ones who read the Bible." After she'd stepped away, Ramón and I broke out laughing, but we didn't laugh for long. In Mexico there's a Doña Paz on every street—Ramón's own mother nearly fits the mold—and the novelty of their fundamentalism soon wears thin.

MILK AND HOUSES

When Ramón and I debarked from the bus on Revolución's commercial avenue, we went into La Farmacia Revolución, or the Revolution Pharmacy, because Ramón's client, the graduate of a computer school, had said that he lived nearby. My eyes were distracted by the cans of powdered milk on the pharmacy's shelves. My wife had told me to buy milk, and I'd come upon what I'd been looking for.

Milk presents the problems of Mexico in microcosm, and milk probably tells more about Mexico than any electoral campaign ever has. For millenia the peoples of Mexico lived in apparent contentment without recourse to any milk other than that of maternal breasts. Except for buffalo, there were no cattle until the Spaniards came; it was they who introduced beef and milk into the Mexican diet. But their effort and subsequent promotional campaigns have been successful in ways the conquerors could never have imagined. Today, half of Mexico's families consume milk, and educated Mexicans, like Euro-Americans, believe that milk is necessary to child-rearing.

But it is difficult to buy an honest measure of many things in Mexico, including milk, which is almost always diluted with water. Milkmen from the countryside ply Mexican streets from sun till sun, but according to university studies, about 15 percent of their product is bacterially contaminated even before it is watered down. Tap water in most Mexican cities is unfit for

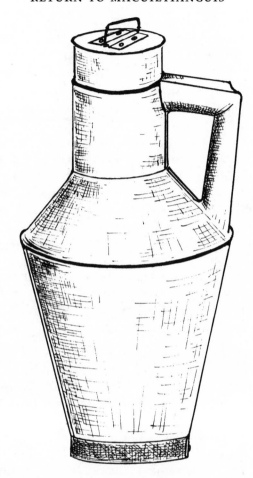

Milkman's Pail

drinking; milk must therefore be boiled to make it safe. Several dairy companies and Conasupo, the government's agribusiness conglomerate, market liquid milk that doesn't need boiling— because it is diluted with treated waters.

Dairymen constantly complain that government price controls make profits on milk unattainable, and they try to divert production to butter and cheese. But even these products are adulterated. A 1988 study by the Mexican National Consumer Institute, for example, showed that only one common brand

205

of butter was made entirely from milk. Other brands, the institute said, contained up to 50 percent goat's fat and soybean oil "among other substances." At any given time, somewhere in Mexico dairymen and government authorities are warring over production quotas and price levels, and as a consequence, milk is usually scarce. Corner grocery stores rarely have it, and supermarkets and special dairy stores only sometimes do. Powdered milk is always available, however, and it has important advantages. It is sanitary, it doesn't need refrigeration, and it has a long shelf life. But because a third of the powdered milk sold in Mexico is imported—Mexico is the world's leading importer of milk—powdered milk is not cheap. Liquid milk in Mexico costs about a dollar a gallon, a fourth of a day's wage. Powdered milk, prepared according to label instructions, costs about $1.75 a gallon, more than a third of a day's wage. The result is that whether they buy it in powdered or liquid form, most Mexicans drink diluted milk.

As I ruminated about milk, Ramón asked for leads. Nobody in the pharmacy had ever heard of the address where his client lived. We stepped out onto the street momentarily and then Ramón wheeled, darting back inside. I followed him. He removed the graduation photo from its envelope and passed it to one of the young women who were loitering at the counter, on the customer side. They smiled and giggled and passed it to the counter's other side. Ramón asked if anyone knew the young man pictured in the print. Several of the girls did. They didn't know his name or his street address, but they knew that when he came to the bus stop near the pharmacy, he came from the direction below. We set off in that direction, showing the photo as we went.

Despite my jeans and my Celtic face—reddish hair, green eyes, and a turned-up nose—people didn't stare at me as we walked by, even when Ramón stopped to speak. Only one or two urchins noticed that I didn't belong, and fortunately they didn't shout ¡gringo! ¡gringo! as urchins sometimes do. The adults we encountered accepted me as Mexican, I believe, because of the tire pump in my hand. I'd had a disagreeable experience with a rental car the week before in the state of Yucatán, and I'd bought the pump in a bicycle shop downtown as a kind of insurance that my Yucatán troubles wouldn't happen again. The pump was apparently a sort of passport to anonymity. Though Mexico is a racially diverse nation, light-skinned people are usually exposed to scrutiny and curiosity. But who ever saw a tourist carrying a bicycle pump?

Ordinary Mexicans do not fear or resent Americans; that is a trait of the educated class. American movies are the most popular movies in Mexico, regardless of their content. I saw both *Rambo III* and *Good Morning, Vietnam!* while living in Xalapa, at an ordinary theater, for about fifty cents. The most popular T-shirt on the streets of town that year was one that depicted a tennis shoe and bore the cryptic legend "He Is So Nice to Have Good Qualities." But there were others, too, dozens of them, some of which, in their rush to appear American, err in English. One T-shirt showed a water-skiing scene with palm trees, perhaps from Florida. "Just Add Water . . . Fasteners," it said. A blouse widely stocked in self-service stores carried the legend "Original Desing" on its breast. A T-shirt showing an imitation of the Levi Strauss label carried the words, "After many years of research now we have reached the best material recognized by its solid colors and resistance proof to make this good according to the authentic design." Perhaps the best proof that anything American is hip is the enthusiasm Mexicans show for their own products once they've been accepted in the United States. Before it became popular in the United States, Corona was not a Mexican prestige beer. Today, it's hard to find—so much of it is being exported—and Mexico's youth are wearing T-shirts that say, "Corona Beach Club," not *"Club Playero Corona."* T-shirt imitation brought to Mexico a design that said, "Bronx Bad Boys." Mexican imitators-of-imitators brought out a competing design, which featured a drawing of Zapata, surrounded by the English-language legend "Mexico Bad Boys." Americanization is a stamp of acceptability in urban Mexico.

After about ten minutes of walking, Ramón and I came upon a corner house whose front door was open. Just inside, vegetables were spread on the living-room floor. I stepped into the house with Ramón behind, and scanned until I saw a cabbage—well, half a cabbage—among the wares. The lady of

207

the house, who operated her small business without the benefit of scales, sold me the half-cabbage for about eighteen cents. I stuffed the half-cabbage into my backpack; neighborhood markets in Mexico do not offer their customers paper or plastic bags, and those that have them charge a nickel to a dime for each one. Ramón showed his photo to the greengrocer woman, who directed us down one of the streets that formed the corner where we stood.

The street that the greengrocer had indicated was a dead-end street about three blocks long. It was much like the one where Ramón lived, unpaved but rocky. Paved streets in Mexico are usually features of commercial life. Downtown streets are peopled by hereditary members of the middle and working classes; usually, people whose grandparents occupied their sites long ago, before their towns grew to maturity. Downtowns are paved, and their homes, usually located behind or above commercial establishments, are painted and plastered. But most Mexicans do not live in such fortunate circumstances. Because the population is rapidly growing—currently at a rate of about 2 percent a year—most Mexicans live in raw, new neighborhoods that were pastures or lots a generation before. They live without paving or drainage gutters, in neighborhoods whose class composition is a matter of chance, neighborhoods like Revolución.

The tradition in Mexico since pre-Hispanic times is that every married man must build his own dwelling. The upper and middle classes do not abide by this tradition, and insofar as class differences existed in ancient Mexico, they never did. But those who belong to what Mexicans call *las clases populares,* or the people's classes—about 80 percent of the population—still erect their own homes, and their middle-class superiors settle in alongside. A typical street in Mexico, like the one we walked, includes the homes of accountants and doctors next door to the homes of tire-changers and taxi drivers.

From its apparent pace of construction, I judged that the street we were walking had been open for settlement for between five and ten years. A third of its lots were still vacant, and the homes on another third of its lots were still under construction. Most self-builders erect shelters of naked cinder

208

block, settle their families inside, and then, at their leisure, paint and plaster exteriors, and add second stories. Only two or three of the homes on the street we walked were plastered, and one of these, a large, double-lot home, bore the crisp and decorative marks of professional construction. An American-brand auto was parked in its driveway. Both the driveway—even new Mexican homes rarely have them—and the car testified that the homeowner within was a member of the upper-middle class.

That showplace house was number 75. Across the street was number 72, a square house of cinder block, lacking windows, doors, and a roof. House number 70 wasn't a house at all. Only its exterior walls, which came up to the street, had been completed, and its owners had apparently abandoned plans to do more. The site's metal door bore the legend FOR SALE in white chalk. As we passed, the door opened and I peeked in. A man was leaving the place, a bucket in each hand. Behind him, on the turf that had once been the site for a family man's dream, stood two fat pigs, grunting over the slop that had been cast at their feet.

Neighbors pointed us toward the house of the youth in the photo, and when we were near, Ramón showed the picture to a ten-year-old boy. "I know that guy," the boy said, "because he's my brother. But he's not here." The boy told us that his brother was visiting a friend, and he pointed to the very end of the street. We followed him, but at the street's end, we beheld an unexpected sight. Squatters, or "parachutists" as they're called in Mexican slang, had recently landed there. Makeshift tents were spread from the end of the street back into the woodlands as far as one could see. They were made of tar-paper sheets, stretched between green sticks, or of vinyl and nylon banners from electoral campaigns. Somewhere in the distance was a natural spring or a waterline. Children walked back and forth from the rear of the camp, carrying plastic bottles for water. Overhead, between the branches of two great trees on opposite sides of the camp, flew a stringer with a hundred small banners attached. The face of Carlos Salinas fluttered in the gentle wind.

Ramón and I glanced around, knowing more from our shared

experiences than we wanted to recall, now or ever. "Ramón, what in hell is Carlos Salinas doing here?" I asked him. He pointed toward a large sign on the right-hand edge of the camp, a sign bearing the name and logo of a local left-wing activists' group dedicated to founding squatter camps. "If the guys in that organization are still the same," he said, "the banners of Salinas are just for protection from the police." Both of us discussed for a minute the possibility that the squatters' organization, despite its reputation, might have transferred its allegiance to the PRI. We ended our conversation by concluding that neither one of us really wanted to know.

THE LAST REVOLUTIONARIES

More than ten years earlier, when I'd first met Ramón, I was staying in the massive Campamento 2 de octubre, an embattled Mexico City settlement that was home to some thirty-five thousand *paracaistas*, or "parachutists." I had landed there by chance, or by grace. At the time, I was working on my first feature article as a free-lance magazine writer. Lacking appropriate experience, I'd come to Mexico to make contact with a guerrilla movement, only to learn that I'd have to wait longer than I'd expected. I didn't have enough money to finance the delay; hotels were rapidly consuming what I had. When I explained my straits to one of the movement's urban sympathizers, he had taken me to the Campamento, where I'd been quartered with other guests. (I suppose that lodging at the Campamento constitutes acceptance of an *embute* from the left.) For about three weeks, I'd waited for contact from the guerrillas, and in the meantime I learned a good deal about the life and politics of the urban poor.

The Campamento 2 de octubre, named in honor of the students killed at Tlatelolco, had been founded in 1972, five years before my visit. Photos from the period showed simple cloth and tar-paper tents, like those in the camp at Xalapa. In those days of the Echeverría regime, the government typically dealt with *paracaista* leaders in two ways: First, it tried to bribe them into abandoning their plans, and if that failed, it tried to frighten them off. The Campamento's leader, Pancho de la Cruz, was a Oaxacan immigrant to the city, then in his late thirties. The encampment that he had founded, mainly with others from his home state, was large enough that he was able to prosper from its collection plates; every Sunday a general meeting was held, and donations were asked for the expenses of the camp, including a salary for leader de la Cruz. Pancho, who had little formal education and no technical skills, snubbed government agents who offered him bureaucratic posts. When the *granaderos*, or riot police, came to evict the Campamento's settlers, they fought back with stones and pails of boiling water. Six people had been killed defending 2 de octubre by the time I arrived. Young men patrolled its streets at night, alert to incursions by the police.

The Campamento was gray, all gray. Its cinder-block houses were gray, the dust that rose in its streets was gray. On birthdays and other festive events, its residents set tires afire, turning the very sky gray. But the Campamento had progressed, everyone said. All its houses except those in one backside neighborhood had electricity by the time I came. The service was stolen—no bills were being paid—but the Campamento's leadership was negotiating with the power commission for regularization of service. Sewer lines were being laid, also by Campamento volunteers. Fresh water was taken from pipes that ran to every block. The Campamento had built a small plant to produce cinder blocks, and it was manned every day by women volunteers. Neighbors formed teams to accomplish building tasks. A great deal of the construction work was performed by women while their husbands were at work or were on the streets, looking for jobs.

So that they might devote themselves more fully to construction activities, the women established a community kitchen and nursery school. Young women with teacher's training taught at the nursery, held in a roofless building under a canopy made of protest banners. The fare at the community kitchen was simple, mainly beans, tortillas, and eggs—I never saw any meat—but the service was free. At nights left-wing minstrels sang, and sometimes left-wing films were shown. The Campamento's leaders communicated with residents over a public-

211

address system located at the settlement's headquarters, where de la Cruz and his family lived. I was awakened every morning by loudspeakers blaring ballads about Fidel and Che. The announcements and music didn't cease until dark.

But the Campamento was not the Communist cradle that the newspapers or its detractors supposed. Most of its leaders and its settlers, too, were first-generation, de-Indianized urban immigrants, with a similar background and a similar view of the world. One of its strongest elements was distrust of modernity, including socialist ideology: Fidel and Che were heroes because they symbolized the victory of the poor, but so too were Zapata and Villa, who had never read Marx. Pancho de la Cruz saw himself as a successor to the Mexican Revolutionary tradition, not as a follower of anyone. Socialist speakers were welcome when they came to express solidarity with the encampment, but they were not allowed to establish organizations there. When members of the Communist party began winning converts in a corner of the settlement, Pancho and his followers forced them to secede. He and his cronies not only banned ideology, they banned alcohol, too. Little corner stores sprang up all over the Campamento, but the leadership's edict was respected; none of the stores sold beer.

Daytimes I walked the streets, usually in the company of a muralist who had settled in the camp. I watched *colonos*, or colonists, as they slaughtered the pigs they raised on their lots, and in what almost always became a block celebration, in great vats prepared *chicharones*, or fried pork skins. For the first time, I tasted an unheralded Mexican staple, cactus leaves, which women pare of their spines with fingernails and a knife. Boiled or fried with a pinch of lime, to counteract the plant's natural sliminess, sliced cactus leaves resemble green beans, in both texture and taste. The fruit of the plant, called *la tuna*, was skinned for eating raw, like watermelon.

At night I slept in the Campamento's medical clinic, a facility operated by leftist volunteers. I slept in its examining room. Three peasants from the Huasteca region, near the city of San Luis Potosí, slept in its waiting room. The three peasants, all young men in their twenties, had come to Mexico City to raise money, by begging, for a rural squatter camp at home. Early each morning they left the Campamento carrying empty tin cans and leaflets explaining their cause. Night after night, I watched as they sat at a table counting aloud the coins they had collected. At other camps, similar scenes were enacted every night: Mexico City was thick with left-wing beggars at the time; there was one on almost every bus. Strikers asked for funds, student organizations asked for funds, everybody who was in rebellion went to the streets seeking financial backing. Mexicans gave generously. The peasants brought in about fifty dollars every night.

One night one of the three peasants told me what had happened to him at home. "We had taken over the land," he said, talking about the *ejido* he and his peers had tried to form. "Then the state police came in their van, a blue van, and took three of us off. They drove for a while, and then they stopped and took one of us out. We listened, and we heard a shot. Then the cops came back, but the first of us didn't.

"They drove some more, and then they took the second guy out. I was left alone. I listened and heard a shot, two shots, I think. The cops came back again, but the second guy was gone. They didn't tell me what they'd done to him.

"They started driving again. I was afraid. I didn't know what to do. Then I told myself, 'What would Kalimán do?' " Kalimán is a superhero in comic books, not a figure like Fidel or Che. "They took me out and made me walk over some ridges, and down into a little dry creek. I tried to act like I wasn't afraid, because that's what I think Kalimán would have done. And when one of those cops looked at his shoe, I did what I think Kalimán would have done. I hollered real loud, to scare them, and I ran up over the bed of the creek. They fired their guns behind me, but they fired into the air."

The peasant waited a few minutes and then went back to the road to hitchhike home. The driver who gave him a ride also stopped to pick up the other two peasants, who were hitchhiking, too. The policemen, it seems, had only intended to give the rebels a fright.

The peasants from San Luis Potosí were only one step removed from the guerrillas I was waiting to see; indeed, back in San Luis Potosí several members of their organization had

213

blocked a highway, asking motorists for donations at gunpoint. I finally made contact with the guerrillas I'd come to see after the urban sympathizer stopped by the Campamento to give me an address in a Mexico City neighborhood called Proletarian Revolution. "Go there," he said, "and tell them you want to see 'the Uncle,' el Tío."

A taxi dropped me at the address, a brick wall with a windowless metal door. My knock was answered by a short, dark young man in jeans—Ramón—whose eyes grew large when I mentioned "the Uncle." He took me to his quarters, a room at the back of the house behind the wall, and we discussed my mission. "The Uncle" was a code name for Florencio "Güero" Medrano Mederos, the last of Mexico's guerrilla leaders. "Güero" was a man in his early thirties who had been involved in land-tenancy conflicts for more than a decade. During one Christmas of his youth, he later told me, twenty-seven of his relatives had been in jail for participating in land seizures. Güero had sought to escape their circumstances by joining the Mexican Army, and then by migrating to Mexico City. He encountered new difficulties there. "Several times I went out to buy tortillas and couldn't find my way back home. All the streets looked the same to me, and I couldn't read the signs. Nobody would give me a job because I hadn't finished primary school," he said. Güero ultimately joined a group of traveling handicrafts hawkers, and while with them was befriended by university students who taught him to read. *Quotations from Chairman Mao* was his text. After he'd known them for about a year, the Maoist students arranged for their prized peasant convert to visit the People's Republic of China. Years later, members of Güero's movement would tell me that he received military training there.

Both before leaving Mexico and upon his return, Güero had aided the ill-fated guerrilla movements of Lucio Cabañas and Genaro Vázquez. In 1973, Güero tried to expand the Maoist effort to urban settings. He, his brother Primo Medrano, and a cousin nicknamed "Ful" founded a squatter camp in Cuernavaca, about an hour's drive south from Mexico City. The Campamento Rubén Jaramillo, named after a peasant martyr of the sixties, attracted some fifteen thousand settlers and lasted

214

nearly two years in extralegality under Güero's leadership. Troops marched into the camp when local authorities began issuing land titles to its residents. Primo Medrando was killed while firing on them with the Campamento's only weapon, an M-1 rifle. Güero and a handful of followers fled to the wilds and began organizing a better-armed revolt.

Ramón said that it would be necessary for me to meet Güero before going into the hills, and that, for security reasons, I'd have to leave the Campamento in the meantime. He accompanied me to collect my bags and say my good-byes—the people in the Campamento didn't know why I'd come and didn't ask why I was leaving—and took me downtown to a hotel. Then Ramón left, telling me to wait for further contact.

At about ten o'clock the next morning, a terribly thin young man with curly black hair came to my room. He was wearing an ordinary short-sleeved shirt, a pair of Mexican blue jeans made of a light denim, and tennis shoes. He was born nervous, I believe. He couldn't sit still, his eyes were always darting about, his hands always in motion. He introduced himself as "Flaco" or "Skinny," and said that he'd come to lead me to the *Tío*.

"Do I take my bags?" I asked, not knowing how many days we'd be gone.

"Don't bring anything," he said, without further explanations.

Flaco took me to a bus station and, with my money, bought tickets. The bus we boarded bore a sign saying PACHUCA, an industrial suburb of Mexico City. We rode for about an hour, neither of us speaking. My assumption was that in Pachuca we'd board another bus, headed for the mountains somewhere, and I was worried about what the hotel would do with the bags I'd left behind. But at Pachuca, Flaco set out walking. I followed silently, having realized that he either disliked guiding me or had been told to explain nothing.

We walked toward the edge of town. As we went, the streets rose until, after about half an hour, stark, sandy hills were in view, and I was huffing from the incline. Two or three blocks before the streets ended, Flaco turned onto an unpaved block, and halfway down it, knocked on a huge sheet-metal door. He spoke with someone on the other side, and then we entered a sandy lot. Six or seven decrepit cars were parked there; I assumed the place was a junkyard or part of a shade-tree mechanic's shop. Flaco led me to a stucco one-story building on a far corner of the lot.

We entered an open door, and a man in his mid-thirties, muscular and unmistakably *güero*—white-skinned—rose and embraced me. He had clear, deep-set blue eyes and curly, sandy hair, cut short. He had come down from the mountains just that morning. Pasteboard suitcases, still packed, were scattered around the room. A pile of floor sweepings rested in a corner at the foot of a broom, and the smell of dust was still in the air. In the center of the room stood a single chair and an unvarnished table stacked with wrinkled paper bags and fresh tortillas. Along one wall was a narrow cot, made of burlap sacks and lumber. Güero and I sat down there, side by side.

Flaco had gone outside, but we were not alone. Near the table, an Indian woman was bending over an infant daughter. The woman was about thirty, less than five feet tall, with attractive dark spots—sunburn—on the crests of her cheekbones. She was wearing thong sandals, the footgear that Americans call "shower thongs," made out of a spongy rubber. Her thongs told me that she'd probably come to Pachuca not from the mountains, but from a tropical zone, and I suspected that she and Güero had come together. No introductions were made, but I knew enough about Medrano to know that she was *la Tía*, Silvia, his wife. The child was his daughter.

The scene before me wasn't entirely domestic. An M-1 carbine sat on the table with the tortillas, and not more than three feet from Güero and me, at one end of the cot, stood three young men whom I took to be peasants: thin, poorly dressed, and in need of haircuts. The handle of an automatic pistol poked out of the back pocket of one of the peasants' pants, and I sensed that in the room with us there were more than the two guns that I saw. Not that they would have done any good, however. The three young men kept glancing out the doorway, looking for soldiers or police. It occurred to me that if the soldiers or police did come, they'd probably come in such numbers

216

that three guards and even a dozen guns would be too little. I was uncomfortable.

Güero told me that our meeting had been delayed because several days earlier an army search party had marched on the *ejido* where he was headquartered. Forewarned, he and his aides had retreated further up on the jungle-covered mountainside, where only peasants, burros, and outlaws go. He had not come down until allies from the *ejido* had told him that the soldiers had marched off again.

Not even Flaco had noticed, but I'd brought a tiny, half-frame 35mm camera with me, the kind of camera designed for detective work. I slipped it out of my front pocket and asked to take a picture of Güero. But he declined. He'd shaved his mustache in preparation for the trip to Pachuca, and wasn't proud of his denuded face. We chatted a while about a mutual friend in Texas, but about nothing of great importance. That was fine with me: My experience with political chieftains is that they are salesmen, and they say only what helps them to make a sale. Their lieutenants and underlings are better sources of the candid facts.

Back in Texas, I'd heard that Güero had a bleeding ulcer, and I asked about it, mainly because I suspected that he'd come to Pachuca primarily to see a doctor, not me. "We'll get that taken care of in the next few days," he said, as if he did have medical plans. But if he saw a doctor, the cure didn't work. About a year later, on a remote *ejido* in the state of Veracruz, I'd stand by, merely listening, as Güero argued with an aide over the urgency of treatment. "Look, don't worry, somebody will kill me before this ulcer gets a chance," the guerrilla leader told his aide.

After our pleasantries were exchanged, Güero sent one of the peasants to fetch Flaco, who reappeared in a moment's time. Güero opened a billfold bulging with both pesos and greenbacks, and handed a bill to my guide. Then he dictated a note to Flaco—Güero could read, but he couldn't really write. In a scrawled hand, Güero wrote his name below—he signed it with flourishes, as Mexicans always do. I had obtained my passport to the rebel zone.

217

The money that Güero gave Flaco was for paying a guide's expenses on a trip I'd take to the hills. But when Flaco returned me to the hotel, he said nothing about seeing me again. The next morning, Ramón was at my door, a denim Mexican backpack strapped to his shoulder. A couple of hours later, we were riding a bus to Tuxtepec, in the state of Oaxaca.

There are of course no transnational twins, but Oaxaca is about as close to midcentury Mississippi as Mexico can get, a poor, southern agricultural state whose dark-skinned people have for centuries been oppressed. Many of the smaller villages in Oaxaca are ruled by *caciques*—a Mayan word for "chief" or "leader"—who vote for them, buy their corn, own the store where they shop, and keep order with terror. No roads lead to many of Oaxaca's mountain villages. They are so isolated that, for practical purposes, police protection has never existed. *Pistoleros* or gunslingers hired by *caciques* and landlords mete out summary punishments to their patrons' enemies, and a few of their own. I am not a fearful man, but there are few sights in life as intimidating as that of a couple of men in cowboy hats and boots eyeing you from the window of a pickup whose gun racks are loaded with automatic weapons. *Pistoleros* are the Mexican Ku Klux Klan.

They have been standard characters in the cast of Oaxacan life for more than a century, at least since the passage of the land reform laws of 1857, which essentially outlawed pre-Hispanic forms of tenancy. Before the Conquest, land belonged to communities whose members tilled individual plots but never thought of selling them: Other members of the community had equal rights to land, and outsiders could not enter in. There were no buyers or sellers of land, only tillers. Land was cultivated for family consumption, and given the technology of the era, larger-scale operations weren't possible. No donkeys, horses, oxen, or other large draft animals lived in the Western Hemisphere before the Conquest, and largely because of their absence, pre-Hispanics had neither carts nor plows.

Land was tilled with hand tools, a flint or obsidian machete, and the *coa* or *xul*, a fire-hardened stick. Pre-Hispanics cleared the land, dried and burned unwanted vegetation, and poked holes in the ground with their *coas*. Into each hole they dropped two or three grains of corn, and usually beans or squash seeds. The resulting fields, called *milpas*, produced the staples of life. In good years, if a farmer had produce to spare, he might barter it for luxury goods at a regional market, but money did not exist. Cocoa beans and feathers filled with grains of gold were sometimes used as mediums of exchange, but they were of limited value because there was no labor market. Men built their own homes, women spun thread and made clothing, and almost no one was for hire. Other than a few domestic servants, who were often slaves, and a few artisans' assistants, almost no pre-Hispanic Mexicans belonged to a proletariat. Mexico was a land of tillers who were largely self-sufficient.

The conquistadores appropriated huge tracts of land for themselves and usually turned them to the production of export crops—sugar, tobacco, cocoa, and the like—using captive or slave labor. As the Indian population dwindled, new lands became idle. Other Spaniards and members of the mixed or *mestizo* caste followed them in developing a cash economy. By the late nineteenth century, even German coffee growers and American hemp planters were getting in on the act. In Oaxaca during the 1870s, cattlemen were the expansionists of the cash economy.

Colonial and early-day Mexican governments favored non-native interlopers in agriculture not only for reasons of racial and political policy, but also because the Europeanizing enterprises were more productive. The Spaniards brought draft animals and the plow. Their successors brought technical know-how and implements of every kind. Their plantations may not have produced the corn that Mexico's masses needed to survive, but they did produce crops that brought foreign currency to finance government purchases abroad, and to pay Mexico's chronic national debt. The only inherent drawback in the workings of the plantation system, from the government's point of view, was a shortage of arable land. Planters not only needed great expanses of land, but they also needed flat lands, since plows and oxen can't work the mountainsides. Flat, rich lands became a premium over which Indians and their European and *mestizo* rivals fought. By outlawing communally held lands, the reforms of 1857 allowed individual members of Indian com-

munities, or *comuneros,* to sell their tracts to land-hungry planters. *Pistoleros* forced Indians to sell—exactly as Klansmen forced
freedmen to sell or abandon their farms—and prevented the
traditional order from coming back. The Constitution of 1917,
by creating *ejidos*—farms owned by the government but en-
trusted to tillers' groups—had promised the possibility of restoring the past. But laws are only as good as the force that
backs them, and that is what has given rise to Güero's guerrilla
group.

PEASANTS IN ARMS

The roads leading into Tuxtepec are usually congested with
trucks from the mountains, carrying cords of timber, and trucks
from the coastal plain, carrying sugarcane: Tuxtepec is home
to both a sugar refinery and a paper-making mill. It's a pictur-
esque town, cut through by the slow-moving Papaloapan River.
Tuxtepec's streets are lined with palms and veterinary stores.
The town is a trading center for ranchers, whose cowboys ride
to town on bicycles. But in summer months Tuxtepec is a steam
cabinet, and for a century now, the town has not been exactly
proud. It is known to history as the hometown of Porfirio Díaz.

Tuxtepec had become an important place to Güero because
it is a regional transportation hub. Buses in Tuxtepec run to
northern Oaxaca and southern Veracruz, and though Güero
couldn't safely travel by bus, his lieutenants and his peasant
followers did. Tuxtepec was a town where conspirators from
the remotest areas of the region could rendevous in a half-day's
time. For the next ten days, Ramón and I coursed northern
Oaxaca's mountains and plains, visiting villages so small and
remote that they're not listed on any but topographical maps,
the kind of map that soldiers, dope-dealers, and surveyors use.
But our travels always took us through Tuxtepec. Tuxtepec was
the explanation for Silvia's thongs and Güero's boots: She spent
most of her time in the tropical town, while he moved about
in the higher country beyond.

The region was ripe for Güero's agitations, the *ejido* of Miguel
Allende—I must still call it by a pseudonym—for example.

220

Miguel Allende was a relatively new *ejido*, less than five years old, where about twenty families lived in palm-thatched homes with walls of cane and sticks. Though Miguel Allende's inhabitants no longer spoke an indigenous tongue, most of the *ejido*'s homeplaces consisted of two structures, a kitchen–dining room and a sleeping room where hammocks hung. Ramón introduced me to a dark, squat, graying man who spoke in a near-falsetto voice. He was the mayor of the community, one of its founders. In 1971, along with two hundred other landless peasants, he had petitioned for the formation of an *ejido* on the square mile of land where Miguel Allende sat. For five years, representatives of the peasants' committee had signed papers —the verb "to sign" had become a part of local scatological slang by the time I arrived—and kept appointments with the governor's office and Agrarian Reform Ministry. More than once they'd gone to Mexico City to make appeals. But their efforts got them nowhere. Their petitions were neither granted nor denied.

In early 1976, a few militants, armed only with hatchets and machetes, occupied the land and cleared it for planting a spring corn crop. But as soon as they'd begun, two or three *pistoleros* built huts on the terrain just below, between the *ad hoc ejido* and the highway to Tuxtepec. When the corn plants were knee-high, the *pistoleros* turned cattle onto the *ejido*'s fields. Most of the crop was destroyed. The community survived by communally dividing the surviving harvest and, I suspect, from the proceeds of a hidden patch of marijuana as well. Rather than face a new cycle of challenges from the *pistoleros*, several families abandoned the *ejido*, migrating to the towns or returning to former stations as *jornaleros*, or agricultural day laborers. Those who had nowhere to go sent for Güero and stayed on the land.

The guerrilla showed up alone and emptyhanded, but with promises of guns and a tractor. He asked in return that the whole village join his Maoist organization, the Partido Proletario Unido de America, or United Proletarian party of the Americas. The settlers of Miguel Allende discussed the proposition for a week in meetings held under their open-air, palm-thatched town hall. A vote was taken, and Güero's supporters won. Six dissident families left the *ejido*, and though fewer than twenty families remained, they began preparing for the inevitable confrontation with the *pistoleros*. Güero sent a tractor and a cache of arms, mostly M-1 carbines.

On the evening of May 1, the men of Miguel Allende gathered in the *ejido* assembly hall for an attack. There were seventy-seven of them, twenty-two with guns, and the rest with only machetes and hoes. They grouped in a crescent on a ridge above the hollow where the *pistoleros* had built their huts. A warning shot initiated the fighting.

"They shot back, about twenty rounds," the mayor told me. "We started giving them thunder from all sides and they skipped out, running for the highway. We got one as he ran off. He just lay there and we waited, not shooting anymore because we were short of ammunition. After dark, a pickup pulled up down there, and two men laid the *pistolero* in the back and drove off. We don't know if he was alive or dead."

It had been about six months since the shooting when Ramón and I arrived. Nothing had been heard from the *pistoleros* since. A crop was coming to harvest, and new families were asking to move in, before fall planting. Several of those that had fled the *ejido* before Güero came had tried to return, too, but the mayor and his followers had kept them out. If the original petitions were ever granted by the authorities of agrarian reform, the would-be returnees would have a legal right to plots. But I doubted that anyone would enforce the law: The *ejidatarios* were now armed, and unlike the soldiers and police, they were always in Miguel Allende.

A five-hour walk and a muddy river separated another village we visited from the Tuxtepec highway. The village was set in foothills where few vehicles, other than the tractors Güero had sent, had ever passed. One of the more prominent of the some 350 residents of the place had been killed during the disputes over the hamlet's affiliation with Medrano, and a force of seventeen state policemen had come to town. They had taken over its central building, the municipal hut, and converted it into their barracks. A flagpole stood outside the palm-thatched structure, on a dusty little plaza or square. Each morning four of the policemen, carrying rifles and uniformed in blue, came

222

outside to raise the flag, and about sundown four policemen came to bring it in for the night. Otherwise, they did not leave the barracks. I sneaked into town by a trail that brought me to its edge, and with Ramón and a local guide, worked my way to the residential hut nearest the barracks. From between the cracks of the hut's stick walls, I photographed the cops as they did their daily official duty. Ramón and I spent more than two days in the town, and though I was the only *gringo* for miles around, my presence was apparently not betrayed to the interlopers in uniform. Güero had issued orders that the locals were not to harm the cops, for fear that if one were killed, the village would face reprisals from an even larger force. A revolution was theoretically in march in the town, but both sides had fallen into a truce.

I had lunch one day with the residents of a hut on another side of the municipal square. We ate in the kitchen–dining room area typical of the region. I noticed long strings of red meat hanging from beams in the hut, as in a butcher shop, and asked my host, a young man in his twenties, how he could afford to buy beef. "Well, ever since Güero sent us the guns," he said wryly, "we've been able to hunt." The beef came from cows he and his comrades had killed on a nearby ranch.

The residents with whom I dined drew water from a nearby creek. They slept in hammocks, and because there was no electricity in their village they illuminated their hut with lanterns. Dishes were washed in ceramic-coated steel platters, or in buckets, items bought in town. In most of the villages, knives and spoons were available, but I rarely saw a fork, for a reason that didn't immediately come to mind: The fork is a latter-day European invention. Until recent years, the Oaxacan countryside's chief contact with Western civilization had occurred at the time of Conquest, five centuries ago, when Catholic missionaries established churches in the area. Conquistadores and friars didn't use forks, either, because the fork hadn't been invented yet. Before the Spanish Conquest, Oaxacans had used their tortillas for spoons.

No newspapers arrived regularly in any of the places where we stayed, and some had no stores of any kind. We were in a region of Mixteca and Chinanteca origins, but all of the men

223

we encountered spoke ample Spanish, and most of the women did, too. Primary schools in the better-established towns taught the language. A few *ejidos* had been formed by peasants from across the region, and on those some people spoke native languages, and others didn't know how. Language wasn't a cultural dividing line. Religion was. Most of the towns had a Catholic chapel of some kind, even if it was only a palm-thatched hut. But priests didn't visit often, and Protestant missionaries had come instead. Whole villages were split into factions, Jehovah's Witnesses in one camp, Pentecostals in another, Catholics off to the side. The chief obstacle that Güero's lieutenants faced in organizing a town wasn't the specter of incursions by *pistoleros*, the army, or police. Instead, it was uniting men who disagreed about God. Ramón and Güero's other spokesmen had been forbidden to say a word about their views on subjects like the afterlife.

On my second day in the occupied village, I met a young man who spoke too knowledgeably about Mexican and American political affairs. After twice inspecting the signature on my pass from Güero, he told me that he was not Hector Calzado, as the villagers believed, but Pablo de la O Castoreña. I recognized the name from newspapers. His sister, Maricela, was then in prison for her role in one of the urban kidnappings that had helped to finance the tractors and guns that Güero supplied. Pablo was living alone in a wall-less *palapa*, or hut, about five hundred yards outside the village, in case he should have to fight or run. In the *palapa* that night, he told me the story of his presence there.

He had come to the village on the lam. Some three years earlier, he had been working in a brickyard in Cuernavaca when his sister had persuaded him to drive the getaway car in the kidnapping of the wife of an expatriate American investor. The kidnapping had gone off without a hitch, but in the sixty-six days that followed, the American refused to pay his wife's ransom. Ultimately, a settlement had been reached: Some sixty-six thousand dollars was paid, and the industrialist's wife, a Mexican national, had signed over the titles to several pieces of rural property that Güero's group, acting through an archbishop, had donated to the poor. Pablo was then sent to the

United States to take charge of smuggling a shipment of arms into Mexico, where gun ownership is legally curtailed. About eighteen months before I'd met him, Pablo had been halted at a Mexican border checkpoint, driving a pickup with some eighty rifles strapped to its underside. Border guards took Pablo to a Monterrey jail for questioning.

Knowing what awaited him, he'd decided it would be less painful and more valorous to die. He had passed his belt around his neck and over a shower pipe in his cell. "Just as I was losing consciousness," he told me, "the damn pipe broke." When guards discovered his attempt, they hauled him into a room for a *calentada*, or warmup. Tying him to a chair, they forced water, lemonade, and alcohol down his mouth and nostrils, a technique generally known in Mexico as a *Tehuacanazo*, because the mineral waters of Tehuacán, Puebla, are often used. For a while the cops forced a hose down Pablo's throat, pinched his nostrils shut, and filled his stomach with liquids. Then they punched him in the abdomen repeatedly, until he vomited. The *calentada* was repeated two or three times over the course of about four hours, until Pablo promised to tell all.

The guards took him upstairs to a room where he was unbound. Pablo told them that he traded in guns for profit, but the cops knew he was lying. They decided to take Pablo downstairs for another warmup.

"I knew that I'd rather die than to suffer through that again," Pablo told me, "and I knew that if they kept up, I would talk." He looked for an out. "We were going downstairs and the handcuffs were still off. So I told them that if they didn't shoot me right there, I would make a run for it." The cops didn't unholster their weapons, so Pablo ran. Shots rang out behind him, striking a passerby in the street. But Pablo kept running, and that is what had landed him in the *palapa* where we talked that night. Later, I dug up clippings in Monterrey newspapers, confirming some of the details of Pablo's escape. Had it not been for those clippings, I might have doubted the tale he told.

A few mornings later, I was awakened by the sound of voices. Ramón and I were in another village, and had slept in a vacant *palapa* on a *petate*, the straw mats that in many Mexican rural communities haven't been superceded by that European invention the bed. The voices I heard were those of elder *ejida-tarios*, conversing with Ramón. The topic was an *ejidatario* named Alfonso, a founder of the *ejido* and its first proponent of relations with Güero. But Alfonso had changed sides, the elders were saying. He had tried to sell *ejido* membership to landless peasants, a common but illegal practice of corrupt *ejido* and squatter-camp leaders. Suspicions about Alfonso had been confirmed, they said, several weeks earlier, when he came back from Tuxtepec with a set of knee-high boots and a feathered cowboy hat. The elders figured that Alfonso was passing information to authorities or to the owners of a nearby ranch. "Where else would he get that kind of money?" one of them said. "The rest of us barely have enough to feed the cockroaches." The proposal the elders were putting before Ramón was that Alfonso should be killed.

The visitors in the hut, seated around a small table, noticed that I had wakened, but they paid me no mind. A little boy and a dog wandered in and sat down together on the hut's dirt floor. They, too, were ignored. The elders wanted Ramón to approve of their conclusion about Alfonso, but he was reserved. "What about his family?" he asked. The men told Ramón that their prospective victim had no children in the village. He lived with two sisters, one of whom was mother to an already-orphaned child. Ramón thought a minute, then assented. "But don't provoke him in any way. Wait until you can ambush him in the jungle," he said.

The conversation that I'd heard had so unsettled me that I'd decided it was time for me to leave. But I'd heard that the itinerant priest was in town, and despite my vows to journalistic objectivity and nonintervention, I wanted to warn him of the murder that was afoot. Through a villager, I sent word to the priest, asking for a meeting. He said that I'd have to meet him in Tuxtepec the next day, an arrangement that suited my plans very well. We met at an off-street diner in the market town.

The *padre*, Father Antonio, was a white-skinned man with an urbane accent, about forty years old. He told me that he had formerly been an athletic director for a Mexico City parish whose faithful had come from among the rich. He'd arranged his transfer to Oaxaca because he'd wanted to work among the poor, and he'd gotten more than he had bargained for: 24 villages scattered around Tuxtepec, in the same territory where Güero Medrano was organizing. After chatting a few minutes, I realized that he knew many of the people I'd met. But he knew them from a different angle. In one of the Chinanteca towns I'd visited, the priest said, chickens were still sacrificed. "The people would like to be thorough Catholics, I guess," he said, "but they don't understand that they must give up their old ways."

There was no need for me to mention Alfonso. The priest already knew, and had decided not to intervene. "Alfonso brought a pistol to mass last week, and I threw him out," he told me. "I went by his house to persuade him to give up the *ejido*. His sisters agree, but he's determined to show that he cannot be scared off." I asked the priest, nearly pleaded, that he talk to those on the guerrilla side. "What good would it do?" he asked me. "They know and I know that Alfonso tried to make side deals on the *ejido*. People here in Tuxtepec have told me that he offered to make them members for a fee."

The *padre* had ordered Cokes for both of us. When they were served, he pointed to his glass, as if in toast, saying, "¡Aguas negras de imperialismo!" "Sewer waters of imperialism!" and he laughed. Then he began to tell about the hardship of life on the *ejidos*, and the reasons why in his two years in Oaxaca, he'd become an admirer of Güero and his men. "You know," he said, "the Revolution for Independence was led by a priest, Miguel Hidalgo, who had Indian parishioners like mine. Hidalgo didn't wait for the whole Church to develop a full-blown social conscience, and sometimes I wonder what I should do." His reference, I thought, contained its own counsel. Hidalgo and his followers rose in 1810, a decade too soon. Hidalgo was shot within months. When independence came, its leaders were reactionaries, not Jacobins like Hidalgo. The Spanish had begun to experiment with democracy, and Mexico's prominent people took the opportunity to seat an emperor in New Spain.

During the next eighteen months, I made two more trips into Oaxaca to watch Güero Medrano and his men. On one of them, I marched with the leader and his peasants all night long, as they took hostages as insurance against an attack during a land takeover. Because no Mexican printshop was willing, or could be trusted, Medrano's monthly newspaper was published in Texas. I keep up with the movement's gossip through the paper's editor-smuggler. Among other things, I learned that Alfonso was not killed, because he skipped town, that Pablo de la O got into a shootout with the state police and went on the lam again. I was told when Güero's second child was born, and shortly afterward, I was told when Güero died. *Pistoleros* wounded him near the mountain village of Yolox. Ramón Pérez brought a doctor from Mexico City, but the pair arrived about half a day too late. Local supporters buried el Güero Medrano, and a few days later the army caught up with him at last. To make sure he was dead, soldiers dug up his cadaver, photographed his face, and rolled him back into the ground.

GOING BACK HOME

Ramón Pérez had returned to Mexico City with the doctor and had taken the subway to the stop nearest a relative's home. As he walked up to the house, two men from Gobernación appeared. Half an hour later, Ramón was locked into a cell, he didn't know where. Within a few hours, he had recognized voices he heard at his door. His younger brother, Narciso, was in the same jail, and so was Rafael or Rafa, the brother just older than Ramón. Narciso had been taken from his room, the little place where I'd first met Ramón, along with another townsman who'd moved to Mexico City to attend school. The army had taken Rafa, another young man, and the village schoolteacher, a female, in their Oaxacan hometown. The jail where Ramón found himself, wherever it was, was filled with Güero's supporters, and a few innocents besides: Three of his suspect townsmen had had no dealings with the guerrilla band. Every now and then, Ramón would hear screaming, and his turn came, too. With kicks and blows, his interrogators confirmed what they already knew. Whoever had talked first, it seemed, had informed them fairly well. The problem was, the exercise was punitive, nearly pointless. Neither he nor any of the others believed that Güero's movement would rise again.

The movement that Güero headed had been built on his charisma, his strength, and his material supplies. His appeal has been overpowering: When I played a taped interview with Güero for my wife, her comment was, "What a masculine voice!" Güero was young, handsome, and bold, and he also seemed to know very well what he was doing. His vigor and his strength expunged the doubts with which he was sometimes received.

Güero's life and movement did not alter the conditions of peasant life. Forty-five percent of Mexico's *ejidos* are embroiled in boundary conflicts today. Peasant revolts and *pistolero* attacks haven't ended, either. According to the Autonomous University of Chapingo, between December 1, 1982, and October 1, 1988, 720 Mexican peasants were killed in land struggles, 235 of them in Oaxaca. Between 1983 and 1988 in the northern part of the state of Chiapas, for example, some 24 peasants were killed, 108 were wounded, 82 were jailed, 22 were kidnapped, and 323 disappeared and are presumed dead. Ramón and other survivors of Güero's movement knew that rural discontent wouldn't subside, but they had begun to doubt that their struggle could ever win. Eleven days after he was jailed, the men from Gobernación returned Ramón to the streets where they'd found him, and like his comrades, he spent a few weeks mourning and nursing his broken ribs, then began to map out a new life. Ramón Perez is a Zapotec. He decided to go back to Oaxaca, the center of Zapotec life.

I'd known little about the Zapotecs until after Güero's death, when Ramón showed me the culture's present capital, the city of Juchitán, where the leaderless guerrilla went for a time. Juchitán is a poor town, bereft of material grace. It has only one service station, and supermarkets are yet to appear. Pigs roam freely in the dusty garbage that blows in Juchitán's streets. Though the town's population is about seventy thousand, no daily newspaper is published there.

To understand why neighbors and natives take pride in Juchitán, you almost have to study Zapotec. Juchitán is three towns for the bilingual: one whose streets and landmarks are named in Spanish, after heroes of the *mestizo* federal government; one in which the same places are named after local residents, in Zapotec; and one in which the two languages have tried to find a meeting ground, producing terms that only Juchitecos comprehend. For example, Avenida Melchor Ocampo, or Melchor Ocampo Avenue, is named after a leader of the movement to unseat mid-nineteenth-century emperor Maximilian. Locals call the street pasu Necho Lón. *Pasu* is a Zapotec corruption of the Spanish word *paso*, or passage. Necho Lón is the Zapotec rendition of Nemesio Leonardo, the name of a man who lived on the street. Avenida Benito Juárez, named after Mexico's only Indian president, himself a Zapotec, is called pasu Na Cheya, *na* being the Zapotec equivalent of Mrs. or *señora*, and Cheya the equivalent of the Spanish name Cliseria, the name of a former resident of the street. An alley called Limón or lime is locally known as pasu Ta Fino Guelaguidi, or, in English, Mr. Rufus Sandal Street. But deriving that translation requires both Spanish and Zapotec. *Ta* is the Zapotec equivalent of Mister or Señor. Fino is the Zapotec rendition of the Spanish name Rufino, or Rufus. *Guelaguidi* is the translation of the Mexican word *huarache*, or sandal, a word not common as a surname. A man named Rufino probably lived in the alley, but whether "sandal" describes his occupation or a mere nickname, Juchitecos no longer know.

Naturally, in a context like this, Juchitán goes by other names, too. The town was called Ixtacxochitlán by the Aztecs, a name meaning "place of the white flowers"; this mouthful evolved into the shortened form Xochitán, which the Spanish later adopted under the present spelling. But the locals called it Lahui Guidxhi, "the center of the people" or "the center of town." When the conquistadores came, they prefixed the name of Saint Vincent Ferrer, San Vicente, to the Aztec simplification they spelled as Juchitán. After the defeat of Emperor Maximilian, the town was renamed Juchitán de Zaragoza, in honor of a hero of the day. It officially retains that name, but Juchitecos do not call it that. For them, the town is Shavicende, a name derived from *sha*, or at the feet of, and the Zapotec corruption of San Vicente or St. Vincent's name. Changes like these lead not only to confusion but to mistakes. There's a chapel in Juchitán to Nuestro Señor de la Exaltación, or Our Lord of Exaltation. But the Zapotec name assigned to the shrine is yu' du' Saltación, a name that, if it means anything, means "the Church of Jumping."

Juchitán's central market officially occupies a two-story building, a block long, on the backside of the city hall. But cars can't enter any of nine blocks on streets south of the civic plaza, either: Vendors block the way with their stalls. As at Mexico City's La Merced and at most traditional Mexican markets, government planners can't build fast enough to keep commerce under a roof. Everybody in Juchitán, it seems, has something to sell.

Ambulatory vendors jostle in the streets, carrying shoestrings or ballpoint pens or boxes of matches in their arms. Broomheads stand in booths at eye level, supported by sticks of whittled mesquite. Pineapples and avocados perch waisthigh on stools and tables; sun-dried shrimp and snapper bask in galvanized tubs. Flower vendors squat on plastic buckets, tying their wares in bouquets and wreaths, and on the pavements, bound with strands of twine, armadillos, iguana, and hens wait to be bought and slaughtered. Eight types of tortilla and six types of tamal are consumed in Juchitán, and on a good day, you can find them all for sale by women of the market streets.

Juchitán's women look like packages of a brand-name product, in different sizes. That's because they're dressed nearly alike. The regional custom is that when a young woman marries, she dons two traditional garments, the *huipil* and the *enaguas*, nearly every day for the rest of her life. *Huipiles* are pullover or buttonless blouses, with square or rounded collarless necklines. In Juchitán, they're made of cotton, or synthetics or silk, and their fronts are almost always stitched with quadrilateral patterns, large squares, diamonds, and the like. The *enaguas* is an ankle-length skirt, usually with a wide strip of lace at its bottom end. Despite the heat of coastal Juchitán, many women wear a petticoat beneath. On festive days, they add a white lace headdress to their two-piece daily garb, and they drape their necks in gold jewelry. Despite the town's poverty, gold-plated items are mainstays of the jewelry shops on the indoor market's second floor. Juchitán's women are especially fond of earrings in the shape of the fruit fly. As far as I

231

Juchiteca in huipil

can determine, the entomological aesthetics of Juchitecas are not shared by women anywhere in the Western world.

Juchitán's men are almost invisible. They're to be seen only at work or at home. Some are artisans at different crafts, depending upon the neighborhood where they were raised. Men born in the area called Neighborhood 8, for example, tradi-

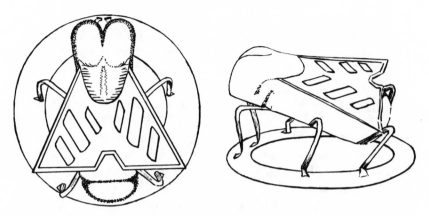

Design from Juchitán Earring

tionally make items of palm. Those of Neighborhood 2 produce roofing shingles or tiles, and those of Neighborhood 7, hammocks or pottery. Several hundred men catch buses to jobs at a Pemex refinery in Salina Cruz, thirty miles west, while others, especially from the south and west sides of town, go fishing on boats moored in Laguna Superior Bay. But most of Juchitán's men are peasants. They work their fields with oxen, and bring their harvests home in oxcarts. They celebrate the festival of Saint Isidore the Plowman because most images picture him with oxen like they drive. The farmers leave home at dawn and return in steaming midafternoon, during siesta time: Juchitán, like most Mexican towns, closes its commercial district for three hours at midday to allow families to dine together at lunch; stores stay open until eight o'clock at night. Men are scarce in Juchitán's stores and streets, because commerce is a monopoly of their wives. The males aren't striking figures. They dress in ordinary cotton pants and shirts, and until the fifties, most of them didn't wear shoes. In most Juchiteco homes, ladies' wear is kept in an adorned wooden trunk. But men hang their clothes on hooks in the walls.

Some students of Juchitán argue that the town is a matriarchy. Women are the chief providers of cash, because they sell what their families produce. In homes where married men work

233

on industrial jobs, there's a tradition of signing one's paycheck over to one's wife. If a young man wants to marry, he asks permission of his mother-in-law. If she consents, he then pays a mock homage to Mexico's more macho customs by arranging the *rapto* or "kidnapping" of his bride, who, of course, has been in consultation with her mother about the whole affair. Civil and church weddings do not take place until after the *rapto*, which both families celebrate. At a *rapto* celebration I attended, the men sat soberly on a porch, like wallflowers at a dance. The women, who danced together more often than with men, were drunk and rowdy. "Women are not superiors in Juchitán," a native female intellectual told me, "but we do have a more equalized relationship than elsewhere in Mexico." In Juchitán, only the dead are accorded more respect. The city's cemeteries consist not of graves, but of *casitas*, or "little houses" of concrete block and plaster, usually big enough to host five or six living guests. Most flowers sold in Mexico are given to the dead, and that's especially the case in Juchitán. Every Sunday families sweep their *casitas* and place flowers in their urns. "Juchitán is a hard, poor place to live," one of my local informants told me, "but it's the best place on earth to die. Nobody ever forgets you here."

One of the reasons that Ramón went to Juchitán was to see its politics work. The town had elected a mayor who represented a four-party Communist coalition called the COCEI, or the Worker-Peasant-Student Coalition of the Isthmus. The COCEI had for several years been, and still remains, the chief political voice of Juchitán's Zapotec majority. But its mayor was jailed, and after several killings, troops occupied the town for the second time in a decade, restoring the PRIista rule. Ramón was frustrated, not only because the COCEI was outgunned, but also because he could not make himself understood. As a matter of principle, the COCEI conducts its meetings in Zapotec, Ramón's native language. But Ramón speaks highland Zapotec, and the Juchitecos speak a coastal or Isthmus version of the tongue. The two dialects are mutually unintelligible, the product of a geographic dispersal that occurred nearly a thousand years ago. Ramón Pérez was an outsider in Juchitán because he could communicate only in Spanish, the language of the Conquest. After about six months, he decided that he'd best go home.

THE VILLAGE

In Güero's movement, Ramón had been known as "Tianguis" because he is a native of San Pablo Macuiltianguis, a village of some five thousand, high in the pine forests of Oaxaca's Juárez mountain range. San Pablo Macuiltianguis is a place of historical complexities, beginning with its name. San Pablo, or Saint Paul, is a prefix added by the Spaniards to the town's Aztec name. Macuiltianguis is a combination of two words in Mexica or Náhuatl, *macuilli,* meaning "five," and *tianquiztli,* meaning "plazas" or "markets." The town got its modern, official name, San Pablo Macuiltianguis, in the mid-sixteenth century, when conquistadores passed through with their Aztec guides. But the conquistadores were evangelizing and their guides were merely translating. Then, as now, when talking among themselves, inhabitants of the hamlet call it *Ta Gallu,* "five plazas" in their native Zapotec tongue. When dealing with people who don't speak Zapotec, they call it Macuiltianguis, or Macuil, for short. Only the telephone and postal services refer to San Pablo Macuiltianguis by its full name, and telephone service hardly matters: There's only one phone in town, at a general store.

Macuiltianguis is a revealing place because it has resisted modern economic and political forms. Because of its mountainous isolation, land-grabbers never wanted the town or its fields. Laws abolishing communal property were ignored. Macuil was an *ejido* before the Spaniards came, and it was not dissolved, as most collectives were, during the Porfirato. At the time of the Revolution, Macuil's tillers were already in possession of lands. They had always been. Today, as always, every adult male citizen of Macuil has a right to a *milpa,* or cornfield, a right to pasture animals on commune lands, and a right to an equal share in the town's income from a sawmill and the sale of timber rights to a paper mill in Tuxtepec. Citizens also have a right to participate in the town-hall meetings where most civic decisions are made. They have unusual duties, too.

All male citizens must participate in *tequios,* or municipal-works projects, and they must accept *cargos* when their times come. A *cargo* is a municipal office—mayor, secretary, treasurer, policeman, some fifteen jobs in all—that requires full-time work. The town's *sindico,* for example, takes charge of streets, garbage service, and building projects. The *juez de llaves* is chief of maintenance at the town's Catholic church. The chairman of Macuil's educational committee oversees cultivation of plots set aside for the benefit of the schools.

For administrative purposes, Macuil has for centuries been divided into five neighborhoods, or *barrios:* That's how the town got its name. The *barrios* rotate the responsibility of providing men to fill *cargos.* Neighbors propose the names of prospective officeholders to a town assembly, which assents to the choices or requires the submission of new names. Civic and church service is a sacrifice, because *tequios* and *cargos* are unpaid. It need not be a sacrifice, but the people of Macuil have preferred to operate that way. Anthropologist Eric Wolf has described the functioning and ends of the system of salaryless religious service, common in many indigenous communities. Macuil's civic service works the same way:

> . . . Each year, a different group of men undertakes to carry out the tasks of religious office; each year a different group of men makes itself responsible for the purchase and ritual disposal of food, liquor, candles, incense, fireworks, and for all other attendant expenditures. A tour of religious duty may leave a man impoverished for several years, yet in the eyes of his fellow citizens he has added greatly to his prestige. This spurs men to renewed labor toward the day when they will be able to underwrite another set of ceremonies; and a man will sponsor several such ceremonials in the course of his life. Each tour of sponsorship will add to the esteem in which he is held by his fellow men until—old and poor—he reaches the pinnacle of prestige and commands the respect of the entire community. . . . Thus old age itself becomes a source of prestige for Indians; an old man is one who has labored in the interests of the community for many years. . . .
>
> Each year, religious participation wipes out considerable sums of goods and money; each year part of the surplus of the com-

munity is consumed in offerings or exploded in fireworks to please the saints. The system takes from those who have, in order to make all men have-nots. By liquidating the surpluses, it makes all men rich in sacred experience but poor in earthly goods. Since it levels differences of wealth, it also inhibits the growth of class distinctions based on wealth.

Macuil's political system, like that of Monterrey, can be judged by the honesty with which it selects leaders, and by the behavior of its most obvious public servants, the police. Local election fraud is unknown, for three reasons. First, men who hold *cargos* are generally selected by consensus, not by a vote. The entire town assembly must assent to a *barrio's* final nominee, or else discussion continues—and the *cargo* goes unfilled in the interval. Second, the hardship imposed by *cargos* encourages evasion, not candidacy. Were ballots cast in Macuil's municipal elections, candidates would stuff *tacos* to ensure the election of opponents, not of themselves! Third, there is only one candidate for each *cargo*, the candidate named by the *barrio* whose turn has come to shoulder responsibility. Macuil's policemen are all unprofessional, as I realized one night when I came upon two drunks, staggering in the street. One of them wore the cap and carried the flashlight of the town policeman, and the other introduced himself as the policeman's assistant. But law enforcement, such as it is in Macuil, is a success, largely because the town's social cohesion and economic security protect it from malaise.

Murder is practically unknown. During the forties, one local allegedly killed another, and twenty-five years ago an outsider who'd fallen in love with a local woman reportedly shot her native boyfriend. Once in a blue moon, someone will charge a neighbor with theft. The city's policeman makes an investigation of his own, and if he thinks the charge is founded, he and his assistants will apprehend the suspect. They then interrogate him. This is done by tying a rope to one of the suspect's thumbs and stringing him up in the town plaza, in view of everyone, until he confesses or astounds onlookers with his valor. A restitution agreement usually follows confessions, but other remedies are available. In the most recent case—more

237

than five years ago—the alleged thieves were outsiders who'd moved to town. The policeman brought the matter of punishment before a citizens' assembly, which ordered the outsiders to move on. Suspects who don't confess are remanded to the state capital for a big-city, "professional" interrogation, sentencing, and confinement.

The chief police problem is dealing with drunks. By day, if the town policeman encounters someone who is rowdy or unconscious, he goes to the public-address system's microphone and asks family members to take their wayward relative home. At night, the policeman and his assistants wrestle or carry drunks back to their houses. If no one is home, they lock the drunks in the town's two-cell jail, until daylight or relatives come. Drunkenness can become a breach of the peace if men fight, but it is rarely regarded as a crime. It is not a traffic offense, because in Macuil there is no traffic. A half-dozen citizens own cars, but they must park them on the municipal square because most of the town's streets are too narrow for vehicles to pass. Macuil's system of justice is rudimentary, but it is not corrupt. No one can recall a policeman asking for, or accepting, a bribe. In Maquil there are no minority rights, but as in few places in Mexico, the will of the majority is rarely thwarted.

For years Macuil's natives died within yards of the spot where they were born. Nobody ever left town. The village produced objects of clay, alcoholic beverages of sugarcane and maguey, clothing, rope, fireworks, sandals—almost everything that was to be had. No roads connected the heights of the Juárez mountains to anywhere below, and the trek out—three days to the city of Oaxaca—was too slow for medical emergencies and almost too steep for commerce. Nearly half of the town's children died before the age of five, usually of infectious diseases, malnutrition, or dehydration, and Macuil's people lived in dread of droughts, which inevitably came. Dryness meant poor harvests, and in chilly Macuil only one corn crop was possible each year. The specters of frost and drought created pressures for an exodus, but in Macuil there was no easy way out, and nowhere to go. That began to change on the eve of Pearl Harbor, with the passage in the United States of a labor import or *bracero* program, and with the opening of a highway near Macuil in 1952.

In 1940, a group of Macuil's young men went to the city of Oaxaca, and from there to the United States as *braceros*, or temporary laborers. The tales they told and the goods they brought founded a tradition of going north: Virtually ever male older than thirty has been to the United States, and most women beneath that age have gone, too. Most of them have lived in Los Angeles. In the cities they passed and on the farms where they worked, Macuil's men became aware of the relative poverty of their town, and of their abused status as Indians. The first generation of immigrant workers all came home to marry or to establish their mature lives, but they also brought an ambition to see their children compete in the world at large. They demonstrated their own ambition by casting aside the tradition of local dress. The men had worn loose-fitting white cotton clothing before. They began wearing cowboy shirts and jeans, the garb of the *mestizo* class. Some of them planned a new order of family life. Ramón's father, for example, banned the speaking of Zapotec in the home. When the highway came, it put the urban world as close as a morning's bus ride. Macuil was eight miles from the highway, closer than any neighboring town. That closeness transformed village and regional life.

The highway meant that though Macuiltianguis didn't have electricity, its city hall could have a public-address system, powered by a motor and gasoline lugged in from the road. It meant that town residents could buy batteries and radios, though in the early years not many of them could afford to: The public-address system still plays music all day long, in deference to the radioless past. In 1963, pumps and piping brought over the highway allowed Macuil to establish a safe municipal water system. Electric lines reached town five years later, and following them, a secondary school.

Because Macuil was the nearest town to the highway, and sat on a wide, smooth, year-round road, it also became the stopping point for anthropologists and government specialists whose job was modernizing indigenous life. Outsiders launched a dozen schemes, ranging from an outdoor movie theater run by Gypsies to a communal implements factory that

239

failed. One of the plans, since abandoned, was that of educating an indigenous elite. It was an ambitious undertaking, because in Macuiltianguis there was no elite to draw upon: Everyone lived at about the same level of poverty, and there were few books in any home. A start was made by sending the best fourth-grade students to boarding schools. Three girls went to the city of Puebla. None could tolerate the separation, and all were returned home. Three boys were picked, too. Ramón Pérez was one of them. Dressed in a khaki uniform, he was sent to a military school in the city of Oaxaca. When he'd finished the program, he stayed on for secondary studies with relatives who'd moved into town. He became a part of Macuil's shifting population, a young Okie of our times. After junior high school, he went to Mexico City to study at a technical school. He was not the first there, either. One generation had already preceded him into the diaspora. But city life didn't sweep Ramón's generation off its feet.

The cities, he and his peers believed, had turned workmen into robots, public servants into thieves, and children into orphans from nine to five. On both sides of the border, in Mexico City as well as L.A., men were unequal in rank, usually from the moment of their births. In the industrial world, time, work, and seasons had been squeezed of their pleasures, producing a dry and tasteless fruit whose only virtue was abundance. Leisure didn't begin when the rains came, nor did it last as long. Work was paced by machines or foremen, not taken at one's own speed. In the village, men spent their nights promenading from one general store to the next, toasting their friends to drinks of *mezcal*. Nobody walked in California, and in Mexico City the bars of poor folk were buckets of blood: Macuil's diasporans were accustomed to poverty but not to the slums. Most of Ramón's peers married hometown brides, but in the cities their children were surrounded by *mestizo* or *ladino* playmates, and the Zapotec of the supper table did not go outside. On playgrounds and in the streets, children learned an impudence that was new, and they brought home a word, used to draw a line between them and their ancestry, that is taken as an insult in Mexico. They referred to their parents *indios*, or Indians.

The diaspora created problems at home, too. Macuil's leaders were shorthanded. Rather than disenfranchising the exiles and inviting newcomers to town, they decided to buy time. Several *cargos* were abolished, including those of the Comité de la Liga Feminil, or Women's League Committee, which had operated a kindergarten; there were no longer enough preschool children to justify the draft. The town also abolished the Youth Society's *cargo,* which had been used to procure a young man for ringing the church bell at 5:00 A.M., noon, and 5:00 P.M. But the most unsettling reform was one that allowed diasporans to hire seconds for *tequio* and *cargo* duties. Sons put their fathers to work as seconds, undermining the hierarchy of age. A few elders expressed misgivings about the new order, but the majority were already compromised. Most parents received money from the children who had left home.

Money orders for dollars and the exodus of the young put an end to Macuil's self-sufficiency, and to many of its rustic ways. Cigarettes were no longer made of home-grown tobacco, rolled in corn shucks. They were bought at the stores. Nobody grew wheat to make festive breads, or cured leather, or made lime, or baked clay for roofing tiles. Towns farther from the highway became satellites of relatively cash-rich Macuil. Potatoes were brought from Atepec, coffee and *tepache,* a sugarcane wine, from Comaltepec, storage baskets from Maninaltepec, earthenware from Quiotepec, beans and flour from Abejones, and cheese from Jaltianguis. For the first time in history, labor was imported, from Luvina, just across the vale. Elder residents of Macuil no longer had as many sons and daughters at home to help at planting, harvest, and weeding times; the *milpa* became a petty-capitalist enterprise.

Several of the nearby towns did not have primary or secondary schools. Parents in those towns didn't have the means to pay for children's room and board, but seeing Macuil's success, they longed to have their children learn Spanish and acquire literacy, too. Out-of-town students became a class of domestic servants in Macuil. They traded services for their keep. Most of the immigrant students were Chinantecs, who spoke neither Spanish nor Zapotec when they came to town. The culture and language that they took home at the school year's end was as much Zapotec as Mexican. A chain of bewilderment arose: from the Chinantec towns to Macuiltianguis, from Macuil to the United States.

Even the routines of the hearth were disturbed. For as long as Ramón and his generation could remember, mothers had kept the same schedule every day. You could set your watch by it. About eight o'clock every night, after supper was served, they put a pot of corn, lime, and water on the hearth to boil. When they arose at sunrise, they strained the corn and washed it of its lime and skins. Then they gathered at the grinding mill. They were back at home by 6:00 A.M., forming tortillas of *masa*, or meal, with their hands. Nobody in Macuil liked the taste, texture, or color of the machine-made tortillas sold in other, bigger towns. But the men and women who were parents to Ramón's generation remembered when *masa* had been prepared with manual grinding machines, and their parents recalled the days of stone implements for grinding, called *metates*. Macuil's mature residents viewed change in a relative light, not as the harbinger of the end of an era, and when women from other towns knocked on their doors with fresh handmade tortillas to sell, they bought. But the younger people, especially the males, feared for Macuil's folkways and the security of its past.

These conditions were not unique to Macuiltianguis during the seventies, and they are not unique to Mexico today. The general picture drawn of Mexican society is of one in transition from a rural to an urban existence, and that picture is accurate in gross terms. But it fails to account for population growth, and it is usually based on figures that can't bear scrutiny. In 1960, according to official data, about half of the Mexican population lived in rural areas. By 1970, only 40 percent of the population was reported as living in rural settings. In 1980, the rural population percentage reportedly fell to 20 percent. But these figures are misleading. They create a false sense of urbanity by defining as rural only those settlements with populations of less than twenty-five hundred. By these terms, Macuiltianguis is a city! (A similar statistical problem exists in the United States, whose Census Bureau also defines as urban any settlement of twenty-five hundred or more. By those terms, Plains, Georgia, is a city!)

A more realistic but still skewed sorting of census data, one that classifies as urban only settlements of five thousand or more (Macuil is still a city, by those terms), indicates that in 1960, about 60 percent of Mexico's population was rural. By 1980, according to that definition, the ratios had reversed; 40 percent of the population was rural, 60 percent urban. Mexico's population had increased during that period by about 200 percent. Both factors, the rural/urban shift and the population explosion, present frightening perspectives, even as exercises in blind math. The changes mean, for example, that if there were 100 people in all of Mexico in 1960, and 60 of them lived in rural areas or settlements, today's economy must provide land for 20 new tillers, or a total of 80, an increase of one third. Either that, or Mexico's cities, which in 1960 would have housed 40 inhabitants, must today provide jobs and homes not for 120 people, but for 140. If land is scarce or the cities fail to provide jobs, three consequences are possible, and at least one of them must occur: either immigration or starvation or social unrest. Ramón and his generation were weighing these alternatives when Güero Medrano appeared.

Ramón was a student in Mexico City, and was also working at an industrial plant, when he first received news of Medrano's risings in Oaxaca. The news was brought to him by a townsman who was studying at a trade school in Tuxtepec. Two weeks later, Ramón and another peer paid a visit to Güero in a little Oaxacan town. They had heard and read about socialism, and Güero confirmed that they knew what it meant: To them, it meant that the whole world could be a commune, a Macuiltianguis, writ large. Ramón and his companion joined on the spot. In the months that followed, they sought and found co-conspirators and sympathizers in their hometown. Güero's movement was popular because it promised to extend the communal ways of the region, not relegate them to the denigrated "Indian past." It was also popular because Macuil's diasporans were on the bottom of both Mexican and American society, and moving up was tough.

243

One of the unspoken causes of the popularity of socialism in Macuiltianguis was the psychological distance between its young men, and Indo-Americans in general, and the Westernized Mexicans who in urban settings were their supervisors and bosses. Most Indian children are strictly raised. They are taught the virtues of deference and silence. Westernized Mexicans treat male children as the centers of family life. They do not defer, they expect and command. As adolescents, the economically privileged do not learn to identify with the poor, as most Indo-Americans must because they are the poor, nor do they learn to blush with shame or discomfort, as most Americans do, when witnessing material misery in Mexico. Instead, they learn to justify the exploitation that denies ordinary Mexicans a dignified wage. As white teenagers once did with blacks in Mississippi, they treat female Indo-Americans as prostitutes, males as procurers, and even the elderly as objects of pranksterism and abuse. An antisocial sadism, justified by racial lineage and economic status, becomes the order of their lives, and it never really leaves them, though with age, young men of privilege learn to exploit, as planters in Mississippi did, with the manners of grace. Viciousness turns to paternalism, but the principle of congenital superiority remains. Indians in Mexico do not often speak of the Westernized class, because a part of what they see as their dignity involves overlooking that difference: They are like the American blacks in former times who did not speak of black and white. But Westernized Mexicans speak of the underclass all the time, in frankly racial terms. Indians are the butt of their jokes. "The reason Mexico has problems and you don't," a Mexican businessman once confided in me, "is that you Americans killed your Indians, and we let ours live."

Most of Ramón's townsmen-comrades, of course, never planned to place themselves at risk. Though he had given up school and a job to go with Güero, and others had not, he expected more of himself. After all, he'd been raised to be a member of the village elite. Back at home after Güero died, he forgave bygone disappointments and, with his peers, began living a traditional routine. The young men took their turn at the nightly pilgrimage of *mezcal*-toasting that their fathers were beginning to leave behind. But the newer generation did its drinking differently, its members believed. Most of them joined a loose group that called itself "Los Choskys, A.C.," or "the Chosky Civic Association," though it was chartered nowhere. Chosky was no Mao. He had been the town drunk, a man who, the kids told me, had the good fortune to die with three sheets to the wind. The scandal of the Choskys was not that they became young drunks—that was anticipated—but that when they got tilted, they reverted to their student days, charting socialist republics in the air. Because there was constant interchange between members of the younger generation in Macuil, Mexico City, and Los Angeles, the group quickly acquired money. Members donated funds to build and stock a substantial library for the town. They named it after the Cuban hero José Martí, and they stuffed its shelves with the works of socialist theory that they had failed to master for themselves.

But farming and idleness and the rites of *mezcal* were not enough to satisfy Macuil's young men. In groups of two and three, they began going north, to join their peers in the United States. Ramón became a part of the migrant stream. He was a cherry-picker, a busboy, a carpenter, and a printer in the United States. Like most Mexicans, he never stayed. For nearly eight years, he ran a circuit, going north and coming back. At home, he took over the carpentry shop that his father had abandoned for a janitor's job at the town school. He built the booth in which Macuil's only telephone sits, and he made furniture for local sale. As the tradition commanded, whenever someone died, he built a casket for free. Survivors provided him with the lumber, "usually the worst wood they had," he recalls, and with flashlight batteries whose life had expired. With the carbon the batteries contained—which shoeshine boys use to make polish—Ramón painted his caskets the traditional black. His woodshop tied him to the folkways of the town, but not in as gratifying a way as in his father's time: There were more deaths per carpenter now, because carpenters had left town, while the elderly stayed.

Ramón lived in his parents' home on his return stays. It was an example to him of how he would have lived had he never left Macuil. A large rectangular building, big enough for five bedrooms, was its sleeping quarters. The building was made of adobe, plastered in white, with a roof of *láminas,* or corrugated steel sheets. A large room, divided from the rest of the quarters by curtains that hung from the roof, stood at one end. It was subdivided by another set of curtains. In each section was a bed, a wardrobe, and other dressing-room furniture. On the opposite side of the building was another bedroom, narrow but with a partitioning wall and door. In the middle of the building was a huge, cavernous room. Straw baskets filled with dried corn stood against its walls. A large round table was in the middle of its hard earthen floor. Chairs surrounded the table, and a cassette player sat on top. On one of the walls of the living room, the family altar hung.

Abutting the large rectangular room, forming an *L,* was the building for cooking and dining. Of similar construction, it had two rooms, one for the hearth and the other for preparing and consuming meals. A long wooden dining table sat there, the center of family life. In one corner stood the gas range that his mother used during rainy season, when firewood was scarce. Next to it was a sink, fed by a single, cold-water pipe. On the other side of the hearth was a separate room enclosing a commode, which drained downhill to a river, and a shower where hot water ran. The boiler sat outside on a sidewalk between the bathroom and the *fregadero* where Ramón's mother washed clothes. Beyond was her garden, where a dozen varieties of spices, vegetables, and flowers grew. The woodshop sat on the opposite side of the yard, attached to the sleeping room. Behind it was a pen where turkeys were kept for slaughter on festive days. Chickens walked where they wanted, here and there. In the middle of the yard was an open-air shed. Under its roof were the thousands of adobe blocks that Rafa had bought for building a home. Rafa now lived across the street in a house rented from absent in-laws. Family nearness was comforting, and in Ramón's view, so was the yard: Most houses in Mexico don't have them. There was no heating in the house, as there had been in houses where he'd stayed in the United States, and Macuiltianguis grows cold. But Ramón hardly noticed, when he was home. In familiar surroundings, one adjusts.

At times Ramón wished for a way to stay in Macuil and settle as his father had. But two obstacles stood in the way. The first was that he was distrusted outside of his circle of peers. A useful custom had died on the day the army marched in, and Güero's cadre were widely blamed. Despite Mexican laws to the contrary, most of Macuil's menfolk owned rifles. For decades they had strapped the guns on their backs when they went to chop firewood or work in the fields. They used their rifles to fell rabbits and other small game. But when the soldiers came looking for guerrillas and encountered armed farmers instead, they invoked the law and dispossessed those who had left home with rifles that day. Macuil's menfolk no longer carried rifles on their forays to the fields, for fear that the army would come again. Their fears and memories meant that Ramón's returns were no longer welcomed by many people in town.

Indeed, he was skirting disenfranchisement. The incursion by the army had caused such consternation that when the troops had left, a town assembly had met to discuss stripping Güero's followers of their birthrights. The assembly did not reach an agreement on its first night, and because consensus, not majority rule, is the local ideal, it met again, on a second and a third night. Ultimately, most people decided that, as one old man argued, "we have to accept our children, even the bad ones." No action was taken. But ill feeling continued.

Ramón also couldn't stay because of a debt he felt that he owed to Rafa, the older brother who was jailed in the wake of Güero's death. Rafa had faced Macuil's hostility rather than fleeing north. When he had gotten out of jail, he'd come home to take out a *milpa*. He had married a local woman who had done her time in Los Angeles, as a cook in a fast-food diner. She believed that life would be easier in California, but when others went, Rafa stayed. He had been trained in Mexico City as an industrial electrician, and his educational level, though not his technical skills, landed him a local job with a federal farm agency. With the job came the luxury of a car. But before long, Rafa's neighbors tested his determination to stay, by assigning him to a *cargo* that would last for fully three years. He quit the job and accepted the *cargo*, though it meant that he would have no income other than what he could earn in off-hours from the family woodshop. The labor-saving tools that Ramón brought on each trip home helped Rafa's family survive. Even though Ramón wanted to stay in Macuil, he didn't think that he could endure Rafa's fate. People abused his brother, he said. He also complained that he couldn't find a mate. Ramón was nearing thirty, and he had no girlfriend in town.

On one of his returns home, an anthropologist came. She was a graduate student at the University of Veracruz, and a woman of about his age. Her reason for coming to town was to study its migrant chain. But she had other reasons for wanting to interview Ramón. María Eugenia Otero was an urban leftist in a small Indian town, wanting to share ideas with those who might understand her views. Villagers had told her, in a hushed way, the story of the time that the army had come to town. They'd told her that the Pérez brothers would know why. María was no guerrilla but a socialist from books, the type of woman who in Mexican academic circles was regarded as on her way up in life.

María attracted Ramón in ways that local women could not. She spoke with erudition. Ramón knew one townswoman with whom he could converse about the news and books, but she was preparing to wed. María was assertive and opinionated, especially about women's liberation, a cause that Ramón didn't espouse but, because of its leftish origins, didn't entirely disown. She was ambitious and hard-working, and perhaps most important of all, she was physically distinct from the women of his town. Mary, as friends called her, had the look of Veracruz. Everyone in Macuil noticed her hair. It grew out at an angle, rather than falling straight down, and it was thick with wavelets that mountain Zapotecs don't have. Almost from instinct, he gave her a nickname, *mi negra*, or "my Negress." She accepted the nickname as a compliment, and that's the way it was intended. In her home state, *Negra* and *Negro* have become terms of flirtation and romance.

Mexico calls itself a *mestizo* nation, as do most countries in Latin America. But racially, Mexico is more like Colombia or Venezuela than like Argentina or Paraguay, and the word *mestizo* has a double meaning. In general use, *mestizo* means "born

248

of parents of different race," and in that sense, Mexico is a
mestizo nation, but the term tells us little, because it does not
specify the parent races. *Mestizo* historically meant "born to a
Spanish and an Indian parent," and in that sense—a sense that
Mexicans still adopt to describe themselves today—it is more
often wishful than real.

Indo-America suffered a holocaust when the Spaniards came,
but most of the decimation was bloodless. Plagues killed people
by the millions. The Spanish brought measles, chicken pox,
smallpox, and probably malaria, diseases that had been unknown before, and for which Indians had not developed resistance. The indigenous population was reduced in the span
of a century from some 15 million to 25 million—nobody knows
for sure—to about three-quarters of a million. Even the most
conservative estimates place the death rate at six-sevenths of
the total population. Every family had members to mourn.

As the indigenous population sank, mines and plantations
faced labor shortages. Spaniards brought African slaves to cover
the labor shortfall. Census figures for the colonial era show that
from 1570 to about 1650, blacks outnumbered whites in New
Spain by a ratio of three to one. Even afterward, when the
balance shifted, the black population remained half as great as
the population of Caucasian descent. What these ratios mean
is that Africans probably contributed as much to Mexico's gene
pool as Spaniards ever did. But Mexico remained a predomi-
nantly Indian country. Even at their peak, Europeans and *criollos*, or native-born persons of European descent, accounted for
no more than eight one-thousandths of the total population.
The country's indigenous or Indian population was always 60
percent or more of the total, but as the decades passed, a mixed-
race population came to life. By 1810, it constituted New Spain's
second-biggest population block, of nearly 40 percent. With
independence in 1821, both immigration and the keeping of
racial records waned, but most scholars believe that today Mexico's majority is of mixed race. But it is not necessarily *mestizo*,
as Mary is not *mestizo*.

During the colonial years, one's status at law depended upon
pedigree, and the Spaniards developed a dizzying set of codes
to keep track. An Indian who had a European grandparent, for

example, was termed a *mestindio*, an Indian with an African grandparent, a *mulato lobo*, etcetera. Ultimately, all these codes proved unworkable, because the number of possible racial permutations is infinite. But those codes shed light on the word *mestizo*, and on the way that Mexico works today.

According to the codes, colonial authorities could grant or deny certain obligations, immunities, and privileges, based on findings of race. For example, Spaniards and *criollos* had access to the professions. Nonwhites were barred. Indians could not own guns or horses, but they were entitled to communal lands, and were at times exempted from taxes that Spaniards and *criollos* had to pay. As in the United States, it was illegal to hold whites in slavery. The enslavement of Indians or of persons of mixed ancestry was sometimes restricted and sometimes banned outright, depending upon changing historical circumstances. But African slavery was always legal. A *mulato pardo*, as a child born to an African and an Indian parent was called, could not be legally enslaved, but could also not partake of the landed status accorded the Indian population by Spanish law. Most of the mixed-race population lived in a legal netherworld, more at liberty than the Africans, but not as protected as the Indians or as privileged as the Spaniards.

A mistaken theory about "dominant blood" led the Spaniards to design codes in which Negritude or African ancestry was always a negative factor. For example, most of the codes permitted the Spanish entitlement of persons whose great-grandmothers had been of the indigenous race if their parents and grandparents were all of Spanish lineage. But some of the codes denied European status to anyone who admitted African ancestry of any kind. Liberalization of the codes allowed for the European entitlement of ostensible Spaniards who could show an absence of African ancestry back to the generation of their great-grandparents, i.e., a generation later than those whose ancestry was measured on the Euro-Indian scale. Because the Europeanizing provisions of the codes were not realistic—thousands of legal nonwhites were accepted as white in everyday life—their chief effect may have been to encourage evasion of the law. The codes left modern Mexico a legacy of contempt, and also a disconcerting phrase, *"mejorar la raza,"* or "to improve the race." Improvement, in the context of the phrase, means whitening or Europeanization.

The term *mestizo* designated a category in the old racial codes. An ostensible Spaniard was called a *cuarterón* under the codes if he had a black grandparent, and a *castizo* if his nonwhite grandparent had been Indian. The child of a black and a white parent was called a *mulato,* as under the racial codes once in effect in the United States. The child of a white and an Indian was called a *mestizo:* The term that Mexico uses to describe itself means not only "born to parents of different race," but something much more precise. The grandchildren of *mestizos* were eligible for European privileges if their parents were both white, but the grandchildren of *mulatos* were not. *Mestizo* was an official term that implied an absence of African ancestry in a country where blacks were nearly as numerous as whites. As a term to describe the Mexican nation as a whole, it greatly exaggerated Spanish lineage. It also associated Mexicanhood with an economic strata, that of the overseers' class. *Mestizos* were the foremen of the mixed-race and Indian populations. A recent study of 145 ranches and plantations near Córdoba, Veracruz, in 1788, for example, shows that "the Spaniards registered, in their majority, were owners of ranches. . . . The *mestizos* many times appear registered as foremen of a ranch owned by a Spaniard. . . . In respect to the 145 ranches, we found only three of them as property of indigenes. No Indian was foreman on any ranch in which the owner was a Spaniard." The term *mestizo,* when it originally came into Mexican use, implicitly depicted Mexico as a nation that had been somehow denied the privileges of first rank, but as one that, in the span of two generations, could almost magically acquire European (and therefore improved) standing. It made the same sort of claim that Mexico's modernizers have been making in political life ever since.

The legacy of African slavery in Mexico is strongest in two coastal states where plantations were vast, Veracruz and Guerrero. Both states are home to towns whose populations are largely black, and the traits of African ancestry are widely distributed across their general or *mestizo* populations. Even today, as Americans call people from Indiana Hoosiers and those from

251

Nebraska Corn Huskers, the people of Veracruz call themselves and are called Jarochos. The music of the state, known to Americans by the song "La Bamba," is called Jarocho music, and the original words of "La Bamba" were apparently written about a man of *jarocho* status. Few Mexicans know it, but the word *jarocho* was a racial term, like *mestizo*. It meant the same as *indio pardo*, a reference to offspring of an African and an Indian parent.

Veracruz has a reputation in Mexico, as Oaxaca does. Oaxacans are seen as Indian conservatives, stuck in archaic ways. Jarochos are viewed as daring individuals with a lightning survival sense. The Veracruz myth dates back to the seventeenth century, when Africans were being imported, the races were mixing, and both *negros* and *jarochos* were running away from branding irons. The thick foliage of the state's mountains offered refuge from the oppression of the plantations on the coastal plain. Thousands of runaway Indians and slaves gathered in misty enclaves to live by raiding the commercial traffic at their feet. These runaways were called *cimarrones*, or "untamed creatures," when they stayed in the wilds, and *léperos*, or lepers, when they came into the towns, forming a part of the class of catch-as-catch-can. They were an early part of the Mexican underclass, a class that at various times in the country's history has constituted a numerical majority. They were a decisive, somewhat dangerous people, independent and relatively unafraid. Mary Otero, like most people in Mexico, cannot trace her peerage beyond two generations. But she does not deny that she probably descended from Mexico's desperate *lépero* class. She instead takes pride in the possibility. *Cimarrones* and *léperos* had the wits and mettle that work wonders even in the contemporary world.

Of course, it made no sense to regard Mary as a *negra* or *parda*. Her racial aspect was a barrier to her advancement only in the same ways that Ramón's Indianness was a barrier to him. They were excluded from certain levels of Mexican society, levels that didn't interest them. There are, for example, no dark-skinned soap-opera stars or fashion models in Mexico, and Mexican history has known only one Indian president. The faces that appear on newspaper society pages are usually white,

252

as are those of governors, diplomats, and Cabinet men. Stock-brokers and industrialists are white—far out of proportion to their presence in the population—and until the banks were nationalized, dark-skinned tellers were rare. Official, prestigious Mexico is mainly white, even though others can enter in. But Ramón and Mary's preparation as leftists, more than birth with dark skins, had accustomed them to thinking of reaching their goals by the strength of persistence, not by luck, or mercy, or being carried in the flow.

Mary saw an opportunity in the sojourns Ramón made to the north. She wanted to interview Macuil's diasporans, not only in Mexico but also in the United States. The idea was one that would require her to live for several months among the illegal immigrants in Los Angeles, and she doubted that U.S. authorities would permit her to enter the country: American authorities require potential visitors to show money as proof of solvency. Though it was hardly the sort of proposal that she could ask a thesis committee to approve, and though she knew her family would be scandalized, she decided to accompany Ramón on his next trip north. A year after the two of them left Macuil, her daughter was born in Los Angeles. Mary named the child Haydée, after Haydée Santamaría, the Cuban Communist. A few months after the child was born, the family returned from the United States. Ramón wanted to settle in Macuil, but Mary found its rustic ways confining: In Macuil, among other things, women weren't accorded full citizenship. While they discussed alternatives, a summons came. Ramón was asked to take a *cargo*. He refused, saying that it wasn't his neighborhood's turn. He promised to accept a *cargo* the following year, but before it came, he received bad news. The town assembly had removed him from the citizenship roster, with no explanation and no plan for making amends. Friends and relatives denied knowing why he'd been disenfranchised, but he was willing to guess. Over the years, he had offended three local sensibilities. He had participated in a political movement in which the town had no immediate stake; he had married an outsider; and he'd said no when a civic duty called. The assembly's decision showed none of the favoritism that permeates ordinary affairs of government in Mexico: Ramón's fa-

253

ther was mayor when it was made. It was a sudden and strident decision, and it crippled his will to resist.

In Xalapa, several years later I watched Ramón age and change. Without any instruction, he had earlier developed an interest in literature. At every meeting, he had told me of a new book. He had read Kafka and de Maupassant, Raymond Chandler and even Goethe. At nights in cherry-picker camps in the state of Washington, he'd pecked out stories of his own with a secondhand manual typewriter. His tales, mostly about incidents in Maquil, had taken my breath away. But he quit writing, and he quit talking about books. His conversations centered on his photographic outings, on collections and sales. He worried over the details of photography, and small flaws in the pictures he took. Yet his pictures, unlike his writing, showed no art. Politics became for him the science of the impossible. When Mary and I discussed the topic, he listened but did not talk. Mary was enthused by the Cardenistas. Ramón didn't register to vote. Shamefacedly, he marched in his union's contingent of the Labor Day parade; if he didn't, he faced a fine. But as the months passed, he began speaking of the PRIista union as "we," not as "they." Ramón "Tianguis" Pérez, the former guerrilla, was buckling under the weight of modern life. The rustic rebel was becoming the urban man-on-the-street.

A NATURAL CURE

A few days after the 1988 national elections were held, I accompanied Ramón on a visit home. Our first stop, at my insistence, was at Macuil's city hall, where, as the law dictates, election results were posted on a bulletin board. The town was nearly unanimous: Cuauhtémoc Cárdenas had polled 96 percent of the vote, 843 of 881 ballots cast. The PRI polled 31 votes, or 4 percent. The PAN was represented by only seven supporters, and other parties got no votes at all. There had been no hanky-panky in Macuil on election day. Instead, its leaders had tried to guard against fraud by others. They had refused to entrust their ballot boxes to the soldiers who came for them.

A delegation of local officials drove the boxes to the district counting center themselves.

But Macuil was empty, as even the voting tallies showed. A village that had housed five thousand only three years before had been reduced to about two fifths of its usual number. Drought and immigration laws were the reason why. The lax provisions of the U.S. amnesty program for illegal aliens had drawn new migrants northward, and other citizens of Macuil had remained in L.A., waiting for amnesty papers to be approved. The back-and-forth flow had stopped, and most people were at the current's northern end. When I walked the streets at night, for the first time I failed to meet young men who said, "You're from the United States? Gee, I was just there last week." Only one bit of good news was circulation in Macuil. Two weeks earlier, ten young men had quit college and jobs in Mexico City, and had come back home as a group. Most of them were working in the municipally owned sawmill. I talked to their leader, and he told me that their return had been "an act of conscience." Ramón's other brother Rafa was their model, he said. The young men had come home to stay, ready for whatever discipline and life Macuil held in store for them.

Ramón and I found his brother Rafa in the kitchen of his rented house, a place more spacious and better furnished than Ramón and Mary's quarters in Xalapa. In one sense, at least, Rafa was prospering more than his cityfolk kin. But Rafa was pale and gaunt, and he looked twice his age. His head was wrapped tightly in a bandana. That morning he had arisen from his sickbed for a *tequio*, planting seedlings in a burned-out patch of pine forest. He had a fever of 102, and he'd had it on and off for ten days. He was in a difficult mood. When I mentioned the hamlet's election results, he said, "Yes, some people still believe in asking the government to change." Like Ramón, he hadn't voted.

Rafa was also buckling, but in a Zapotec way. He no longer believed in doctors, though when his children were sick, he still sent them for medical advice. At the urging of his wife, he'd agreed to let a *curandera* treat his fever, and his submission was complete and sincere. It wasn't a question of money. Two government clinics in Macuil treat patients for free.

255

His *curandera* had a theory about the cure she was working. She believed that Rafa was the victim of a delayed reaction to a *susto*, or fright. A couple of years earlier, he'd been pitched from a horse in his front yard. His son had been thrown, too. The boy wasn't hurt, but the horse kicked Rafa in the ribs, causing him to faint from *susto*. I was present one morning when the *curandera* came. She entered Rafa's bedroom, made the sign of the cross, muttered a prayer, and washed her hands in alcohol. Then she prepared a mud pack of *catalán*, a local liquor, and dirt from the spot where Rafa landed on his fall. She placed the mud on his abdomen, wrapped in a band of white cloth. The treatment was supposed to draw the fever from Rafa's body, but the fever came and went that day, its eleventh day, as it had on days before. Rafa's grandmother said that she'd seen men in his condition, and that *susto* wasn't the cause. She said that he had an intestinal infection, and predicted that it would last from seventeen to twenty-five days, no matter what cures were tried.

But the *curandera* had a stronger remedy, and a chicken was selected for sacrifice the next day. Early in the morning, Ramón and I paid a visit to Rafa's bedside. His strength had fallen low. We could barely hear the words he spoke. But he wouldn't listen to our advice, and we didn't have any desire to watch a chicken bleed. We left town, leaving the problem to his *curandera* and his wife. The situation reminded me of Macuiltianguis, and of Mexico. Nothing Rafa was willing to try was working in his favor, and he was lying on a European bed awaiting a distinctly Indian death.

Two weeks passed, and no letters or telegrams came from Macuil. In Mexico, no news is not good news—what it usually means is that the communications networks have fouled up again. Ramón began to worry about Rafa's fate. One afternoon he telephoned Macuil, leaving word for his mother to call us. She spoke to us about two hours later. Just a few days before, she said, on what would have been the twenty-first day of Rafa's illness, he awoke in good health. His grandmother's prediction had been justified.

Cultures, like men, don't live forever. But some of them endure longer than anyone expects. Five decades ago, when

Macuil's young men first began to go north, the town was infected with the germs of change. Today, it is shuddering with ill health. It seems to be on the edge of extinction. But it and the rest of Mexico were beaten down even lower during the century of the plagues. Macuil can repopulate, and it will: Rafa is only a year older than Ramón, but he has four children; Ramón has one. Even those natives of Macuil who ultimately go into the diaspora have not necessarily been absorbed. They can conquer, too, as they did in Campamento Rubén Jaramillo and in 2 de Octubre. Indo-American culture is neither passive nor static, as romantics and its detractors claim. When times are favorable, as during the boom, the culture ingests new elements, and tries to extend itself beyond its poverty-stricken confines, as Güero's men did, enlarging their *ejidos*. When adversity comes, as it did with the bust and in one corner of Oaxaca when Medrano was killed, the culture doesn't roll over and die. It goes back to its wellsprings, stares death in the face, and thus far has always lived to tell the tale and to multiply: Even when defined by the narrow criterion of language, there are more Indians in Mexico today than ever. From the time of Cortés to the present, those who have wanted to Europeanize Mexico have faced a barrier: Mexicans don't necessarily want to change. All of the accomplishments of Western medicine, for example, can be reduced to meaninglessness in any peasant's hut.

Return to Xtampak

ABOUT three o'clock in the af-
ternoon, "Vicente" turned the white Volkswagen to the left,
off of the highway and onto the dirt road. Vicente is Keith
Vincent Dannemiller, thirty-eight, an American photographer
who lives in Mexico. He looks every bit the part of the *gringo*
—blue-eyed, six feet tall, bearded and with a ponytail—and
nobody in Mexico can pronounce his name, hence, Vicente. I
had known him when he lived in Texas, and we had renewed
our acquaintanceship in Mexico. I was writing an article about
the Yucatán Peninsula, today's states of Campeche, Yucatán,
and Quintana Roo. Vicente's job was to provide the photos.
We were heading down the dirt road to a little-known ruin
called Santa Rosa Xtampak that had been abandoned by the
Mayas about a thousand years before.

The Mayan culture was the most extensive in pre-Hispanic
America. It included parts of El Salvador, Honduras, and Belize,
all of Guatemala, the Yucatán Peninsula, and part of the modern
state of Chiapas. It was arguably the most advanced; the Mayas,
for example, invented the zero, years before it was known in

India. It was also one of the most pacific. There was no Mayan empire; unlike the Aztecs, the Maya did not subjugate their neighbors. The Mayan world rose perhaps as early as 500 B.C., and lived a long life, until about A.D. 900, when the people who lived in its centers suddenly disappeared.

A contemporary encyclopedia describes the Maya this way:

The ancient Maya Indians created a spectacular civilization in southern Mesoamerica. In many ways their achievements surpass all other native American groups—certainly their superb monumental remains are more numerous. Some historians have compared the Maya to the ancient Greeks, noting that both made great intellectual advances, designed aesthetically pleasing works of art and passed their civilization on to other peoples.
. . . The genius of the Maya is revealed in their extant monuments at the Classic era sites. Here are handsome limestone temples with mansard-type roofs topped with decorative combs; stone-faced pyramids that usually served as a base for temples; cut-stone buildings . . . ball courts, gateways, plazas, carved stone pillars (stelae) and water-reservoirs—all constructed without metal tools. The Maya, who invented and utilized the corbeled vault or arch that is the hallmark of their Classic architecture, were the only pre-Columbian Indians who used any form of the arch.

The Yucatán Peninsula is a hot, nearly flat expanse of tropical rain forest, or jungle. Its mean annual temperature is 77 degrees, 2 degrees hotter than the Baja California desert. It is called the Yucatán Platform on physiographic maps, because it has no rivers or mountain ranges. The area is home to every pest that you'd imagine in your worst nightmares. Before coming, Vicente and I had been told that if we saw men who were missing forearms or forelegs, we should think of snakes, not industrial accidents or war. There's a snake in the Yucatán's jungle whose bite gives its victim about a minute to live. Natives carry machetes when they go outdoors in the countryside; if they get bitten, they lop off the affected limb. Yucatán is a terror to explore on foot, and it's dull country to drive. All the traveler sees is miles and miles of dense, shoulder-high foliage. Unless you've got anthropological or archaeological interests, or enjoy frying on Caribbean shores, I can't see any reason to go there. Hernán Cortés took a look at the Yucatán nearly five hundred years before Vicente and I did, and he decided the same thing.

Cortés had orders to establish a trading settlement in the Yucatán in 1519. He landed at Cozumel and Isla Mujeres, and at Campeche, on the peninsula's western coast. His reconnoitering told him that some of the natives were hostile, that drinking water was scarce, and that there was no gold in the region. He decided to conquer central Mexico instead. The Conquest of the Yucatán didn't begin until 1527, six years after the Aztec territories were pacified, and it lasted not two years as in Central Mexico, but nearly five decades. Native resistance, bugs, disease, mud, and heat discouraged wave after wave of conquistadores, who were poorly rewarded for their victories, anyway. There was nothing in the Yucatán to sack. The only possible fountain of wealth in the peninsula was the labor power of its natives, and because they were not centrally organized, they were difficult to vanquish. Even after the Conquest, the Yucatán's isolation and climate kept it on the fringe of Spanish and Mexican life. The area didn't join Mexico until two days before the War of Independence was won, and twice afterward it seceded. Until the Cuban Revolution, the Peninsula's commercial ties were more with Havana than with Mexico City, because no road led from the Mexican interior to the Yucatán, and Cuba was closer by sea.

The Yucatán has always been reluctant to Westernize. The confusion of Oaxaca, where towns have at least two names, doesn't exist on the peninsula. The state of Yucatán, for example, has 106 municipalities, only seven of which have been given Spanish names. Nor do Maya individuals adopt Spanish surnames, as have indigenes elsewhere in Mexico. By the usual standards of measure, the area's Mayan majority has been oppressed. The first Maya-speaking governor of the state of Yucatán, a founder of the Socialist party of the Southeast and a tribune of the Indian caste, Felipe Carillo Puerto, was executed in a local military coup in 1924, only a year after he'd taken office. No Mayan-surnamed governors were named in Yucatán until 1970, nearly fifty years later. Today's Mayan-speaking population, half or more of the total, remains isolated from modern life in small towns and in the countryside. Henry Kissinger says that the "objective conditions" for revolution exist in the peninsula, as much as in its neighboring Central American states, and a CIA report leaked in 1988 postulated that stability in the area depended upon the success of Mexico's dubious programs of agrarian reform. But agrarian reform hasn't been a problem in the Yucatán since the forties, when the henequen plantations faded away. The peninsula has plenty of idle land, waiting for machetes to clear it. If the Maya revolt anytime soon, it will be in defense of the culture that their forebears bequeathed.

The ruin we'd come to see, Santa Rosa Xtampak, was first described in 1842 by the adventurers John L. Stephens and Frederick Catherwood in a two-volume work called *Incidents of Travel in Yucatán*. The two travelers visited some forty-four lost or forgotten ruins, and gave the world its first broad picture of Mayan civilization. Stephens was an American writer, thirty-five years old in October 1841, when he and Catherwood set sail in New York for the Yucatán Peninsula, aboard a freighter loaded with cotton, gunpowder, and turpentine. Catherwood was a British illustrator and pioneer photographer, then in his forties. For six months, the pair battled ticks, mosquitoes and fleas, malaria, and other fevers, while taking notes and making drawings and daguerreotypes of contemporary Mayan life and ancient ruins. They visited some forty-four lost or forgotten Mayan sites, including all those that have become tourist spots today: Chichén Itzá, Palenque, Uxmal, Cancún, Cobá, Kabáh, Palenque, and Tulum. They had become heroes to Vicente and me about two months earlier, nearly as soon as we'd read their book. They were our heroes not only for the work that they'd done, but also because they had survived the Yucatán. We'd come to the Yucatán once before, and unlike Stephens and Catherwood, we'd been turned away. Tropical afflictions had sent us running for home.

We'd paused in Ticúl on our first visit. Ticúl is a market town of some thirty thousand about fifty miles south of Mérida, the capital of the state. It is a charming place. As in most towns on the peninsula, motorbikes outnumber cars. Bicycles outnumber motorbikes. Pedestrians outnumber people using any form of transporation. Life moves slowly, at a salutory or "Good Morning" pace. We found that if you ask for a taxi in Ticúl, you'll be directed to a pickup with a canopied bed and wooden benches. Ticul's "taxis" go to Mérida, not from street to street. If you merely want to go across town, you hire a *triciclo*, or tricycle, a three-wheeled pedal-cart, complete with chauffeur. It costs about fifty cents an hour. While I was sitting in a restaurant for supper, a group of townsmen passed on the main street. They were skipping and singing and dancing. Their leader, a potbellied man, carried a basket atop his head. Protruding from it was the snout of a pig. "What's going on here?" I asked a waitress. She thought a minute, as if to say, "Why, don't you know?," then explained that the procession was an invitation of a kind. Somebody was having a party. The pig's head announced that there would be food to eat.

I didn't go to the party. Two other things were on my mind. The first was a test of Ticúl's unchangedness. One night Stephens had watched the locals gamble at a game called Lotería on the porch of the town's city hall, facing its central plaza. When darkness came, I went off in that direction, as if to keep an appointment with him, 150 years late. A group of people were gathered on the porch, men in straw hats and women in the white *huipiles* that are the region's native dress. They stood facing a long table on which colored playing cards were spread. Pictures of common objects and mythical creatures—a frog, an arrow, a mermaid, for example—were printed on the cards. A man stood on the other side of the table, just above a wheel on which similar images were pasted. People placed coins on the cards, the man spun the wheel and then stuck a knitting needle into its surface; those who had bet on the pierced image were winners of the round. It was the same game that Stephens had played. I placed two bets, one for him and one for Catherwood, and waited for the wheel to spin. I lost my stake. I probably should have taken that as a warning to leave town.

Bad luck was coming, because of bad bugs. That was the second matter on my mind. We'd been in the Yucatán for only two days, but mosquitoes don't know what "welcome" means. That afternoon, one of Vicente's eyeballs had begun to streak in red. We knew what to fear, an epidemic called hemorrhagic conjunctivitis. It inflames the eyes, impairs vision, and, because cold symptoms come with it, imparts misery to life. Mosquitoes spread it, and so does contact. Conjunctivitis lasts only four to eight days, but it's not the kind of passing ailment that any photographer can like. Before turning in at our hotel, I'd stopped by Vicente's room to check on his health. One corner of the affected eye looked as if it had been dabbed with red paint.

My wife, Miriam, had made the trip with me. When we arose the next morning, Vicente decided to stay in Ticúl until the hour when doctors' offices opened. Miriam and I decided to see Santa Rosa Xtampak. We had no precise directions, just the words of an American archeologist we'd met at Chichén Itzá the day before: "Take the first white road south of Bolonchén, and follow it until it ends." A "white" road, he'd told us, is a road that's been covered with caliche, safe for travel even when the ground is wet. We'd set off in my yellow Volkswagen for the village of Bolonchén, about an hour away.

We found the white road, about three miles south of Bolonchén. It was an uneven, rough, one-lane road, dwarfed and nearly hidden by the foliage at its sides. During a muddy spell, wheels had made ruts on the edges of the road, creating a midmargin hump that at places scraped the bottom of my Beetle. But the drive was a pleasure. Yellow, white, and green butterflies gathered by the dozens in spots of the road, and showered our car like confetti when we passed. Once or twice, when I stopped to inspect worn or washed-out sections of the roadbed, we heard birds singing in the silence. No people or any signs of habitation were nearby, and on only one stretch did we see any fields. Most of the terrain was jungle, unimproved. We came to a large tree that grew in the middle of the road, which went around it on one side. The tree, we later calculated, was a halfway point. The distance we traveled before the road's end wasn't much, about nineteen miles. But not until Vicente and I made our return would I learn just how long even half that distance could be. Driving it had taken us ninety minutes.

Near the end of the road, we came upon two men. They were on top of a *palapa*, or palm hut, thatching its roof. The hut was nothing more than posts and roof. No sides had been erected yet. I got out of the car to ask further directions to the ruin. The two men climbed down to take a look at me. One was a hatless, thin, and tall older man, with very dark skin and gray hair. If he spoke, his voice was so low that I didn't hear it. The other man was short, square, and stout. He wore a straw hat, and there was sweat on his brow. He was younger, about forty. He pointed toward the end of the road and told me that when I got there, I should turn right, not left, drive to the road's dead end, and walk toward a hill. He said that if I could find the trail, the ruins weren't far away. I thought about snakes and about the instructions he'd given, which weren't as simple as I'd have liked. "The only thing is," he said, "the guard isn't there right now." I thought about meeting policemen on my way out of the ruin, and it occurred to me that having a local man in tow might be good insurance against all kinds of things. He agreed to accompany us, and said so long to the older man—his father, it turned out—in a language that I didn't understand. When he was seated in the car, he introduced himself. He was Heliodoro Huchín Cauich—naturally, a Mayan. His ancestors built Xtampak.

As we drove toward the ruin, Helidoro told us about himself. He is a native of Bolonchén, but his father had been born near the *palapa* where I'd found them working that day. The surrounding area was several years ago granted to them and other families as an *ejido*. But most of the *ejidatarios* had abandoned the settlement because for the second year in a row there hadn't been enough rain. There were no wells, either: No rain meant no water to drink. Heliodoro swore that the puddles that I'd seen were recent, the product of a storm yesterday. The rains might begin, he allowed, but he complained that it was probably too late to sprout the grains of corn that he'd planted back in May and June. "How much corn have you got saved up at your house?" I asked him. "About a year's supply," he said. I found myself thinking that although a peasant's life is rough, not many urbanites have a year's survival in the bank.

The hill we climbed was steep, and the ascent was without any visual reward. The jungle was so thick that we couldn't see below. Trees, vines, and shrubs blocked every possible view. At one point during the climb, Heliodoro stopped, held aside some vines, and asked us to step off the path. When we'd done so, he showed us a white hole in the ground. It was like a bottle, made of limestone. A material that looked like soft concrete covered the ground for about a foot around the opening of the hole, whose purpose was obviously to store runoff water. I looked down into it; it was dry. "This must be a *cenote*," I said, trying to show what I'd learned from books. "No," Heliodoro said, "*cenotes* are formed when underground limestone collapses, making a big hole. This is a *chultún*. *Chultunes* are man-made." He sounded like an archaeologist, not a peasant. "How do you know?" I asked. "Well, I try to keep up," he said. "Last year I attended the First World Congress of Mayanists." After he said that, our conversation moved to a different level.

Heliodoro reminded me of another man I'd met. About six months earlier, Miriam and I had visited a set of ruins at an out-of-the-way location in the western state of Michoacán. Only two other people were at the site, a young Mexican archaeology student who'd been hired to guard it, and a sandaled peasant about sixty years old. When we had arrived, they'd been discussing an archaeological monograph that the peasant had brought. He showed us a fragment of a clay idol he'd found at his home, about a mile away. "Will you sell it?" Miriam asked, not because she really wanted to buy but because the man's motives were of interest to her. He declined. Then he showed her the journal he'd been reading. "Why are you reading this?" she asked. "Because," the old peasant said, "I was born near here. I want to know who I am."

Heliodoro had made a similar passage. He'd grown up wanting to leave Bolonchén, and he'd gotten as far as the city of Campeche, where his wife and school-age children live today. But he'd come back home to help found the *ejido*, and his interest in Mayanism had grown like the vines. He spent his spare hours studying, but his studies were woefully incomplete. For one thing, he hadn't been able to learn how to count past ten in his native tongue; everybody used Spanish words. In Juchitán, I'd noticed the same thing. Numbers above twenty are counted in Spanish there. Heliodoro's current campaign,

265

he told me, was trying to persuade the government to open Santa Rosa Xtampak as a tourist site. Besides having a cultural interest, Heliodoro figured that restoration of the ruins would provide jobs to him and his fellow *ejidatarios* during spells when the rains failed. But as Heliodoro knew, half the people in Mexico are trying to convince the government to restore a ruin, and the competition is tough.

Mexico is among other things a country of ruins grander and more numerous than anybody but a handful of specialists suspect. According to its Instituto Nacional de Antropología y Historia, Mexico has more than eight thousand pre-Columbian archeological sites. Fewer than 150 of them are open to the public. The others are unadvertised, unmapped, and secret. A few, like the Yucatán's fabled Oxpemul, haven't been seen in more than a hundred years. They're lost in the jungle, because the explorers who found them were lost themselves. Archaeologists who know the location of an unadvertised ruin do not disclose their information freely, because looters are waiting to hear. They also don't think that finding ruins is nearly as difficult, or nearly so important, as raising the funds to explore them. "Get me a helicopter, put me down anywhere in this jungle, and in a day or two I'll find you a ruin," one of them told me. What he said sounded like a boast, but it probably wasn't. There are some eight hundred unexcavated Mayan cities in the state of Quintana Roo alone, and new finds are made every year, across southern Mexico. When the Mexican Department of Tourism began clearing land to develop the new resort at Huatulco, INAH's archaeologists gave out a scream. Nobody else knew, but there were 180 pyramids in the area where hotels and an airport were being planned. In early 1988, bridge-construction crews in Mexico City unearthed a sculptured ceremonial stone, ten feet in diameter. On May 12, the blades of bulldozers working on a road-construction project near Chilpancingo, in the state of Guerrero, struck the peaks of five pyramids. A month later, men who were digging a cistern in Chilpancingo struck an ancient tomb. A newspaper reported the find of "a false arch, commonly known as a Mayan arch, that was built with limestone and with an entrance on the west. In it, in addition to human remains, were found a

decorative vase and other objects, most of which were spirited away by the workmen."

Miriam and I had been struck by archaeology almost the moment that we set eyes on a peculiar figurine in Xalapa's archaeology museum. It was a small image of baked clay, about four inches long and four inches wide, made in the shape of a jaguar. Four wheels were attached to the jaguar's feet, as if it were a toy. About a dozen of these figures are known to exist, and they're regarded as important because they exemplify pre-Hispanic Mexico's only use of the wheel. But they're probably not toys, the archaeologists say. The jaguar was a symbol of the underworld, where the dead lived, and the wheeled jaguars were found in the tombs of adults. The figure that caught our eyes was a relic of the Totonac civilization, which rose and fell in the state of Veracruz, and it carried a label saying that it had been found at a place called Nopiloa. But when I asked museum curators and archaeologists for Nopiloa's location, no one would say. Though Miriam and I understood the reasons for their noncooperation, that didn't stop us from wanting to see the site from which the relic came.

So we did what the grave-robbers do. We searched detailed topographic maps of the state until we found a location with Nopiloa's name. It was near a town called Joachín. Though only dirt roads ran to Joachín, we loaded my Volkswagen and set off. When we got to Joachín, we asked about the ruins. Nobody knew anything. But they pointed us toward Nopiloa, and we continued the trip. The topographical map didn't show nearly as many roads as we passed; it was out of date. But after a while we came to a crossroads where two palm-thatched buildings were set. One of them was apparently a country store. Several men were sipping soft drinks outside. "Where is Nopiloa?" I asked them. "This is Nopiloa," one of the men chuckled, gesturing in a semicircle. I looked around, but only sugarcane fields were to be seen. "Well, where are the ruins?" I asked. The men seemed not to understand. "I'm looking for pyramids," I explained. The men laughed. "There is nothing like that in this poor farm country. Boy, you must be way off track," they said. "Are there any hills nearby?" I insisted. They gestured in the direction that lay behind the store, and we resumed our trip.

About a mile down the road, a chain of hills came in view. As we approached them, it became clear that a couple of them were sharply inclined. I got out of the car and looked. A palm tree stood at a peak of one of the hills. It's probably just legend, but people have told me that the pre-Hispanics planted palms atop their pyramids, and that the descendants of those trees have sometimes survived until this day. We drove until we came to a peasant's hut, and I pulled up in front. A shirtless man was lying atop a *petate*, or straw mat, just outside the front door. I asked him about the hills. "Well, I don't think they're pyramids," he said, "but some people from the university did come here, about two years ago. They took away a big stone frog that had always been here. The first machine they brought wasn't big enough to lift it, because the thing weighed twenty tons." I'd seen the frog he talked about—actually, the image of a mythical creature resembling a turtle—in a courtyard of the Xalapa museum. We had found the archaeological Nopiloa, and all that remained was a look at close range.

The peasant accompanied us, and we scaled several of the mounds. We climbed one after another, until Miriam's strength flagged and my lungs gave out. They were not hills, I was sure. But there was no obvious proof that they were pyramids, either. Their sides were covered with nothing but dirt and weeds. No cut stones, no signature of human workmanship was at hand. Except for one clue: several rectangular, casket-sized depressions in the ground at the base of one of the mounds. "Somebody has been digging here," I told our guide. "Yes, a few months ago people came at night," he said. The relic-looters apparently were also on Nopiloa's trail. That afternoon I left the ruins disappointed at the mounds that we'd found, but convinced that there were pyramids underneath. I kept telling myself that God didn't make hills that steep.

Two months later, in a private collection, I located an old archaeological report; in Mexico, finding old books is no mean feat because public libraries are poorly stocked and few. The report said that in April 1957 federal policemen had arrested some men whom they'd found in possession of pre-Hispanic artifacts, which, by law, are all property of the government. The men had taken them from Nopiloa, a site that until then the archaeologists had not touched. To discourage further looting, archaeologists spent about eighteen months at the site, mainly digging at the base of its mounds, where burials were often made. They struck stone foundations at one mound, and kept digging until they struck foundations again. Many of the pre-Hispanic peoples for religious reasons destroyed all their possessions every fifty-two years, when the end of a celestial cycle was thought to occur. They did not level their pyramids at these times, but instead constructed new ones above the old. Nopiloa had been built twice. The archaeologists of the fifties had not excavated all of it—that's why the looters were coming back—and nothing promised that the pyramids on which I'd trod would ever see sunlight. The experience had dulled my desire for unrestored ruins, and when I'd been told about Xtampak, I'd made it clear that I wasn't going to climb sandhills again. "Don't worry," the American archaeologist had told us, "there's a three-story building in Chenes architectural style, perfectly exposed to view." Stephens had seen the place, and he said that it was "the grandest structure that now rears its ruined head in the forests of Yucatán."

After seeing the *chultún*, Heliodoro, Miriam, and I climbed a few minutes more until we reached a plateau that, I suspect, had been created by human labor. We were at the top of a hill, and the surface before us was as flat as a parking lot. Vines hung down from trees, and thin tree trunks stood in the way, but almost immediately we came upon a huge white limestone building, so big that we couldn't see all of it from where we stood. We approached it slowly. Its three stories were stacked so that each succeeding level was narrower than the one at its base, leaving room for a terrace or walkway around both of the higher stories. Trees had grown onto the terraces, and the action of their roots had sent cascades of building stones and dirt sliding down the walls. At two or three places, the landslides had covered the probable locations of doorways, and from the ground it was possible to ascend to the second story by scaling the rubble alone. Other trees had planted their roots in the rubble, and vines hung down over it all. I scanned the building before me and my memory of the drawing that Catherwood had made for *Incidents of Travel*, and I found the smooth panels above and between the ground floor doors, panels that even before his visit had lost or been stripped of their monstrous stone embellishments; a feature of Chenes architecture had been door openings decorated to look like the mouths of snakes. We were looking at the building from its west side, the side that Catherwood had drawn. I walked to the right or south side of the building, to be sure of its size. It was fifty yards long!

Heliodoro led us to the building's south face, which I estimated to be about twenty-five yards wide. Landslides had seriously affected it. We had to climb over grapefruit-sized rocks to reach the entrance of two rooms, but we didn't go inside.

Between the two rooms were two smooth panels, and in the rubble below, Heliodoro turned over two large stones, each about as big as a block of ice. Their sides bore pictographs, though we couldn't determine what images they outlined. These stones were all that remained of two pictorial panels that Stephens and Catherwood had seen and copied; they, too, had been unable to make sense of their designs.

We returned to the building's west side, and Heliodoro led us up to an entrance. A beam of wood ran across the top of its door. It was plastered into the masonry at both its extremes. The beam was dry and weathered, but despite its thousand years of abandonment, it showed only a few insect holes, probably because it had been hewn from a resin-rich *chicozapote* tree, the kind of tree from which chewing gum, originally a Mexican concoction, was once made. We stepped into the room. Its floor was covered with plaster or limestone dust. Its ceiling formed a corbeled or Mayan arch. Its walls were bare, showing only the joints between its square-cut stones. This room led through a doorway to a similar but smaller room, on whose eastern side a narrow stone stairway opened. We were preparing to ascend to the second story when we noticed a problem: A wasp's nest hung from the roof, just above our path. Heliodoro went outside, picked up a dried palm leaf, and brought it to me. I set it on fire with my cigarette lighter. He fanned with his hat until the leaf became a torch, and then he walked beneath the nest, raised his arm, and singed the wasps until they fell to the floor. We stomped on them until they were dead. Then Heliodoro reached up to the nest, pulled it down, and stuck it in his shirt pocket. I couldn't imagine why he'd do that.

We began ascending the stairs. As we rose, we passed through a space of total darkness; the staircase made a 180-degree twist. It delivered us to the second-floor terrace, facing west. By another stairway, we reached the terrace of the third floor, where, holding onto vines and bracing ourselves against trees, we made our way around the north edge of the building, to the eastern or front side. There we descended to the second story for a look at indecipherable legends carved onto two stone towers, one on each side of a great exterior stairway, ten yards wide. Picking our way up the remaining sections of its steps, we eased across the third floor, stopping to enter and view several rooms as we went. The floor of one of the arched rooms, about 10′ × 15′ in size, was covered with fruit seeds about as big as my thumb. "Who's been using this place for storage?" I asked Heliodoro. "No, those seeds were brought here by the bats who lived in this room until about a year ago," he said. In each of the rooms we entered, a hole about a foot wide had been dug in a corner. Dirt from the diggings formed mounds around the holes. The holes were filled with rocks. I couldn't tell how deep they had been. Heliodoro said that the holes had been dug by grave-robbers, looking for gold or relics. I wondered what they had found, and was startled to realize that we live in a world where we can be mugged a thousand years after our deaths.

At the northwest corner, by handholds and footwork, Heliodoro and I climbed onto the building's flat roof. From there, sixty feet above the ground, I could see the horizon line. Heliodoro pointed off to some hills in the distance. "There is another set of ruins over there," he said. But from the mounds that I could see surrounding us, each one probably concealing a building or pyramid, I knew that I'd never have time to explore all of Xtampak, let alone the ruins in the distance. At the moment, I was also more curious about something else: "Heliodoro," I asked, "what are you going to do with that wasps' nest?" "Why, I'm going to eat it," he told me. He explained that he'd fry the nest in cooking oil, remove its larvae, and mix them with salt, onions, and peppers. "It will make a good snack," he said. Santa Rosa Xtampak is a part of Mayaland, where the mysteries of the present rival those of the distant past.

After we climbed down, Heliodoro accompanied me as I scaled a nearby *montículo,* or mound, mainly because I wanted to see if it was a mere hill or hid a pyramid. I wasn't impressed. It wasn't nearly so steep as the mounds at Nopiloa, and in its rubble I found nothing that revealed human workmanship. The mound was but a pile of rounded stones, none with square-cut or finished faces. The problem, I decided, was that the pre-Hispanics didn't build their pyramids as I would have liked them to. They had substructures of dirt, faced with stones; they were not all-stone buildings. The millenium that has passed since Xtampak's abandonment had created a rubble of dirt and rocks whose original relationships are no longer apparent. I found myself thinking that perhaps Xtampak, like Humpty Dumpty, couldn't be put back together again.

Just for good measure, I scaled a second mound. As I rounded its northern edge, about thirty feet aboveground I saw a corbeled arch, rising six feet above the debris. I climbed on rocks and vines until I came face-to-face with it. It enclosed a room whose walls were visible for nearly three feet beneath. The room was filled with rubble, and in a way, I was glad. Whatever treasure it contained had not yet been spirited away.

Mayan Arch

It would take a couple of days to empty the room, and relic-robbers, from what I can gather, do not undertake laborious projects. Xtampak still had vaults of history waiting to be opened. Maybe, I told myself, someday one would reveal the mystery of the Mayas.

Xtampak had not been a city. Nor was Chichén Itzá, Palenque, Uxmal, or any of the other known Mayan ruins. The agriculture of the time discouraged the rise of cities. Typically, the Maya cleared a section of jungle and cultivated it in corn for three years, until its poor soil gave out. They'd then let it return to the jungle for about twenty years. This slash-and-burn agriculture required each tiller to have access to about six times as much land as he seeded in any year. The Maya population was therefore sparsely distributed, and it still is today. For religious purposes, the Mayas established centers like Xtampak, which tillers visited at ceremonial times. Priests and their servants inhabited them. This essentially ceremonial class lived on tithes or tributes. Its buildings were probably raised by men whose labor was drafted, as in Macuiltianguis, by a *tequio* or *cargo* system. In places like Xtampak, archaeologists have found idols and altars that were pulled from their moorings, hurled to the ground, and sometimes buried. The Spanish did such things when they came to Mexico, but the Mayan centers were abandoned long before the Spanish came. Some archaeologists suspect that Mayan civilization was ended by a tillers' revolt. Tired of supporting a pompous and parasitic priestly class, the tillers did away with them and continued a simple form of worship on their own.

After ousting their priestly class, the Mayas lived without a central government for about a hundred years, until they were invaded and conquered, about A.D. 1000, by a people believed to have been the Toltecs of central Mexico.

The new rulers of the Maya were militarists who established their seat at the former ceremonial city of Chichén Itzá. The city's original inhabitants had been ruler-priests, but they had been more priestly than rulerly. The buildings they left were, like Xtampak, composed of small rooms, divided so that one section, usually a mere cubicle, received little light: The presumption is that the cubicles were for meditation. The new rulers constructed buildings whose signature was the conference room, the architectural stamp of committee society, of a collective ruled by small groups or elites.

The Maya did not like the new order any more than that of their own priests, and about the year 1200 they overthrew the Toltecs and their exotic gods like Quetzalcóatl, the Plumed Serpent, king and god. Leaders of the revolt established a dynasty at Mayapán, which received support from the Mexica or Aztecs. But the Mayapán rulers, too, were ousted by the Mayas about 1450. For a second hundred years, they lived an apparently contented, stateless life, until the Spanish came. In 1761, they rose against colonialism under the leadership of Jacinto de las Santos Uc, who called himself Jacinto Canek, in honor of a previous rebel. The Spaniards quickly captured Canek and Cistel, his headquarters town. They took Canek to Mérida, and in a ceremony on its main square, with pincers pulled the flesh off his living bones. Cistel was plowed in salt, and ceased to exist.

Mexican rule wasn't much kinder. During his stay on a *hacienda*, Stephens recorded the following scene:

> Early one morning we were wakened by the sound of music from the church. The priest was imparting the benefits of his chance visit by celebrating a mass. A little later we heard a different kind of music. It was the lashes of a whip upon an Indian's back. At each blow, despite the efforts he made to control himself, he let out a little cry. His whole expression showed submission and with the final lash, his face seemed to give thanks that he'd not received more. Without saying a word, he crawled over to the overseer, taking his hand, kissing it and then retiring. No evidence of disgust was shown on his face. These people who in their time were so fierce are today so certainly humbled that they have a proverb among themselves: "Indians don't hear except through the buttocks."

Less than one hundred years after the Canek revolt, the Maya rose against the Mexican Republic. The new rising, called the War of the Castes, was probably the most bitter conflict in Mexico's modern history. In 1846, Maya tillers marched on peninsular towns, murdering all their white and *mestizo* inhabitants, including children and the aged. Their revolt coincided with the American invasion of northern and central Mexico and our blockade of the port of Veracruz, by which the Mexican government had communicated with the Yucatán. Unable to get military supplies from Mexico, Yucatán's governors futilely offered sovereignty of the peninsula to both Spain and the United States. So alarming was the situation that the Church offered to sell all its possessions to help buy guns! Not until 1848 was Mexico able to send arms, and by then all of the peninsula except a narrow strip along the northwestern coast and the city of Mérida was under Maya control—and Mérida was under siege. But as the troops of Emiliano Zapata would do during the Revolution of 1910, in June the army of tillers took a break: It was planting time back on the *milpas*. Federal forces moved in and secured Mérida, and as they took captives, they sold them into slavery. Not until 1902 would the whole of the peninsula return to Mexican control. The War of the Castes, the rebellion against Mayapán, and the original destruction of the priestly class that ruled in cities like Xtampak form a pattern, confirmed over the centuries. The pattern is that of an agrarian people determined to reclaim independence and local rule.

After viewing the ruins of Xtampak a first time, Miriam and I returned to Ticúl to check on Vicente and his diagnosis. He'd seen two doctors. The first had told him that nothing could be done for his condition. The second had prescribed eyedrops and an antiviral tablet. Vicente's affected eye was blood red, but since one eye was still clear, he decided to take a look at Xtampak. Rain poured on us as we again drove the nineteen-mile white road. By the time we reached the ruin, clouds had shut out most sunlight, and dusk was coming in. Vicente wanted to try to shoot pictures at daybreak, but I didn't want to put my car through the punishment of the white road again. We consulted Heliodoro, who offered us his new *palapa* for the night. He brought us two matrimonial-size hammocks, and built a fire of corncobs and dry wood. The smoke kept mosquitoes away, and Miriam and I slept well. Vicente was in pain.

Whenever he moved his eyes, he felt as if there were sand under the lid of the afflicted one. And as we'd all noticed, his other eye was beginning to streak red. When morning came, he could barely see.

We visited the ruin for only a few minutes, but as we were leaving, I glanced down at my shoes. They were covered with a half-sticky red-brown clay. I looked at the area surrounding my feet, too. The rains had washed surface dirt away. The ground was scattered with pottery shards. They gleamed in the morning light. I examined several of them, slivers about an inch wide and three or four inches long. Most of them were about three-eighths of an inch thick. Their texture was coarse. One of the pieces was dark-stained at its lower end, as if its oven had burned too hot. I couldn't determine whether the pieces had been parts of pots or plates or cups, or perhaps of ceremonial objects. But my hands nearly trembled. I am an American. I had never found anything, however insignificant, that was a thousand years old. In the United States, we believe that history began when Captain John Smith established a colony in 1619, and our countryside doesn't present us with much evidence that that isn't the case. Like most Americans, I was accustomed to thinking in a historically insignificant time frame.

After visiting the ruins that morning, we had fled to a luxury hotel in Chetumal, on Quintana Roo's border with Belize. On our first morning there, all three of us awoke with bug bites on our legs and torsos. I took mine for chigger bites, and paid them no mind. Vicente did much the same. But one of Miriam's legs was so swollen that she couldn't bend her knee. We applied the usual remedy, calamine, and waited another night. Again we arose with bites. Our conclusion was that the hotel's carpeting was infested, and Miriam and I moved to a tile-floored room. No new bites appeared immediately, and as soon as we could, the three of us left, this time for Xalapa. For the next four months, Miriam periodically awoke with a new outbreak of stings. Four dermatologists and one general practitioner examined her, each offering a different diagnosis and cure. None worked. We tried cattle dips and a remedy for humans based on poisonous and caustic lindane; nothing worked. Ramón advised us to soak tobacco in alcohol, and to rub the resulting solution on the bites. That, too, failed. Miriam did not accompany Vincente and me on our return, because she'd had enough of the Yucatán.

Vicente sped down the white road, about twenty-five miles per hour. We came to the tree at midpoint, and just beyond, to a stand of Johnson grass that rose above the roof of the car, a sure sign that no vehicle had passed by in a few weeks' time. But a light rain had begun to fall, and we were hurried lest we get rained out again. About a mile beyond the tree, Vicente hit a bump in the road. The Volkswagen veered over to the side of the road and stuck. Vicente opened his door and stepped out. His leg sank knee-deep in a white bog. We'd hit a wallow of quicksand. Hurricane Gilbert had passed since we'd first come down this road, and its rains had turned the countryside to mud. And mosquitoes. The repellant we had brought kept them from lighting on us, but they still buzzed by. We fanned ourselves frantically as we tried to devise a means of escape. But nothing worked. We couldn't mount the jack because its mount on the underside of the rented car—I'd left my own Volkswagen at home—had been bent out of shape. In a desperate and unwise attempt to give us a chance, I let the air out of the passenger side's rear tire, hoping to gain traction that way. When that measure failed, I set out walking in the rain. By my reckoning, we couldn't have been more than seven or eight miles from Heliodoro's house. I figured that I could return to Vicente and the car in about three hours.

As I walked, the rain washed the mosquito repellant away. I became the object of whole swarms of the pests. I smoked until all my cigarettes were gone, hoping the stink would repel them. Then I adopted a bovine defense. Picking up a palm leaf, I flayed it back and forth, around and around, imitating the action of a cow's tail. It seemed to work. I kept walking. The terrain around me was uncultivated land, all jungle, and in places at roadside, it formed a marsh. Stagnant water stood six inches to perhaps three feet deep. From time to time, my presence disturbed animals I could not see but could hear as they ran. At one point, I heard a crash as loud as a person would make, entering or leaving the thicket. I looked toward the jungle from where it had come, fearing for my own safety. I saw nothing but could hear the sounds of a large creature swimming in the marshlands just beyond. No human being would swim there, but the jungle is thick with javelina, or wild pigs.

After about two hours of walking, I sighted a man on horseback. When he drew near, I noticed that he was riding a mule, not a horse. He wore sandals and cotton pants, a raggedy cotton shirt, and a straw hat. A narrow-gauge shotgun was strapped on his back; peasants in Yucatán carry arms as men in Macuiltianguis once did. The man told me that he was looking for a dry entrance to his *milpa*, and he pointed toward it, back down the road. He hadn't visited the plot, he said, in about a month. It had been too wet to get in. He also said that Heliodoro had gone to Campeche to talk to archaeologists about damage that Xtampak had suffered in the hurricane. But he assured me that if I kept walking I'd reach the *palapa* where Heliodoro's father lived, and he promised me that after looking at his *milpa*, he'd join in helping dislodge the Volkswagen. "How far is it to Heliodoro's place?" I asked the peasant. He shook his head from side to side, the way people do when they have bad news to break. "It's a long way," he said.

A little further down the road, I came to a smooth stretch of land, the site of the *ejido*'s *milpas*. Though the sun was going down, I could see corn plants standing in the fields to my right. Between me and them was a swamp at least twelve inches deep. Its water was discolored. A brown substance seemed to seep in from its bottom, where plants were decaying. Tadpoles swam in the water, and I was sure that mosquito larvae lived there, too. I kept fanning and kept walking. The road almost disappeared at my feet. Weeds had covered its surface from side to side, and some of them were tall enough to reach my shoulders. Soon I was able to pick out the road's course only by its reflection of the fading light. Its white surface led me on.

It was fully dark when I stumbled into Heliodoro's yard. A dim light was shining from within, probably from the fire of a hearth. Since Heliodoro's father might be startled, and might be armed, I decided not to go hunting for the hut's door. Instead, I hollered in a loud voice, "Hello! Hello! *¡Bueno! ¡Bueno!*"

And then, in that same voice, I began explaining my circum-stances. It occurred to me that I might be shouting in vain: I didn't know whether Heliodoro's father understood Spanish or not. About a minute after I'd finished my speech, he emerged from the hut, bent and slow-moving. When he reached me, he explained in his Mayan accent—a flat accent, similar to that of English-speakers—that he couldn't be of much help. But he stood with me at roadside while we waited for the mounted man to come.

It was now so dark that I couldn't see twenty feet in front of me. I decided that I wasn't going back to the car until I knew where the mounted man was. He might be hiding in the bush, waiting for me to pass on my return; he had a gun and might rob me. In a flash, it also occurred to me that if the Mayas wanted to resume their War of the Castes, Vicente and I would make ideal victims, for there would be no non-Mayan witnesses to our fate. After I'd fretted an appropriate time, two figures appeared out of the darkness, both mounted on mules. One was the man I'd met back near his *milpa*. The other was Teodoro Huchín, a cousin of Heliodoro, about twenty years old. The three men began to converse in Maya. I offered to pay if they'd help pull the Volkswagen out of the bog. I heard Heliodoro's father say the numbers "eight, nine, ten, eleven, twelve" in Spanish, and he mentioned Bolonchén. From what I could sur-mise, the two mounted men wanted to know how long it would take them to reach the village if they left the *ejido* to help me. Then all three of them dispersed, leaving me in the road alone.

I cursed myself for not having moved to Mexico when I was younger, to learn Maya and Zapotec and Náhuatl and the other languages of rural life. After a few minutes, Teodoro appeared on foot. He went into the old man's hut, then came out carrying a torch. He passed by me, silently smiling in the light of its flames. Then he returned to the shadows of another hut, about fifty yards away. A few minutes later, he came out, leading two mules. The mounted man from the *milpa* appeared on his mule, too. Teodoro told me to mount the spare beast, which he called a *caballo*, or horse. I climbed atop it. My saddle was a stack of two or three burlap bags. The man from the *milpa*, whose name was Salvador, took the lead. I rode in the middle,

280

with Teodoro close behind. None of us could see a thing, but the mules knew where to go. The ride was bumpy, and my mule's backbone rubbed gratingly against my wet jeans.

From what I could make of the skyline, we were near the *milpa* when my mule bolted to the right in a gallop. Before I could halt him, we'd gone more than fifty yards down what seemed to be a dirt trail. A black silhouette in the shape of a *palapa* was in view. When Teodoro reached me, I asked him who lived in the *palapa*. "Nobody does. That's where we shell corn," he said. The mule had fond memories of the place because whenever he went there, he was well fed. Apparently, he had decided that with an unfamiliar rider astride, he might get away with stopping at the feeding trough. But the harvest was in peril, Teodoro said. My "horse," as he called it, had long ears and coarse hair and it stood not more than four feet from the ground, just like Teodoro's and Salvador's "horses." Several times I asked Teodoro questions about his "horses," and I learned, for example, that they weren't shod. They were mules, but Teodoro had apparently never learned that word in Spanish.

After about an hour and a half of riding, we came upon the Volkswagen. It had been six hours since I'd left. I was glad to dismount; the ride had worn the skin from a patch on my rear end, and I was oozing blood like hamburger meat. Vicente had passed the wait in ease: He had cigarettes, water, and a radio. Teodoro unsheathed his machete and felled a small tree. He and Salvador passed a rope through the Volkswagen's sunken wheel. They tied the rope to the tree trunk or limb. Using it as a lever, the three others pushed upward on the rope, until the Beetle cleared ground. I shoved huge rocks into the bog beneath the wheel. We repeated the process on the front wheel, which had sunk several inches into mud. I got inside the car, started it, and drove onto the dry part of the white road. We were out of the bog.

A representative for the rental-car agency had shown me the tools for changing a wheel, and since I'd let the air out of one tire, we needed them. I took the jack and the shiny new lug wrench from their place behind the seat, and, outside, laid them by the flat tire. But when I put the wrench onto the wheel lugs,

I found that the wrench was too big. It was the appropriate size—for a bigger car. "Jesus, this is Mexico!" I said in disgust. Vicente tried the lug wrench, to make sure that I hadn't panicked. "Yep, this is Mexico," he said, as exhausted and peeved as I was. We thanked the two Mayas for their assistance, got into the Volkswagen, and closed its doors for the night. It was hot, but we couldn't open the windows because we had used the last drops of our insect repellant. We somehow fell asleep, and when we awoke about daybreak, we found more than fifty mosquitoes inside the car. They'd entered through its ventilation system. The windshields were fogged with mosquitoes looking for a way to get in. I got out of the car and placed onto its scorching roof the damp clothes that I had changed before retiring. In case it rained again, I planned to have a dry change of clothes. I also began putting big rocks into muddy holes in the road. In case we ever got the flat fixed, I didn't plan to get stuck again.

About nine o'clock, a big truck pulled up behind us. Teodoro was inside. Its occupants had come to help us, with a jack. But we didn't need a jack, we needed a tire iron, and the one that they carried was like ours, of the wrong size. The truck's owner demanded an exorbitant fee for extending additional help— he'd found an opportunity to *chingar*—and we acceded. Vicente got into the truck, and the group of them headed back to Bolonchén. Three hours later, they returned with a bicycle pump, and in ten minutes we were ready to roll again. That's when the pickup came along.

The pickup was a red-brown Chevy, 1968 model. Its roof was rotting away. When the pickup moved, the roof flapped atop the doors, like a covering of canvas. But I trusted the pickup, because I'd seen it on the road before. It belonged to a former peasant from the state of San Luis Potosí. He'd been in the Bolonchén area, working as a mechanic on farm machines, when the *ejido* had been chartered, and though he spoke not a word of Maya, he had cast his lot with the Huchíns and their neighbors: Land has an overwhelming appeal to landless Mexicans of peasant extraction. The man from Potosí explained that he'd gone to Bolonchén to take refuge from the hurricane, and hadn't been able to return until that day. He was going to the *ejido,* and offered to take us along. We parked the Volkswagen and jumped inside the pickup's decrepit cab. Teodoro crawled into its bed, behind. Two other men, also *ejido* partners from the north, rode in the back with him.

When we got to the *milpas,* naturally the men wanted to see their crops. They removed their boots and shoes and waded off into the marsh. Teodoro went with them, also barefoot. They returned a few minutes later carrying samples of corn and peanuts. Only their bean crop had been drowned, and the three were in high spirits. They'd had better luck than the Huchíns, whose crops were nearly submerged. The pickup's owner took us to the ruins, and waited below for our return. He built a fire to keep the mosquitoes from biting while he waited.

While Vicente with Teodoro photographed the ruins, I looked for damage caused by the hurricane. It wasn't a pleasant job, because gnats were thick on the main building's two lower stories. Only the breeze at the top story drove them away. The force of the hurricane had uprooted trees from the building's terraces, and in their fall, some had unearthed stones. A corner of the second story on the south side had turned into a rubble below. Interiors had experienced collapses of a kind. Here and there, sections of wall had tumbled, leaving gaping holes, especially above doorway beams. Somebody—probably Heliodoro—had swept the dust into a corner, and stacked the fallen stones in heaps. The dislocations apparently unearthed fragments of various kinds, for in each room, I found a neat stack of pottery shards. Some of them were painted, and others bore the marks of impressions made in wet clay. As I looked over the destruction that Gilbert had wrought, I realized that all decisions about salvaging are made in a race against time. Neither we nor the ruins will be here always.

When we passed the *milpas* on our way back toward the Volkswagen, the pickup stopped again. Normally, Mexicans wait until corn has dried before bringing it in from the fields. But the Potosí men wanted to take corn on the cob back to Bolonchén. Teodoro stayed with Vicente and me. He was thirsty. The men from San Luis had brought plastic bottles full of water, but Teodoro did not ask to share. Instead, he sat on his haunches beside the fetid marsh, dipped his palms beneath

283

the water, and drank. Nothing I'd seen in months impressed me nearly so much. Teodoro is able to fend with the jungle. He and his kin would make marvelous, invincible soldiers. Had the rest of Mexico remained on the level of economic development that is the Yucatán, I realized, like another peasant country, Vietnam, Mexico would have been able to send its conquerors home.

Afterword

UNDERSTANDING Mexico is, in part, a job of self-understanding. There can be no objective standards for evaluating Mexico, because our appreciation of foreign countries depends upon our assessment of ourselves. The secret to Mexico lies not only in looking at Mexico's daily life and history, but in looking at our own as well.

Americans believe that the individual life is the highest good, and that life makes sense. We believe that we are the masters of our fate, that choice and effort set both men and nations apart. When we look back on our history, we conclude that individuals and nations can get what they want, if only they try.

We also put great stock in the competency of the mind. We tend to believe that for every problem there is a solution, that nothing is beyond human understanding or control. "Where there's a will, there's a way" is a truism with us. Because we value life and because we believe in ourselves, we have promised the world that someday we will vanquish heart disease, cancer, and mental illness. As a nation, we finance huge centers for medical research, and as individuals, we go on low-cholesterol diets, make a sacrament out of vitamins, and jog at every sunset and dawn.

Mexicans do not do any of these things, because they don't believe in them. They don't believe that life is fair, or that it makes any sense at all. They don't believe that the mind can grasp whatever is put before it, or that the human species can become the master of the universe. The enormous difference between Mexico's basic outlook and our own shows itself in the two cultures' attitudes toward suffering and death. Those Mexicans who have witnessed our efforts to protect and prolong our lives suspect that what we are really trying to do is cheat death. Even Mexican doctors take that attitude: Forty percent of them, for example, smoke cigarettes, while only 5 percent of American doctors do. When Mexican patients are told that they are terminally ill, they usually accept the news with steely stoicism. The usual response of Americans is disbelief and rage—what the medical community calls denial. The finality that we shun, Mexico embraces. Many Mexicans believe so fervently in an afterlife that in villages like Macuiltianguis, it is customary for the bereaved parents, on the night following the death of an infant, to host a dance in celebration of the child's ascension to heaven. Mexicans do not abhor and dread death, as we do, because for them death is a moment in an infinite web of time. But for us, all things must have a beginning and an end, and most things—including our civilization—are presumed to have but a brief past. Our belief in the power of newness is a trait that distinguishes us even from our Western kin.

Our national myth says that a little more than three hundred years ago, a group of oppressed Europeans came to the shores of what is today the United States, sorted through their heritage, cast out what was noxious, and began building anew with what was decent, democratic, and sane. The United States has always been a part of Western civilization, but not all that the West represents is necessarily a part of us, we say. The Conquest and the Nazi Holocaust, for example, are not events for which we accept blame. Europe perpetrated those crimes, not us. Americans are the innocents of the West because we were born again in the waters of the Atlantic that we crossed. We believe in that baptism and rebirth, just as fervently as the followers of Jim Bakker and Jimmy Swaggart believe that they've been born again. Like adolescents and the newly baptized, we look with optimism to the future, believing that we've cast off our past.

As individual Americans, we've almost all had friends or coworkers who have taken the evangelical route. They come to us bright-eyed with hopes for a new kind of life, abjuring old vices. They tell us that they are still a part of our world, but that not all of our world is still a part of them. They usually invite us to follow them on their path of "salvation," but we usually show reserve. We are reluctant, because we suspect that John will always be John or Jane will always be Jane. When a particularly notorious member of our community, porn publisher Larry Flynt, for example, professes "a new life in Christ," we react cynically, saying that leopards don't change their spots. We are cautious in judging individuals, shrewd and not easily carried away. Our daily lives have taught us that our skepticism is wise. As individuals, we know that not all new beginnings are real.

Mexico has been baptized, too. Its conversion was one of the cultural goals of the Westernizing that was its Conquest. In 1519, when Cortés dropped anchor off of Veracruz, there were no Christians in Mexico. Today, paganism is forgotten, and almost all Mexicans profess the One True Faith. When the Spaniards came, Mexicans spoke some 206 languages. Today, the nation of Mexico speaks a universal language, taught by the Conquest. Only fifty-six native tongues have survived the cultural holocaust, and their future is in doubt. When the Spaniards came, Mexico was a network of theocratic states. Today, it is home to a modern, secular nation. In 1519, there was no private property in Mexico. Today, communal ownership survives only on the *ejidos*. Mexico is a pagan convert to the ways of the West, and like any convert, it can claim to have begun a new life: Most of its leaders make that claim.

For Americans, new birth on this continent was an act of self-realization. As we distanced ourselves from the evils we associated with Europe, we defined ourselves in a free and autonomous way. For us, the experience of the New World

287

was liberating. Our conversion may or may not have transformed us, but we went to our baptism in good faith. We
despised the inequity of Europe, and we sincerely wanted to
change.

Nothing like that happened in Mexico. It was subjected to
the inequities of Europe, and rather than being given a chance
to define itself, it was forced to negate its own soul. For Mexicans, the meeting of Europe and the Americas was tragic, not
liberating, because it brought Mexico's independence to an end.
Mexico's profession of a new faith was exacted by torture, and
though all of Mexico has been converted, not all of Mexico's
conversions are sincere. In the depths of their lifeways, most
ordinary Mexicans preserve much of their pre-Hispanic, Indo-
American outlook and sentiment. Like Moctezuma, they look
upon modern industrial life—the lifestyle created in Europe—
and feel death in their hearts.

To ask, "What makes Mexico work?" is not the same as to
ask, "What makes America work?" because the United States
lives on a single plane, that of Western civilization. Our god is
material progress, and we've chosen that faith for ourselves.
But Mexico lives on two planes, that of Western or Euro-
American civilization, and that of Indo-American civilization,
its own. It leads two lives, one of them imposing and hypocritical, the other oppressed and sincere. To ask, "What makes
Mexico work?" in official circles is to ask questions that can be
answered in the accustomed way, in the way that we would
answer questions about the relationship of oil to Texas, for
example. Our academics and our newspapers are full of answers. They tell us about Mexico's foreign debt, about oil prices,
balances of trade, currency shifts, and electoral campaigns. But
these reports speak only of the life of Westernized Mexico,
about the lives of Herminio Gómez, Manuel Clouthier, Carlos
Salinas, and even Cuauhtémoc Cárdenas. To ask Indo-American Mexico, "What makes Mexico work?" is to ask how the
oppressed culture survives. It is to ask the subordinate and
vanquished, "Brother, how do you deal with the bossman?"
and it is to ask, "Why do you put up with the bossman's jive?"
It is to ask Ramón and Rafa Pérez, Mary Otero, Doña Paz, and
the Huchíns—the majority of Mexicans—who live under the

dominance of Western civilization but nevertheless in the am-
biance of Indo-America, how they manage to keep their sanity.
The answers from this level are enlightening, because they
show us a Mexico that is not a mirror of ourselves.

Fatalism is the faith that sustains conquered Indo-America.
It is a realistic faith, because it stems not from some wish about
transformation by baptism, but from the record and experience
of history. Did Indo-America ask for the Conquest or Emperor
Maximilian? Did Mexico either start or win the Mexican-
American War? Did Mexico plant oil beneath its soil and con-
centrate the capital for exploiting it in consumer-country banks?
All of modernity, nationhood, Christianity, and capitalism were
imposed on Indo-America by the whip and sword. Mexico has
been the victim, not the maker of its modern history. It has
been fortunate only if one accepts the contention of Engels, by
which the West is to be thanked for having saved Mexico from
itself. The Conquest is seen by Western eyes as the father of
progress. But in Mexico, history cannot be read that way.

"There is no evil," a Mexican adage says, "that does not
come from good." We Americans are too innocent to understand this. We do not fear to evangelize for our ideals. Modernizers are our foreign missionaries. Nuclear-power plants are
one of the current designs for our temples. Dripping with the
waters of baptism, we and they preach that human nature is
infinitely perfectible. We believe that if we can safely handle
the nuke—a hypothesis not yet confirmed—then others can,
too. Most Mexicans believe not only that they are too careless
to manage nuclear energy, but that all men are. In their homes,
devoid of appliances and powered by a single electric line, they
do not understand industrial society's constant thirst for energy. Mexico is not a nation of gadgets or the industry that
produces them. Americans have voted for bond issues to finance nuclear plants. Mexico has never put the issue to a vote.
If Mexicans were allowed to decide democratically on nuclear
power, their fatalism would prevail. The optimism that many
Americans feel toward nuclear power is a reflection of our faith,
and of our youth. Whatever nuclear power is, it has not become
a universal solution to a universal problem, as we once thought
Christianity, and now think science, to be.

The faith that led Spain to conquer the New World also introduced America to plagues. The same faith that led the United States to develop vaccines is also what led us to tinker with the atom. We introduced the world to the specter of nuclear holocaust, and it does not matter, from a Mexican perspective, that the Nazis were also working on the Bomb: Nazism was also an expression of the West. We, as Westerners and Americans, presume that technology represents a gain in human affairs only because the Bomb hasn't gone off. Yet the best minds of our century, including some of those who concocted the Bomb, have gone to their graves with the fear that like Icarus, who tried to fly on wings of wax, we may find that our inventiveness leads to our undoing.

Mexican thinkers believe that in the process of creating our immense economic and technological power, we Americans have made not gods, but dumb instruments of ourselves. "American life," philosopher and poet Octavio Paz says, "is a long series of *paras*," or in-order-thats. We send our children to computer camps in order that they may do well at academics, and we want them to excel academically in order to prosper in the world of work and earnings. If they prosper, they, too, can send their children to camps. In our constant straining to better ourselves, sometimes we fail, but we have solved the problem by making our key relationship, marriage, a machine of interchangeable parts. Economically, the system works: We are eight times richer than the Mexicans, according to statistics on percapita income. But our divorce rate is ten times as high, and at the end of our cycle, nothing awaits us but the black hole of death and oblivion.

The American attitude toward death is expressed in our cemeteries. Most contemporary American burial grounds are plane-surfaced. The humps that marked graves in the past are no longer built. Dirt displaced by caskets is carried away. Grand funerary monuments are not to be seen in new cemeteries, either. Most burial grounds prescribe that graves be marked only with plane-surfaced bronze plates, about 6" × 18" in size. The planing of the American cemetery does not obey any aesthetic or religious imperative. Instead, it is done to keep maintenance costs low. Cemeteries must be mowed, and plane surfaces can be trimmed quickly, by machines. Commerce, not families, provides "perpetual care" to our dead, and cemeteries are no longer what they are in Mexico today, places where the living unite in communion, if only on the Day of the Dead. Americans are too mobile and too future-oriented to linger over the past. In contracting to others our reverence for the past, we relegate our own deaths to meaninglessness. Because we do not believe, as the Mexicans do, that "to remember is to live," we do not believe that those who are remembered live.

Indo-Americans extol death, curse it, and make fun of it. They greet it as we might greet an intimate, with a wide range of moods. A mariachi song from the fifties has now become a Mexican classic, because its chorus says:

> Nothing is what life is worth,
> Life is worth nothing.
> It always begins with crying,
> And with crying it ends.
> That's why in this world,
> Life is worth nothing.

Americans would regard such lyrics as evidence of a depressed or morbid mind. Mexicans regard those lyrics as poetic and sage. In a more contemporary and profane *norteño* song, the singer challenges death with the lyrics:

> I now discern the death that calls for me,
> Death, you asshole, you basket of damn bones,
> Quit kidding around!
> Come take me to destiny!
> If it is in heaven, I deserve it,
> Because hell is this corrupted world.

Mexicans regard those lyrics as hilarious. For them, death is the reflex and continuation of life. Its onset can be as easily hilarious as it can be tragic.

It is hard to separate the Mexican idea of life from the idea of intense suffering. Theologians on both sides of the border say that we know that Jesus was human because he suffered on the cross. But the Jesus of Mexican icons suffers far more

291

than his American counterpart. At Mexican stations of the cross, for example, Jesus is more bruised and bloody, more exhausted, than in any American representations. Most visitors from the United States regard Mexican depictions of Jesus as morbid or ghastly, not as mirrors of their own lives. "Your American Jesus," a Mexican friend told me, "is too much like you Americans. He's clean and unscratched." Not to know intense suffering, the Mexicans think, is not to know the human condition. The Conquest merely underscored this belief, which in Mexico had far more ancient roots. For centuries, Mexicans had believed that the only sure way to reach the heavens was to suffer, as a victim of human sacrifice. The bruised and bleeding Jesus is only a paler version of thousands of figures from the pre-Hispanic past.

When Americans suffer, we regard our suffering as the result of correctable causes: lack of knowledge, lack of resources, lack of self-discipline or planning. We believe that deliverance from our woes can come as handily as a capsule. "Upset? Take Com-pōz," our advertisements once said, and even today, the re-laxant Valium is one of our leading prescription drugs. If a friend comes to us despondent over an impending divorce, for example, we are likely to recommend the services of a marriage couselor or psychologist.

When confronted with heartbroken friends, Mexicans are likely to repeat the refrain, *"Para el mal de amores, no hay doctores,"* "For the malady of love, there are no doctors." They believe that some strokes of bad luck are simply insur-mountable—until recently, widows were expected to wear mourning clothes all their lives—and that if redemption is pos-sible, it must be earned by the penance of suffering. Their logic, which says that he who hasn't suffered doesn't deserve relief, has historically led to acts of religious self-flagellation. For four centuries, Mexicans crawled the last mile of their December pilgrimages to the shrine of the Virgin of Guadalupe, often with cactus pads stuck to their cheeks. Priests and government authorities have asked for a suspension of the practice because crawling pilgrims are obstacles to traffic. Not many people crawl anymore, but cactus-sticking still occurs. It has to. It's an ancient practice. The Aztecs stuck themselves with cactus needles to

292

please their gods. Their ancient belief in the value of suffering allows Mexicans to bear hardship, especially deprivation of the creature comforts, with a dignity rarely seen among their northern neighbors.

Because Mexicans see suffering as beneficent, they are dubious of simple accomplishment. They tend to believe that when someone accomplishes something, what he has actually done is fooled himself. They believe that personal success is no more attainable than scientific progress. The entrepreneur is not their new national hero, and the Horatio Alger that Herminio Gómez admires could never have lived among them. When success is evident, Mexicans usually attribute it to luck or destiny. "For he who was born to make tamales," their adage says, "even corn husks fall from the sky." The difference between their attitude and ours shows in what they consider to be the best periods of life. American society is adult-centered. The American of our dreams is between twenty-five and thirty-five years old and is moving up on the career ladder. For Mexicans, the choice time of life is not its middle, but its extremes, childhood and old age, when one is nearest to God and furtherest from the demands of mortals. The difference between our performance ethic and their resignation ethic shows in the reception we give ambition. In the United States, an ambitious young man is every father-in-law's dream. In Mexico, if you refer to someone as ambitious, you have disparaged his character. A person who is ambitious in Mexico does not say so. He says *"tengo ilusiones,"* "I have illusions," as if all desires for improvement were destined to fail. Having illusions is a forgivable human weakness, but in Mexico *ambicioso* means avaricious, and avarice borders on sin. Mexico's fatalism does not, as one might expect, create a dour and saddened environment, but it does temper joy. Even Mexican festivals are best explained by the adage that "pain sings too, when it cannot cry."

Mexicans who are familiar with the United States tend to view it as we ourselves view Jim Bakker and Jimmy Swaggart. "You Americans claim to have achieved democracy," they say, "because your politicians take bribes before they're elected instead of afterward." We as Americans do not recognize bribery as a part of our political system. We call it campaign finance.

We are not proud that our electoral contests are expensive, any more than Mexicans are proud of the shoddy salaries that they pay their police. But we do not regard our sin as inherent or mortal, because we cannot give up our faith. Democracy is one of the doctrines of our salvation; without it, we would be lost. We are the proof that hypocrisy is a sin of believers. We think that we have nearly perfected democracy, and it pains us to look upon its grosser flaws.

Several years ago, I was having dinner at a motel in Ojinaga, Chihuahua, on Mexico's border with Texas, when a young woman interrupted my meal. She had read an article I'd written about Presidio, Texas, the town on the other side of the line. She was a native of Presidio, and was upset because I'd written that Presidio had more in common with Mexico than with the United States. But our discussion soon turned to Mexico, because my evaluation of Presidio was right: What really bothered the woman was what she thought I believed about Mexico. I mentioned a current rumor—neither of us knew if it was true—that Miguel de la Madrid was buying a home in Spain. The presumption we shared was that if the rumor was true, the home would be paid for with funds illicitly gained. "Of course the Mexican government is corrupt," the woman said, "but what harm did a house ever do?" I was baffled. "What do you mean?" I asked. She mentioned the then-contemporary American scandal Irangate. "When Mexican politicians steal, they don't buy guns or missiles that kill people. Only an American could do that. You Americans"—she was now speaking in a truly Presidio vein, as a Mexican—"are crazy, all you want to do is rule the world. We'd be much better off if your leaders bought homes for their families instead." I thought about the proposition, and decided that the lady was right. Hundreds of building contractors and inspectors in Mexico are thoroughly corrupt, but Pentagon contractors are not altar boys and though faulty fire escapes are dangerous, our military hardware is more frightening yet. America justifies its military readiness in the name of defense. But the Soviets are Westerners, too. Mexico and the rest of Indo-America are justly suspicious of us all.

One night in Macuiltianguis, I talked to an old man in a

wide-brimmed sombrero who had joined the youngsters of Ramón's generation in aiding Güero Medrano.

"What is your religion?" I asked the old man.

"Well, I guess it is socialism," he said.

"But certainly you must have been raised a Catholic," I coun-
tered.

"Oh, yes," he said, "that is true. But I got to thinking about
it, and I decided not to be Catholic anymore, because Catholicism is part of the Conquest, you see."

There will always be Mexicans, especially in towns like Macuil, who would like to return Mexico to the glories of its past
kings. But the ways of the West have become the ways of the
world. Only those countries that the West hasn't wanted to
develop—Guyana, for example—and those that have sent the
West packing—China, Iran, Afghanistan—are exempt from
Westernizing. Mexico was picked for development, or exploitation, in the days of Cortés, and it cannot rebel or turn back
to its past. In Mexico there is not much future for a Pol Pot, a
Khomeini, or a Sendero Luminoso, to lead the country back to
ancestral ways, because as Porfirio Díaz noted, Mexico is too
close to the United States. Its oil is today as coveted as its gold
was in the time of Cortés. As Güero Medrano knew, the collective ownership of land is an Indo-American tradition that
favors modern socialism. But had Medrano captured the south
and marched on Mexico City, the leaders of northern Mexico
would certainly have asked the United States to intervene, and
a divided—or reconquered—Mexico would have resulted.
Indo-America has to lead a life of resignation, because it cannot
freely choose. Mexico is a Finland or Hungary on the other side
of the globe; its geography precludes sovereignty.

If cynical resignation makes Mexico work, it is naive determination that makes America tick. The point isn't as ponderous
or as distant as it may seem. It's a matter of everyday life. At
home in the United States, I often receive unsolicited catalogs
from homeowners' supply houses that advertise products under captions like, "You may never have to change a light bulb
again!" "You may never get bitten by a mosquito again!" and
"Do all your work in comfort with this adjustable table and

stool." Such appeals are rare in Mexico. I have a friend in Texas who, to deal with various problems in her life, is simultaneously taking Jazzercise, rebirthing therapy, and acupuncture treatments. Among Mexico's Westernized urban middle class, an organization called Neurotics Anonymous is coming into vogue, and *Women Who Love Too Much* was on Mexican bestseller lists for a year. But essentially, Mexico is still a nation that has not risen to the clairvoyant plane of psychobabble. I do not believe that many Americans take the claims of fix-it and feel-good schemes in a literal sense, but we provide a market for them because we do believe that improvement is always possible. Mexicans, who have reluctantly been trying to remake their world for five hundred years, have discovered that the effort often produces as much harm as good. I am an American; I bought some never-burn-out light bulbs and learned that they will last for years. I also learned that they draw more current than ordinary bulbs do. It takes a nuclear-power plant to feed them. Most Mexicans have learned to live in the dark. An adage of theirs says that "in a house without lights"—because of its poverty and underdevelopment, Mexico is certainly that—"those who inhabit it are as lights." Mexico has learned what limits are, and how to live within them. I think that knowledge makes its people the wisest citizens of our hemisphere.